MANNING THE LAW

This is a study of elite English men of English law and the methods they used to retain and justify their power and privilege, through controlling the story of the legal person.

It looks at how these men of legal authority thought of themselves and their institution: how they studied and explained law; how they put themselves in the middle of it, as the standard human in need of legal regulation and protection; how they put themselves in charge of that regulation and protection; and how they assigned to women an inferior legal role and being.

The main strategy used to do all this was manipulation of the concept of 'the legal person'. From the 1860s to the 1920s the courts declared that women were not 'persons' who could exercise public power – to vote, to sit in Parliament, to gain degrees, to be lawyers. Up to the end of the 20th century, and into the 21st, women's personhood remained precarious in the private sphere, for rape was excused within a marriage and female reproduction remained under state control (as it still does).

The book examines the active exclusion of women from the means of making legal meaning, especially the ability to shape law's central concept and shows the epistemological effects of this sex differential of legal power which are still felt today. Leading legal thinkers who helped to masculinise the concept of the person, to the detriment of women, are still revered. Law's continuing male orientation is neither seen nor acknowledged and the legal person is treated (falsely) as if he had always been and remains anyone.

Manning the Law

Why the Legal Person Remains a Man

Ngaire Naffine

•HART•
OXFORD • LONDON • NEW YORK • NEW DELHI • SYDNEY

HART PUBLISHING

Bloomsbury Publishing Plc

Kemp House, Chawley Park, Cumnor Hill, Oxford, OX2 9PH, UK

1359 Broadway, New York, NY 10018, USA

Bloomsbury Publishing Ireland Limited, 29 Earlsfort Terrace, Dublin 2, D02 AY28, Ireland

HART PUBLISHING, the Hart/Stag logo, BLOOMSBURY and the Diana logo are trademarks of Bloomsbury Publishing Plc

First published in Great Britain 2025

First published in hardback, 2025

Paperback edition, 2026

Reprinted 2026

A catalogue record for this book is available from the British Library.

A catalogue record for this book is available from the Library of Congress.

ISBN: PB: 978-1-50998-347-6
ePDF: 978-1-50998-349-0
ePub: 978-1-50998-350-6

Typeset by Compuscript Ltd, Shannon

For product safety related questions contact productsafety@bloomsbury.com

To find out more about our authors and books visit www.hartpublishing.co.uk. Here you will find extracts, author information, details of forthcoming events and the option to sign up for our newsletters.

For

Eric Stapleton Richards,

David Patrick Brian Fitzpatrick

and

Grant Paxton Thomas

ACKNOWLEDGEMENTS

Writing this book brought home to me how much university scholarship is a collective endeavour. Over many years I have encountered kindness and generosity of spirit: a willingness of scholars to put their own work down to assist another. Finding time to squeeze in someone else's work, when time is so pressing, is an act of extraordinary intellectual altruism. Again and again, I have been able to count on it.

Thank you Eric Richards, who impressed on me at the start of my career the importance of evidence and explanation (rather than description) and then read so much of my writing from then on, improving its clarity and strengthening its claims.

I am grateful to Adelaide Law School and my colleagues for the opportunity to deliver my thoughts on the jurisprudence of John Finnis in a seminar series.

I thank Adrienne Stone, Jayani Nadarajalingam and Jeff Goldsworthy, for the chance to talk about AV Dicey at Melbourne Law School in its brown bag seminar series. I also thank them, as well as Dale Smith and Ann Genovese, for their comments.

I thank Greg Mackie and Chris Symes for the invitation to give the Dame Roma Mitchell Oration at the University of Adelaide where I could talk of the importance of academic freedom and the pressing need to support legal researchers in difficult times.

I benefitted from helpful discussions with a number of intellectual friends. They are Callum McCarthy and Penny McCarthy, Sandra Holton and Bob Holton, Allyson Robichaud, Cathy Caust, Ruth Trenerry and Michael Ekin Smyth.

My family supplied encouragement and support. Thank you Frances Butterfield, Maxine Cape, Ingrid Butterfield, Alexandra Cape, Marian Richards, Lou Nugent, Sally Richards and Stephanie Richards.

I thank Meg Toews for so many thoughtful and convivial discussions.

A number of people commented on parts or all of the manuscript. I thank Kellie Toole for her thoughts on chapter one. I thank Judith Gardam for reading the first chapters and for so many helpful discussions.

Lindsay Farmer read the chapter on Lord Birkenhead and was generous and encouraging. Niki Lacey read the HLA Hart chapter, more than once, and greatly improved it. Kristen Rundle read the Dicey chapter and helped to shape and deepen it. Ian Leader-Elliott read a number of chapters, more than once, and was constantly helpful and incisive. Margaret Davies, as always, read, encouraged, steered and kept me on task. Tom McClure was a superb research assistant, who assisted greatly in the final preparation of the manuscript. Finally, Jim Lyster read everything, more than once. He introduced me to the work of Gerda Lerner. He helped me to develop and sharpen the arguments of the book. And he endlessly encouraged. Thank you.

Ngaire Naffine
March 2025

CONTENTS

TABLE OF CASES

TABLE OF LEGISLATION

1

Introducing the Arguments: Male Control of the Symbol System Through Definition and Explanation

I. Introduction

Britain was once a powerful empire, extending its legal reach across the world, legislating for many countries, and spreading its case law and its legal treatises. This is commonplace knowledge. Britain has spoken to and for many countries, whether they wanted it or not.

And yet there is an implicit view, especially among theorists of English law, that Britain has not been like this. That it has been essentially a cultured and advanced political and legal system, generally respectful of the rights of others, and so worthy of export to other countries: a system from which one can theorise the nature and conditions of law, confident in the knowledge that one is theorising from a civilised place.

This implicit view, I suggest, is to be found in the writings of English and also American legal scholars and theorists, who have sought to work out the necessary conditions of law, what makes law law.[1] In the background of their thinking is a view that they can write and theorise from jurisdictions which know how to do law properly, to make law well, to get it right, to make it fit for purpose, which is to protect and value the rights of each and every individual. They may say that they are theorising the nature of law anywhere and anytime[2] but their theories have a strongly 'Anglian' flavour.[3]

[1] See Ngaire Naffine, 'The Common Discourse of Hart and Fuller' in Peter Cane (ed), *The Hart-Fuller Debate in the Twenty-First Century* (Oxford, Hart Publishing, 2010) 217–25. See also Gerald Postema, *Legal Philosophy in the Twentieth Century: The Common Law World* (Carolina, Springer, 2011).

[2] As does Leslie Green. See Leslie Green, 'Gender and the Analytical Jurisprudential Mind' (2020) 83 *MLR* 893. For the contrary view, that one cannot make sense of law outside of time and place, see Margaret Davies, *Law Unlimited* (Oxford, Routledge, 2017); Lindsay Farmer, *Making the Modern Criminal Law: Criminalization and Civil Order* (Oxford, Oxford University Press, 2016); Nicola Lacey, *In Search of Criminal Responsibility Ideas, Interests, and Institutions* (Oxford, Oxford University Press, 2016).

[3] I borrow the term 'Anglian' from Peter Cane to refer to legal systems whose concepts and institutions derive from English law. See Peter Cane, *Responsibility in Law and Morality* (Oxford, Hart Publishing, 2002).

In this book I argue that the English legal system has been, and in many ways remains, patriarchal, that is male-controlled and pitted against women. It has therefore not been as it sees itself, which is fair and dispassionate, but has favoured one sex over the other, and actively so. I argue further that, in a very English manner, the way English law and its officials have worked against women is with words and concepts: with their definition, manipulation and explanation.

The power of law to define and explain its terms, I suggest, has been used to advance male interests and to suppress those of women. Key words have been used in perverse ways, flouting ordinary-language meanings. In particular, a perversely narrow legal construction of the term 'Person' has been consistently employed to exclude half the population (women) from a wide variety of roles and activities. In a popular sense, women have been legally declared not to be people. There has also been judicial defiance of statutory instructions to read women into male pronouns, as with Lord Brougham's Act 1850[4] which said that the male case would thenceforth include the female case. When this was tested by women, with a view to getting them the vote, the courts said that this instruction did not apply for this purpose.[5] When women were eventually found to be Persons who could perform these public roles, the sex and reproductive lives of women were still monitored and regulated in ways which had no parallel for men as Legal Persons. To the present day, the Legal Personhood of women remains precarious and compromised because of the sustained and continuing efforts of those with legal authority to control and limit female lives, as if that were the natural and normal thing to do.

II. Insiders and Outsiders: The English Legal Establishment

This is a study of a people, of elite English men of English law: how they thought of themselves and their institution; how they studied and explained and philosophised law; how they advanced and developed it. And how they put themselves in the middle of it, as the standard human in need of legal regulation and protection and in charge of that regulation and protection and assigned to women a lesser role and being.

It is a study of legal insiders and legal outsiders and how the insiders employed basic legal concepts and definitions to keep themselves on the inside of law and women on the outside. The main concept employed was 'the Legal Person'. Its definition and its explanation were used to empower the insiders and to keep the others out. The legal insiders were men of legal authority, profoundly convinced of the rightness of their rule, and intent on preserving their position on the inside of law and keeping the outsiders out. The outsiders were women as a sex, as a total population. In this book I will consider the legal techniques employed by the male

[4] Interpretation Act 1850.
[5] *Chorlton v Lings* (1868) LR 4 CP 374.

legal insiders to preserve their insider status, and the insider status of their sex, to retain and justify their all-male power and privilege and to keep women, as they understood women to be, as lesser beings. I will show that the techniques were those of the lawyer and the academic. They made use of definition, explanation and so meaning formation.

I will consider how legal insiders developed and used the idea of the Legal Person or legal subject, to advance their own interests, while portraying themselves as neutral and possibly believing themselves to be neutral; how they made it seem right and natural and even ordinary and commonplace that this was how law should be developed, explained and understood. Through the manipulation of terms, men of legal authority instated their sex as a fundamental qualification for Legal Personhood (and hence most of the goods of life), while insisting that it was the human and the individual who were their principal concerns. Male personification was elided with human personification. And thus the male legal persona was placed at the heart of liberal legal individualism.

So this is also a study of legal 'explanatory systems', to borrow a term from Gerda Lerner.[6] I will show that key terms embedded in these systems, and their repeated invocation over the centuries, have had a strong adverse effect on the quality of legal reasoning to the present day, in the common law world and especially in England, the country which has exerted so much legal influence on other nations, my own included (which is Australia).

III. The Persons Cases

To work out the male logic of male right in law, why it was thought natural, normal and appropriate, I examine a series of cases that turned on the meaning of the term 'Person' in law: the Persons Cases.[7] In the 1970s, Albie Sachs and Joan Hoff Wilson wrote a pioneering book on these cases, *Sexism and the Law*, which remains a classic.[8] In a separate commentary, Sachs explained the cases succinctly:

> [F]rom 1869 to 1929 British judges wrestled with the problem of whether or not women could be regarded as 'persons'. A series of statutes provided that access to public office,

[6] Gerda Lerner, *The Creation of Patriarchy* (Oxford, Oxford University Press, 1986).

[7] *Chorlton v Lings* (n 5) decided that women could not vote in Manchester because of a legal disability due to their sex; *Jex-Blake v Senatus of the University of Edinburgh* (1873) 11 McPherson 784 decided that women could not graduate in medicine; *Beresford Hope v Lady Sandhurst* [1889] 5 WLUK 37, (1889) 23 QBD 79 excluded women from election to the London County Council; *Nairn v Scottish Universities* [1908] UKHL 3, [1909] AC 147 upheld the exclusion of women from voting for parliamentary representatives for the universities of St Andrews and Edinburgh; *Bebb v Law Society* [1914] 1 Ch 286 endorsed the refusal of the Law Society to enrol women; *Viscountess Rhondda's Claim* [1922] 2 AC 339 disallowed Lady Rhondda from sitting in the House of Lords; finally in *Edwards v A-G of Canada* [1930] AC 124 the Privy Council recognised women as persons able to sit in the Upper House of the Canadian Parliament.

[8] See Albie Sachs and Joan Hoff Wilson, *Sexism and the Law: A Study of Male Beliefs and Legal Bias in Britain and the United States* (Oxford, Martin Robertson, 1978). Sachs was responsible for the analysis of the British legal situation.

> entry to the professions and entitlement to vote should be granted to any 'person' who possessed certain qualifications. When women, as part of the emancipation movement of the time, presented themselves to the authorities duly equipped with the appropriate qualifications, they were confronted with the one major disqualification, namely that they were not in fact 'persons'. In every case but the last one the judges [found women not to be persons].[9]

By way of definition and explanation of one of the most basic legal concepts, English men of legal authority sustained the rights of men to inhabit and shape the public world. Through the concept of 'The Person' and their determinations about who was to count as one, the English judiciary, as well as treatise writers and politicians, asserted male power in law and so they advanced their own interests.

In the Persons Cases this was done boldly and explicitly, with a strong sense of right and justification. As Sachs made crystal clear, leading legal officials took to be right and true: that men had a complete monopoly of legal power and decision-making and that they (rightly and necessarily) should be the ones to decide whether this monopoly should be sustained. Thus men of legal authority exercised their exclusive powers through what Gerda Lerner has called 'the meaning-giving process of interpretation and explanation'.[10]

The Persons Cases are both known and neglected: perhaps regarded as a bit of quaintly awkward history. As Nicola Lacey observed about the theorists of her subdiscipline, criminal law, very little of the scholarship has considered 'what is one of the most radical changes in the conception of legal personhood, viewed in modern perspective – the relatively recent acknowledgement of women as legal persons'.[11] And yet the Persons Cases are eloquent about legal men's sense of themselves and why they believed they were the right kind of beings to exercise legal power, and why women were not, and how they transformed this profoundly sexist way of thinking into law. They show how men of legal authority made use of law, and their control of its concepts and terms, its definitions and the explanations of those definitions, to advance their own rights and interests.

These cases are rich in information about the thinking of senior legal men about the inherent fitness for power of their own sex. For the term 'Person' was an effective gatekeeper to public power and the acquisition of knowledge and expertise and authority. The control of the definition of the Person established who could do what as legal actors, and who were disabled.[12] Men of legal influence deployed this concept to populate law. They decided who was inside and who was outside the concept of the Person and hence who was inside and outside of law.

[9] Albie Sachs, 'The Myth of Judicial Neutrality: The Male Monopoly Cases' (1975) 23 *The Sociological Review* 104, 104–05. Later Sachs became a constitutional judge in South Africa.

[10] Lerner (n 6) 5.

[11] Lacey (n 2) 183.

[12] On the uses and effects of this term in law, see Ngaire Naffine, 'Who are Law's Persons? From Cheshire Cats to Responsible Subjects' (2003) 66 *MLR* 346. See also Ngaire Naffine, *Law's Meaning of Life: Philosophy, Religion, Darwin, and the Legal Person* (Oxford, Hart Publishing, 2009).

The concept of the Legal Person has therefore been a powerful and useful tool of patriarchy. And the Persons Cases are perhaps the clearest, most explicit demonstration of the exercise of raw male power, using a legal concept, sometimes coupled with sophistry and euphemism, sometimes just employing bold unsubstantiated assertions of male superiority and female inferiority, and sometimes by an apparently careful, forensic, judicial finding of what was taken to be the correct law.

A further argument of this book is that Legal Personhood was not fully granted to women at the so-called end of the Persons Cases which Albie Sachs dated at 1929, with the case of *Edwards v A-G of Canada*.[13] For years after this decision, a denial of a fundamental legal right to women continued, strongly associated with basic Personhood. This is the right to exclude others from one's person and so maintain what is often called 'bodily integrity'.[14] It was not until the last decade of the twentieth century that the right of the English husband to have forcible intercourse with his wife (rape) was considered unacceptable and so abolished. And there continue to the present day special legal controls over women's bodies, governing their reproductive lives, which have no parallel for men. Again, the right of Persons to exercise bodily autonomy has been denied to women, but not to men.

IV. The Right to be a Legal Person

The right to be a Legal Person, which is at the heart of this book, is not really a right, but rather the legal status that comes into being as soon as a legal right is recognised. Though there are some rare exceptions, non-human animals are not Persons because they are not permitted to bear rights and they do not have standing in a court of law. They are outside of the community of legally-recognised rights holders.[15]

The invocation of the term Legal Person – who can be one and who cannot – is an important source of information about who matters and who can therefore be and act in law. By asserting their exclusive rights to define and explain this basic term in a strongly exclusionary manner (men always in, women often out), those in control of the legal explanatory system chose the strongest, clearest, least mistakable means of asserting male right. The exercise and portrayal of male right, by imposing female non-right,[16] using this concept, showed a deep conviction of the men of law in exclusive male legal entitlement. By saying that women were not

[13] *Edwards v A-G of Canada* [1930] AC 124.

[14] It is at the centre of John Stuart Mill's harm principle which is the starting point of many criminal law courses.

[15] For a sustained analysis of Legal Personhood and how and why it is distributed, see Naffine, *Law's Meaning of Life* (n 12).

[16] The idea of the legal correlatives of right versus non-right comes from Hohfeld. See Wesley Newcomb Hohfeld, 'Fundamental Legal Conceptions as Applied in Judicial Reasoning' (1916) 26 *The Yale Law Journal* 710.

Persons, the men of law chose the boldest means to keep women out of the polity. They said without flinching 'you are not a Person' and so you cannot exercise the powers of Persons.[17]

V. The Sequence of Arguments

The development of the arguments of this book proceeds in the following manner. To understand just how the concept of the Person operates and so how it could be thus deployed, to assert the rights of one group against and over another, I need to say a little about the formal legal concept and its relation to the ordinary language meaning and that is the task of the next chapter (chapter two).

The Persons Cases, which considered whether women were Persons in law, were a series of challenges to male authority by women seeking the powers of men. Necessarily, rights-seeking women had to call on men as the existing rights holders to assist them and represent them and so the women did. In chapter three I begin my analysis of these cases with the spectacular challenge to male legal authority, launched by the prominent political writer and politician, John Stuart Mill in the mid Victorian period: *The Subjection of Women*.[18] In this dramatic piece of political rhetoric and analysis, Mill identified and condemned the great legal power of men over women, saying it was appalling for women but also bad for men.

Here I examine the nature of Mill's challenge to male authority, the response of Fitzjames Stephen (treatise writer, later judge, and uncle to Virginia Woolf) and then the first round of Persons Cases, which I place in the Victorian period. In the aptly titled *Liberty, Fraternity, Equality*,[19] Stephen sprang into action for his sex and against women. He responded in an open, almost aggressive, manner and made no bones about his contempt for women and his contempt for Mill. He insisted that male right should sound in law. The courts were of the same view. When male power was challenged by women in the Persons Cases, also starting in the 1860s, the first judicial push back in *Chorlton v Lings*[20] was bristling with condescension for women and was adamant that women did not have the rights of Persons – here the right of Persons to vote – and that the male case did not import the female case.

This reasoning was used, again and again, to push back on a number of fronts, in order to retain iron male control of institutions.[21] As we will see, the concept of the Person was used to secure exclusive male control of higher education and

[17] For example, in the case of *Nairn* (discussed in chapter four) the House of Lords openly declared that female graduates were not 'persons' for the purpose of a university franchise. Only male graduates could vote for the university's parliamentary representative because only male graduates were considered to be 'persons' under the governing law. *Nairn v Scottish Universities* (n 7).

[18] John Stuart Mill, *The Subjection of Women* (London, Longmans, Green, Reader and Dyer, 1869).

[19] James Fitzjames Stephen, *Liberty, Equality and Fraternity* (New York, Holt and Williams, 1873).

[20] *Chorlton v Lings* (n 5).

[21] See Sachs and Hoff Wilson (n 8). See also Rose Pearson and Albie Sachs, 'Barristers and Gentlemen: A Critical Look at Sexism in the Legal Profession' (1980) 43 *MLR* 400.

knowledge formation, by positively excluding women from obtaining degrees;[22] to secure exclusive male access to the profession (law) which would produce expert legal theorists and practitioners;[23] to exclude women from the franchise to decide on government; to ensure exclusive male membership of the legal and political institutions;[24] even to control the female body.[25] When women sought to improve their status in law, male legal authority was applied to the definition of terms. Legal power was exercised by wordsmiths.

There was no perceived need to be scrupulous with legal method because there was a common desire to preserve the status quo of male power and no-one to effectively oppose it. The common law was used to ensure that women were not Persons for a wide variety of public purposes, excluding them from public life, while the judges insisted that it was not their doing; that they had no view of the rights or wrongs of the challenge. They were only stating or declaring the law; they were deferring to inveterate usage; they were not making law; that was for Parliament. And then Parliament itself was reluctant to act.

The concepts of the Person and also of the Individual worked at a number of levels and in a number of ways. They had strong moral and religious overtones. They suggested deep human sex differences based on biology and psychology. They connoted natural hierarchy and so were highly political. They were understandable to a general audience as well as to a legal audience. They said a lot in very few words. Legal patriarchy did not need to be spelled out in detail. It had only to classify the general population into two major groups, men and women, and then to set them in a certain relation with one another. And so they were instrumental in shaping society quite fundamentally: dividing it in two and then saying how one half should relate to the other.

Chapter four takes us into the twentieth century. Here we observe the Lord High Chancellors, the highest judicial officials, asserting exclusive male legal power in a strong uncompromising manner and again using the concept of the Person. In 1908 Lord Loreburn, as Lord Chancellor, issued his judgment in *Nairn v Scottish Universities*[26] confident that there would be no opposition. The House of Lords thus upheld the exclusion of women from voting for parliamentary representatives for the Scottish Universities. In 1914 Gwyneth Bebb sought to be declared a Person for the purposes of the Solicitors Act and was refused by the Court of Appeal.[27] In 1918 Lord Loreburn proposed an amendment to the Representation Bill to derail the female franchise (here he was unsuccessful).[28]

[22] See *Jex-Blake v Senatus of the University of Edinburgh* (n 7).

[23] See *Bebb v Law Society* (n 7).

[24] For example, women did not obtain equal rights to sit in the House of Lords until the Peerage Act 1963 though one could date it even later, say 2015, when the first female lord spiritual was admitted.

[25] I am referring here generally to laws governing contraception, pregnancy and rape.

[26] *Nairn v Scottish Universities* (n 7).

[27] *Bebb v Law Society* (n 7).

[28] *Hansard*, HL Deb 9 January 1918, vol 27, col 412.

Four years later in 1922 Lord Birkenhead in *Lady Rhondda's Claim*[29] resorted to more elaborate practices to successfully exclude women from the House of Lords and his actions endured in their effects until 1963.

This book also employs three case studies of leading legal thinkers whose lives span the Victorian period to the present day. One is the constitutional theorist, Albert Venn Dicey, who has been called 'the high priest of orthodox constitutional thought in Britain'.[30] The second is HLA Hart, the immensely influential legal theorist of the twentieth century, who produced a theory of law which sought to detach its validity from its morality. The third is the also influential legal theorist John Finnis, who is still writing, who has sought to fuse law and morality. In different ways, each rendered the Personhood of women problematic but was not taken to task for it. Dicey articulated the rule of law, legality and equality, while pressing openly for the continuing exclusion of women from sovereign power. Hart was an important law reformer for women's causes, and a committed liberal, but still envisaged a legal subject with an essentially male physiology. Finnis sought to connect law to what he declared to be life's basic goods, but spoke repeatedly and over the course of his career against the Personhood of women when pregnant. They were not to be recipients of his basic goods, especially the right to exercise free life choices and self-government.

In chapter five I undertake my first case study. I examine the thinking of the English constitutional theorist Albert Venn Dicey (1835–1922), whose life and writing spans the late Victorian period to the third decade of the twentieth century, almost the entire span of the Persons Cases. Dicey shaped English constitutional thought, promoting the rule of law and equality, while pressing explicitly that women should be kept out of the constitutive power. They should not be considered Persons who were permitted to vote. He was against any sort of significant role for women in government. Dicey is a prominent and so useful exemplar of an influential man of law shaping legal meaning and legal power while insisting that women were not really Persons.[31]

Dicey spoke vigorously against the exercise by women of public power and especially against the female franchise. He included these anti-woman sentiments in his famous *Introduction to Law and the Constitution* of 1915 (in the 8th edition)[32] in anticipation of the female franchise. He had already penned an entire book in which he made his case against the exercise of any sort of public power by women.[33] He was particularly concerned that women, as lesser beings, could assume the mighty powers of running the Empire or rather deciding which

[29] *Viscountess Rhondda's Claim* (n 7).

[30] Martin Loughlin, 'Dicey, Albert Venn (1835–1922)' (*Routledge Encyclopedia of Philosophy*, 1998), available at www.rep.routledge.com/articles/biographical/dicey-albert-venn-1835-1922/v-1.

[31] See Mark Walters' recent biography of Dicey which reveres the man himself as well as his contribution to constitutional theory: Mark D Walters, *AV Dicey and the Common Law Constitutional Tradition: A Legal Turn of Mind* (Cambridge, Cambridge University Press, 2020).

[32] AV Dicey, *Introduction to Law and the Constitution*, 8th edn (London, MacMillan, 1915).

[33] See AV Dicey, *Letters to a Friend on Votes for Women* (London, John Murray, 1909).

Englishmen should. In 1918, English women over 30 years of age were granted the vote, nevertheless. (Heeding Dicey's concerns that the female franchise would make women the majority of voters, adult women from 21 to 30 years old were precluded from voting, while 21-year-old men got the vote.)

Dicey is of special interest because his reputation was sustained as a great legal thinker, despite his anti-woman writings. Being against women did not seem to harm him as a legal thinker in the eyes of his peers. Nor was his misogyny considered part of his general work about law, even though it was so strongly enunciated.

In chapter six, I consider how the Persons Cases supposedly came to an end, and why that ending was unresolved and unsatisfactory, both then and now. In 1929, in *Edwards v A-G of Canada* Lord Sankey, in the Privy Council, declared that women were now persons for the purpose of sitting in the Upper House of the Canadian Parliament.[34] The impression conveyed was of considered, steady, rational, modernisation, by responsible legal statesmen as they gracefully relinquished power and welcomed women into the public realm. There is the emergence of soft power,[35] when dissimulation begins to occur and things are not so transparent. There is a distancing from openly misogynist legal practices of the immediate past, and its uses to shut women out of the offices of public power through law. The bringing of women into law, supposedly as full Legal Persons, is treated as a matter of assimilation, and so one can move on with the rest of law with women now slotted in. I call this the 'First Reform Story'. There is talk of reform, a modernisation of women, and so a suppression of the more brutal story, a quiet burial of history.[36]

As Sachs observes, this is how the Persons Cases notionally ended, with celebration and congratulations for the 'legal statesmanship' of the judges and for the sheer pluck of the trailblazing women. Telegrams crossed the Atlantic. Nothing was said about the rawer facts: the imprisonment of women who had engaged in political protest to obtain the vote; the denial of their political status when they were imprisoned; their forcible-feeding. When the Persons Cases supposedly came to an end, legal reputations (such as Dicey's) were retained. The state remained much the same in its priorities and values. Women were added to the male order, but the male order stayed male. After all, it was explicitly male the day before the *Edwards* judgment. What happened next? Were law reform commissions set up to work out what to do? No, in fact little happened in the way of deep reflection; there was no rupture in legal thought; no paradigm shift.

[34] By contrast, England was a long way off this determination for itself because of the highly effective moves of Lord Birkenhead to keep women out of the House of Lords, notably in *Viscountess Rhondda's Claim* (n 7). Birkenhead's anti-woman activities are discussed in chapter four.

[35] This is a term coined by Joseph S Nye, Jr. See Joseph S Nye, Jr, 'Soft Power' (1990) 80 *Foreign Policy* 153. As Nye explained, 'sometimes people influence others by ideas and attraction that sets the agenda for others or gets them to want what you want'. This is 'soft power'. See Joseph Nye, 'Soft Power: The Origins and Political Progress of a Concept' (2022) 28 *Journal of International Communication* 1, 1–2.

[36] On the suppression of the story of women's efforts to obtain legal change, see Erika Rackley and Rosemary Auchmuty, 'The Case for Feminist Legal History' (2020) 40 *OJLS* 878. And see generally the writings of both authors on women's legal history.

The First Reform Story of the admission of women to (Canadian) Parliamentary personhood by the Privy Council in *Edwards v A-G of Canada* is often referred to as the end of the Persons Cases[37] but so much was left in place. True, after ferocious opposition, property, professional and political powers were ceded to women. But that is not the whole of Personhood. Though power was ceded to women in the male public sphere, in the so-called private sphere of sex and reproduction, powers were ceded very differently. In fact much stayed the same. In the most fundamental ways, law continued to erode women's autonomy and bodily integrity and hence their Personhood. The husband retained his right of sexual access to his wife (because of his common law immunity from rape prosecution). And the Offences Against the Person Act made it a crime punishable by life imprisonment should a woman seek to terminate a pregnancy.[38] Put together, these two criminal laws (an exemption for the man and a proscription for the woman) meant that a man had a lawful right to penetrate and inseminate and any ensuing pregnancy could lead to life imprisonment for the woman seeking to end it.[39]

In chapter six, I also consider the Second Reform Story which was told when the husband's exemption from rape law was removed in the last decade of the twentieth century. (There was an apparent domino effect in Scotland, England and Australia, as the exemption was abolished within the span of a few years.) What is significant about these reform cases is not just the slight treatment of what was strictly speaking a major change in criminal law. My greater concern here is that the judges (again) tended to diminish the scale of change; they failed to take stock of the fact that a husband's rape of his wife had probably been lawful up to then and at the insistence of many of the men of law;[40] and they tended to dismiss the past and dissociate themselves from it. There was little appetite to examine what had gone before. There was no stocktaking, no deep evaluation of law and its active protection of male interests at the expense of female interests.

Indeed, there was no serious rethinking of the concept of the Legal Person, to make the legal subject more representative of the whole population. And so, implicitly, the Legal Person stayed a man because he continued to be thought of, and was regulated, as if he never personally divided and reproduced. The separation of

[37] In fact Canada celebrates the Personification of women every year.

[38] In 1938 the case of *Bourne* decided that an abortion was legal if the doctor was 'of the opinion, on reasonable grounds and with adequate knowledge, that the probable consequence' of continuing the pregnancy would 'be to make the women a physical or mental wreck': *R v Bourne* [1938] 3 All ER 615, [1939] 1 KB 687, 694. In 1967 the Abortion Act provided a therapeutic exception to criminal prosecution for abortion offences. For a history of this law, see Sally Sheldon et al, *The Abortion Act of 1967: A Biography of a UK Law* (Cambridge University Press, 2023).

[39] Under s 58 of the Offences Against the Person Act 1861 there is still provision for a woman 'to be kept in penal servitude for life' should she administer drugs or use instruments 'to procure her own miscarriage' unless she falls within the provisions of the Abortion Act 1967. On the continuing relevance of this offence and sentence, see Tobi Thomas, 'Outrage at Jail Sentence for Woman who Took Abortion Pills Later than UK Limit' *The Guardian* (London, 13 June 2023). On the draconian nature of the abortion provisions of the Offences Against the Person Act 1861, see Sally Sheldon, 'The Decriminalisation of Abortion: An Argument for Modernisation' (2016) 36 *OJLS* 334.

[40] See Ngaire Naffine, *Criminal Law and the Man Problem* (Oxford, Hart Publishing, 2019).

abortion law from general criminal law and theory meant that human divisibility was not dealt with in legal analysis. The Legal Person was still theorised as if he always maintained his bodily integrity, his wholeness, his indivisibility; in short he was never pregnant.

Rape law had been amended to protect the bodily integrity of wives. However, in one form or another, pregnancy law (which could not touch a man), stayed on the books and continued to limit the bodily integrity and self-governance of women and so constrained their Personhood. But pregnancy law, which set the rules for a pregnancy's termination, was not treated as law about Persons and their nature, for it was not about men, who remained the archetypal legal subjects.

In chapter seven, I conduct my second case study of an eminent legal thinker, this time the legal theorist HLA Hart (1907–1992). With the Reform Story, there was no reckoning with what had gone before: with the explicit maleness of the Legal Person. So when HLA Hart became a leading jurisprudential figure of the twentieth century, with his *The Concept of Law*,[41] he could proceed with his theorising *as if* none of this had happened. There was no pressing political or historical need to reckon with the recent past, and the active exclusion of women from much of the legal world, its spheres of influence and its population of Persons. Theory of law could be lifted out of these messy facts and be developed as a legal abstraction, with its characters also conceived as abstractions.

When Hart developed *The Concept of Law* in the late 1950s for publication in 1961, the country from which Hart wrote (England) was imagined as a healthy legal system *de novo*. The vast powers of the husband, still embedded in the rules of criminal law, were of no consequence. That the Upper House of the UK Parliament had yet to admit women on the same terms as men was not of note.[42] That women had been completely excluded from the House of Review up to a few years earlier was not attended to. The maleness of law and the state institutions was simply normal and did not call for comment.

As we will see in chapter eight, the prominent legal theorist, John Finnis (1940–), took full advantage of this fact, from the 1960s to the present day. In this my third case study, I consider how the one influential legal man, Finnis, developed a general theory of law, about what he considered the natural fundamental goods which law must respect, and was deeply respected for it, while he simultaneously worked actively against the Personhood of women, by seeking the prohibition of abortion and was not called to account for it by general theorists of law. Finnis was given free rein to theorise the fundamental rights of the Individual, treated as

[41] HLA Hart, *The Concept of Law* (Oxford, Clarendon Press, 1961).

[42] Duncan Sutherland, 'Peeresses, Parliament and Prejudice: the admission of women to the House of Lords, 1918–1963' (2010) 20 *Parliaments, Estates and Representation* 215, 215: 'Only after the creation of life peerages, after 1958, were women admitted to the House, and even then the hereditary peeresses had to wait until 1963 for admission.' See also Duncan Sutherland, 'Ladies in a Lords' House: Women in the House of Lords Since 1958' in Bruce Kinzer, Molly Baer Kramer and Richard Trainor (eds), *Reform and its Complexities in Modern Britain: Essays Inspired by Sir Brian Harrison* (Oxford, Oxford University Press, 2022).

general human rights, while also saying that much of this did not apply to women if they were pregnant, thus the rights were not in fact general rights.

Again, this sustained endeavour to control and constrain women's Personhood did an authoritative legal figure little reputational damage. And ultimately it contributed to the dramatic contraction of women's self-governance, arguably the most fundamental right of Persons, in the US case of *Dobbs v Jackson Women's Health Organization*,[43] which removed women's constitutional right to abortion.

In chapter nine, I consider what remains concerning in legal theory because of the failures to consider the sexing of Persons in law.[44] The fact that men have exclusively exercised legal power, and used it to their advantage, is treated as irrelevant to the general study of law. The male legal power to define and explain has been so normal, so natural, that little need be made of that fact. One of the most pronounced intellectual habits of the producers of legal knowledge, still, is the taking of male power to be commonplace and banal.[45] It is an unstated truth that law has been a single-sex institution, formulating its very subject as a man and not a woman, actively so, emphatically and avowedly. But nothing of interest is to be found in this faulty fundamental legal orientation.

In law and its analysis, male power has been normal, assumed, unremarked, unremarkable, mundane and intellectually uninteresting. And yet it has been the most defining condition of law, the elephant in the room. The intellectual habit of taking male power to be normal is therefore a classic use of soft power.[46] It operates through the manipulation of terms, concepts, attitudes and thinking. It shapes the culture and is the culture. It does not need to rely on the use of explicit laws eroding personhood, though it has not ruled this out (think of lawful wife rape and laws controlling pregnancy).

I go on to explain how this leaves the male Legal Person in place but unconsidered as a man. The classic Legal Person, the gold standard, the one who has been sharply defined and theorised into this concept, historically, politically and philosophically, has been and remains, in many ways, a man, understood in a certain English liberal way, that is as an abstract, rational, choosing, freestanding, autonomous, physically distinct and individuated Individual. The rights and duties which protect and realise what are thought to be the necessary attributes and conditions of the Legal Person have been openly for men, not women, ensuring that women have weak and vulnerable personhood. And if and when pregnant, women are made to feel this keenly. As a consequence, legal theory has

[43] *Dobbs v Jackson Women's Health Organization* 597 US 215 (2022).

[44] See Ngaire Naffine and Rosemary J Owens (eds), *Sexing the Subject of Law* (Law Book Company, 1997).

[45] So what is it to be banal? According to the Macmillan dictionary, 'something that is banal is boring because it contains nothing new, original, or unusual'. The Britannica Dictionary states that banal is 'boring or ordinary: not interesting'. To the Online Etymology Dictionary it is '1857, "anything common or trite;" 1878, "triteness, triviality," from French banalité (17c.), from banal "hackneyed, commonplace"'.

[46] See Nye, 'Soft Power' (2022) (n 35).

hardly grappled with the question of what it means for a woman to be a Legal Person and an Individual (as those concepts have been developed). And yet the Legal Person and also the Individual[47] are basic legal concepts, central characters of law, and the subject of much law and legal theory. They remain strong operational concepts. They matter now.

The practical effects of this weakly theorised Personhood of women are being felt keenly by American women today: most dramatically they entail the withdrawal of rights to reproductive autonomy (the right to terminate a pregnancy) by the US Supreme Court in 2022 (*Dobbs v Jackson*), and with the active and vocal support of one of England's most recognised legal philosophers (John Finnis). The general failure of legal theory to consider the Personhood of women has left women fuzzy Persons and fuzzy Individuals, not quite the real thing.

In chapter 10 I explain what I think is now occurring in legal theory, conceptually because of the failure to consider the history of law's Person, with his explicitly male character, and the failure to reengineer or at least reconsider the Person when women were notionally added. I suggest that there is now in operation a silent (that is undeclared) heuristic device.

For the sake of theory, I suggest, that as a heuristic device, all Individuals are now treated *as if* women had always been equivalent to men, interchangeable legal units, notionally participating in all areas of law, equally authoritative. The actual history is known to be fundamentally different from this. Through law, men were rendered capable as legal actors, they were legally capacitated, and women, upon marriage, largely rendered incapable. The blocking of women at large from education, from legal practice, from professional and political life, rendered them incapable of being authoritative legal insiders who could describe and explain law. All Individuals are still treated as if they were indivisible human units (who never divide in the process of reproduction) and so the facts of human creation and perpetuation are set aside as irrelevant to theories of the Person, though human aggression and vulnerability are not.[48]

In this final chapter I also consider what might be done to improve law and legal thought, given all this. The legal 'inherited background'[49] of patriarchal thinking, of thinking of the Person as a man, is itself blocking important, even fascinating legal research into the effects of patriarchy on law. Persistent background thinking that maleness is either irrelevant or just too ordinary a feature of law, thinking that is rarely explicitly acknowledged in the modern age, is blunting curiosity. Something so normal and ubiquitous is not striking; it does not call for sustained inquiry. It is the excessively familiar wallpaper of law.

[47] A concept to be more fully fleshed out over the course of this book.

[48] See HLA Hart's speculative point (considered in chapter seven) that we are not giant land crabs with impenetrable carapaces and so we need protection from one another: HLA Hart, 'Positivism and the Separation of Law and Morals' (1958) 71 *Harvard Law Review* 593, 623.

[49] On the idea of the inherited background, see Ludwig Wittgenstein, *On Certainty* (Oxford, Basil Blackwell, 1969); Susan Hekman, 'Backgrounds and Riverbeds: Feminist Reflections' (1999) 25 *Feminist Studies* 427.

Law's overwhelming maleness should trigger a number of research questions. What has this basic fact about law done to law and to the understanding of law? How has it shaped law's priorities and the very sense of what law is thought to be and its basic institutions? These are fundamental questions about the nature of law and if pursued robustly, with intellectual rigour, they could tell us a great deal about law.

The consistency with which legal scholars and jurists have neglected these questions about law's maleness is not only anti-intellectual but baffling; perhaps it even speaks of fear. Open curiosity lies at the heart of good scholarship. We are not seeing this here. The male ethnicity of law has been so thorough and so normalised that it can hardly be seen and it hardly registers. To see a judicial bench or parliament of all or mainly men is to see the normal and the commonplace. (A room full of women holding power would be striking.)

The counterfactual of a world in which law came to be made exclusively by women[50] and organised around their lives and interests, positively excluding the interests of men, is still outside of contemplation. But it is that thought experiment which would inform the men of law hugely about the operations of their law. It would let them see what characterises the law they have and which simply seems normal and neutral. Actually Dicey did imagine a world in which women were a little over half the voting population when he did the figures on the female franchise and it horrified him.

VI. The 'Acceptable Prejudice' and Law from Below

'Sex prejudice … is the only socially acceptable prejudice.'[51] This was said in an approving review of Sachs and Wilson's *Sexism and the Law*, and was seen to be the important message of the book, published in 1979. I would also say that it is the only legally acceptable prejudice. This struck me strongly when I was a law student in the 1970s; it continued to exercise me as a doctoral student and then as a teacher of law. In the authoritative law books I was set to read, one could find derogatory statements about women and no-one turned a hair. And this was within a discipline dedicated to the pursuit of truth, equality and justice.

This moral numbness is probably because men have never experienced law as a hostile institution, as a rights-stripping institution, simply because they were men. Men have experienced law as a rights-giving and rights-protecting institution and this is how mainstream jurisprudence has depicted law. It is true that law has not treated all men equally, but being a man, per se, has never been the basis of rights

[50] Consider Gerda Lerner's imagined matriarchy in which women are in control of the explanatory systems: Lerner (n 6).

[51] Lisa Aversa Richette, 'Book Review: Sexism and the Law: A Study of Male Beliefs and Legal Bias in Britain and the United States by Albie Sachs and Joan Hoff Wilson' (1979) 6 *Women's Rights Law Reporter* 145.

removal. So, as I hope to demonstrate, we need to break the scholarly habit of taking as a given that the institutions of power and knowledge have been mainly, if not exclusively, controlled by men, and that men still have more power than women. Male occupation of power should trigger intellectual curiosity among legal scholars.

It is not that men have been ignored. On the contrary. Men of power have been the focus of legal analysis and legal history, which tends to be told from above, but without noting or noticing that these figures are virtually all men. Legal historiography still tends to employ a 'great men of law' approach; it entails a study of the intellectual, political and male legal elites without a consciousness of this top down approach: that it is a top down approach, a perspective.[52] This is a distinct limitation of thought which could be corrected. The fact that the power is held by men, a power which is endorsed and endowed by law, should be of scholarly interest.

The Persons Cases are entirely from above, from a male perspective, and the perspective of a male legal elite, looking back to earlier generations of legal authorities, to the earlier male elite. And legal historiography tends to do this too. Law is told as a story of the thinking of great legal men. Other disciplines have done much the same so that some historiographers have become keenly aware of this preoccupation with the actions of the powerful, causing a sort of downward looking perspective. As Eric Richards has observed, 'the conventional preoccupations of historians with the ruling elites and power elements in society' has been 'to the neglect of the great majority of the people'.[53] The 'common people' have thus been 'denied moral purpose or even recognition'.[54] They have been treated as 'non persons'.[55]

As I plan to show in this book, male power needs to be inspected as the implicit starting point of law's explanatory systems. Male power makes sense of the analysis, is presumed by the analysis, is even celebrated in the analysis (when the greats of the canon are celebrated), but it does not feature in the analysis. It should. Male legal power needs to be seen as the frame of analysis. Were it to feature, an enormous amount of work would have to be done. In fact, the normal analysis of law would grind to a halt as this fundamental work started and proceeded. And it would create a serious difficulty for legal analysis of the principles and nature of law because law is taken to be principled, at least in its ideal form, but this sex-based distribution of power, by and within law, is not principled, is not designed to be principled and it has been endemic.

Anglian law and theory continue to offer supposedly universal theories of the Person and the Individual, and their place in law, intended to cover the whole

[52] This is striking in Postema's history of legal philosophy in the common law world and also in his invocation of 'the moral presence of the past' and 'the true philosophy': see Gerald Postema, 'On the Moral Presence of our Past' (1991) 36 *McGill Law Journal* 1153; Postema (n 1). And it is strongly in evidence in the most recent biography of Dicey by Walters: Walters (n 31).

[53] Eric Richards, 'History from Below' (1975) 1 *Journal of the Historical Society of South Australia* 1, 3.

[54] ibid.

[55] ibid.

population, but because the work has not been done to rethink law's Person, they are still extrapolated from a certain understanding of men. For this is the actual history of the Legal Person and it has not been reconfigured. For centuries the specific case of the male sex has been made the general case of the Person and the Individual, as those concepts have been understood and implemented. This needs to be acknowledged and something done about it, for it is not good for law and it is not good for law's subjects.

2

The Concepts of the Person and the Individual: The Power of Definition and Explanation

I. Introduction

In orthodox general jurisprudence, in mainstream theory about the nature of law, there is a subject of theory. There is a Legal Person, and therefore a theory of the Person.[1] It is very difficult to have a theory of law without a Legal Person: a legal rights and duty bearer; the being around whom law coalesces; its *raison d'etre*. For this reason, theory of the Person is at the heart of general jurisprudence. This Person is the one addressed by law; the one whom law is for. Law as theorised is theorised for and around Persons. And, generally speaking, law is theorised with the Person understood as a human being, though (for commercial convenience or even necessity) corporations have also assumed the mantle of Persons[2] and, latterly, some parts of non-human nature.[3]

Perhaps the greatest political act of law is the making of a Legal Person (simply put, those who can act in law) and, in the same move, the making of legal non-persons (those who cannot act in law). The moral, political and legal significance of the term 'Person' can hardly be understated. The concept of the Legal Person determines who we must treat with dignity and who we need not. It thereby sets the limits of our moral and legal concern for others. Prima facie, only Persons must be treated as rights-bearing ends-in-self, as beings with moral status.[4]

[1] A now classic endeavour to make sense of the Legal Person is Note, 'What We Talk About When We Talk About Persons: The Language of a Legal Fiction' (2001) 114 *Harvard Law Review* 1746. And for an excellent pioneering analysis of the Legal Person, see Alexander Nekam, *The Personality Conception of the Legal Entity* (Cambridge, Harvard University Press, 1938).

[2] An account of corporate personality of considerable pedigree and influence is that of John Dewey, 'The Historic Background of Corporate Legal Personality' (1926) 35 *Yale Law Journal* 655, 660. A more recent explanation of the competing theories of the nature of corporate personality and corporate responsibility is Nicola Lacey, '"Philosophical Foundations of the Common Law" Social not Metaphysical' in Jeremy Horder (ed), *Oxford Essays in Jurisprudence*, 4th edn (Oxford, Oxford University Press, 2000) 17.

[3] See, eg, Erin L O'Donnell and Julia Talbot-Jones, 'Creating Legal Rights for Rivers: Lessons from Australia, New Zealand, and India' (2018) 23 *Ecology and Society* 7; Erin L O'Donnell, *Legal Rights for Rivers: Competition, Collaboration and Water Governance* (London, Routledge, 2018).

[4] For an analysis of the legal concepts of persons and property, and how they relate to one another, see Margaret Davies and Ngaire Naffine, *Are Persons Property? Legal Debates about Property and Personality* (Aldershot, Ashgate, 2001).

II. The Unstable Concept of the Legal Person

The concept of the Legal Person calls for explanation, from the outset. The Legal Person is law's basic unit of analysis, sometimes called the legal subject. Though it is basic to law analytically, an elementary unit, which might suggest solidity, law's person is also highly abstract in that it is made up of a cluster of rights and duties which are in themselves variable and changing and certainly do not have a material form. Over the course of a human lifetime, the rights and duties which cluster together and make us Legal Persons will shift.[5] As babies, for example, we have many rights but no duties. As rational adults we acquire a rich array of both rights and duties.[6] This makes the Legal Person a fluctuating and hence unstable concept, and therefore rather useful for those who wish to manipulate it and use it for their own desires and devices (as we will see throughout this book).

I once described the Legal Person as a kind of chameleon, noting its ability to transform and change shape, to shift between characters and characterisations.[7] I maintain this view. Sometimes the Legal Person can be, and has been, thought of, or even visualised (even by jurists), as a natural or pre-legal being. This being is legally scrutinised for its suitability as a legal subject, and if found fitting, comes into law and is assigned the status of a Legal Person. At other times, the Legal Person has been imagined in a more abstract and legalistic manner, so that this legal being seems only to exist and arise from the rights and duties endowed by law and can be thought of as a purely positive construction of law, not of nature, and is best thought of as a formal legal analytical tool.[8] But as I will explain, the sexual politics of personification never really go away. Men have experienced a great richness of legal life. As I will show, they have been endowed by legal officials with empowering personifying rights, especially in the public sphere, while women have often been deliberately disempowered by the denial of those very same rights.

To clarify the first naturalistic usage. The Legal Person can be thought of as the natural being who is assessed for their suitability for legal existence, is found suitable, and so assigned rights and perhaps duties within a legal personification process. In this process one asks: To whom should rights be assigned? And why? Who, or even what, best *corresponds* to law's concept of the Person? Who either does or does not qualify for these rights and who is therefore of interest to law, as their being is legally assessed? Thus, the one who gets the nod is a sort of natural person ready to be legalised. And we can perhaps think of these rights and duties

[5] An account of the legal person as a cluster concept is to be found in Ngaire Naffine, *Law's Meaning of Life: Philosophy, Religion, Darwin and the Legal Person* (Oxford, Hart Publishing, 2009) ch 4.

[6] See ibid.

[7] See Ngaire Naffine, 'Who are Law's Persons? From Cheshire Cats to Responsible Subjects' (2003) 66 *MLR* 346.

[8] See Naffine (n 5). Here I consider the relationship between what I call 'realism' and 'legalism', a distinction which has been employed by Visa AJ Kurki, *A Theory of Legal Personhood* (Oxford, Oxford University Press, 2019).

as *adorning* the Person, rather than *making* them. (This is tricky when it comes to the corporation, which is more obviously a piece of legal manufacture, but still the question is often put, 'is the corporation *really* a person?')[9] The question – is this being appropriate subject matter for the legal concept of the Person? – makes perfect sense. However it could be said to elide or conflate the natural and legal meaning of the person and it tends to obscure the politics of personification: that someone is deciding who is the right kind of being to be a Person.[10]

The second more abstract and constructionist meaning has an even greater tendency to obscure the politics that go into the making of Persons. With a good deal of imaginative effort, the Legal Person can be thought of in a strictly formal sense, as the being that *only* comes into existence by acts of law, and only once rights and duties are recognised, and who does not exist before or apart from such an endowment. Now there is no matching process between natural being and legal concept. Rather the Legal Person is considered a pure fiction or creation or construction of law, someone deemed into being, brought into existence, by the assignment of rights and duties. In this view, law makes its Person or, more specifically, rights and duties maketh the Person. As FH Lawson insisted, in this mode:

> We must first note and emphasize the separateness and completeness of what we may call the legal plane ... the instruments with which the business lawyer works do not belong to the world of fact ... Legal personality, estates, and contracts are parts of a world of their own, which is in some way related to the world of fact but is separate from it. It is an artificial world whose members are to some extent arbitrarily, though not irrationally, created to serve certain purposes. Thus they can be defined with fair exactness, much more satisfactorily than the facts of everyday life.[11]

Thus to find a Legal Person at any given legal moment, one will look to formal assignments of rights and duties. Absent such assignments, then absent the Person.

As Hans Kelsen advanced this view, '[t]he person exists only insofar as he [sic] "has" duties and rights; apart from them the person has no existence whatsoever'.[12] And there is no formal need to inquire into the reasons for this assignment or non-assignment of rights and duties. The strictly legal task is to determine the legal uses and operations of these assignments. Or as David Derham expressed this strictly legal quality of Persons in laws:

> Just as the concept 'one' in arithmetic is essential to the logical system developed and yet is not one something (eg, apple or orange, etc.), so a legal system (or any system perhaps) must be provided with a basic unit before legal relationships can be devised ... The legal person is the unit or entity adopted. For the logic of the system it is just as much a pure

[9] Elizabeth H Wolgast, *Ethics of an Artificial Person: Lost Responsibility in Professions and Organizations* (Stanford, Stanford University Press, 1992).

[10] As Fuller argued in Lon L Fuller, *Legal Fictions* (Stanford, Stanford University Press, 1967).

[11] FH Lawson, 'The Creative Use of Legal Concepts' (1957) 32 *New York University Law Review* 907, 913.

[12] Hans Kelsen, *General Theory of Law and State* (translated by Anders Wedberg) (New York, Russell and Russell, 1945) 94.

'concept' as 'one' in arithmetic. It is just as independent from a human being as one is from an 'apple'.[13]

Felix Cohen once satirised this stringently disciplinary way of thinking, regarding it as the route to legal madness or superstition:

> Legal concepts (for example, corporations or property rights) are supernatural entities which do not have a verifiable existence except to the eyes of faith. Rules of law, which refer to these legal concepts, are not descriptions of empirical social facts (such as the customs of men or the customs of judges) nor yet statements of moral ideals, but are rather theorems in an independent system. It follows that a legal argument can never be refuted by a moral principle nor yet by any empirical fact. Jurisprudence, then, as an autonomous system of legal concepts, rules, and arguments, must be independent both of ethics and of such positive sciences as economics or psychology. In effect, it is a special branch of the science of transcendental nonsense.[14]

But as I will spell out more fully, later in the book, I think this may be what those engaged in the creation of modern general jurisprudence are doing, or think they are doing. They know that they must have 'a basic unit before legal relationships can be devised',[15] as Derham put it, but they assume, silently, that they do not need to go into the politico-historical making of the Legal Person. For they are dealing with 'theorems in an independent system'.[16] They can just get on with developing theory of law, with their abstract Legal Person in place, which is why the concept of the person is a vital component of general jurisprudence but is rarely the subject of close analysis. Law's Person gets jurisprudence going. It is fundamental to thinking about the nature of law; what makes law law. But it gets very little air-time.

While the first, naturalistic, approach is more obviously based on moral or political evaluations of the being of concern, the second more formalistic or constructionist view of the Person, I would argue, also harbours a moral and political evaluation, but is less explicit about it. After all, the conditions that determine within law whether X is a person are created by those with the say-so over those conditions, those who have the power to define and explain law's Person. And control over definition and explanation of the Person is a mighty power. Its exercise puts people inside and outside of law.

HLA Hart, perhaps the most influential legal theorist of the twentieth century, advanced strongly a legal constructionist or legal use approach to legal concepts, in his inaugural lecture, where he specifically examined the legal personality of the corporation. There he asserted 'the cardinal principle that legal words can only be elucidated by considering the conditions under which statements in

[13] DP Derham, 'Theories of Legal Personality' in Leicester Webb (ed), *Legal Personality and Political Pluralism* (Carlton, Melbourne University Press, 1958) 5.

[14] Felix Cohen, 'Transcendental Nonsense and the Functional Approach' (1935) 35 *Columbia Law Review* 809, 821.

[15] Derham (n 13) 5.

[16] Cohen (n 14) 821.

which their characteristic use are true'.[17] The task of the legal theorist, bent on elucidating the meaning of legal words and concepts, was to determine and examine 'the legal rules which prescribe in what conditions such a statement [such as the corporation is a person] is correct'.[18] What this set aside, for the purposes of conceptual determination and clarification, was an assessment of the reasons for those conditions.

Hart rejected an approach to the definition of legal words that entailed a search for 'straightforward ... counterparts in the world of fact'.[19] Admittedly, Hart seemed to be thinking of the more abstract legal concepts of right, duty and corporate personality. He said that there was nothing in the world of 'fact' to which you could point and say 'there is "a right" or "a corporation"'. Law didn't work that way. Legal meaning was *not* to be found by matching legal terms or concepts to particular facts outside of law. There was no direct correspondence. Law constructed its own concepts, using its own particular legal meanings; as he might have said, it had its own 'language games'.[20] This seemed to ward off the necessity of matching law to life, and indeed warned against it, when it came to the determination of the meaning of legal terms.[21]

III. The Unavoidable Mix of Uses

I suggest that we are always caught somewhere between these two positions. Though Hart tried to move us away from the correspondence view – saying that law's job was not to match legal concepts to the real world of 'fact' outside of law, to make them correspond – there is a powerful tendency to do just that. Especially when it comes to the morally and politically loaded concept of 'the Person', there is a strong legal leaning towards the correspondence approach, and it is difficult to resist. Even the most theoretically-inclined jurist can assume that there is a being who precedes law, who is in the world of fact, who is being assessed for their suitability for legal life and who can supply a good match. Modern legal decisions about whether say a river should be a Person tend to move between the two meanings.[22]

[17] HLA Hart, *Definition and Theory in Jurisprudence: An Inaugural Lecture Delivered Before the University of Oxford on 30 May 1953* (Oxford, Clarendon Press, 1953) 28. And reprinted in HLA Hart, *Essays in Jurisprudence and Philosophy* (Oxford, Clarendon Press, 1983) 21.

[18] Hart, *Definition and Theory in Jurisprudence*, ibid 26.

[19] ibid 5.

[20] This is Wittgenstein's term which Hart is effectively invoking. In *Philosophical Investigations*, Wittgenstein urged us to ask ourselves '[h]ow did we learn the meaning of this word ("good" for instance)? From what sort of examples? In what language games?': Ludwig Wittgenstein, *Philosophical Investigations* (translated by GEM Anscombe, PMS Hacker and Joachim Schulte) (Oxford, Blackwell, 2009) para 77. In other words, we acquire our understanding of words within communities of meaning.

[21] It must be said that Hart was in favour of evaluating the moral worth of law, and did it himself. But moral worth and legal validity were separate things in his view.

[22] In 2017, the Whanganui River on the north island of New Zealand was made a Legal Person which means that it has legal standing, and its interests are directly protected by law: Te Awa Tupua

In other words, both approaches coexist in law and theory and there is often a slide between the two which goes unstated. There are typically philosophical differences between those who favour one understanding of the Person over the other. The correspondence view tends to support a search for the right kinds of being to match law's Person: the right man for the job. The constructionist (or legal use) view is more agnostic about whether there is a right kind of being for personification and the intellectual focus is more on the formal rights and duties which make the Person, and whether at any given moment of legal determination they can be found to exist. But as I will show, the politics are usually there, in the background. When the variable operation of the two approaches goes unrecognised, when it goes unnoticed that legal meaning can vacillate, there is room for obfuscation. This means that harm can be done to those under consideration (as potential candidates for full or partial Personhood) but the infliction of harm may go unnoticed. The casualties of fuzzy legal reasoning about the nature of Persons, and who should and should not be one, can fall by the wayside.

IV. The Fitting Subject

The link between the factual being and legal being is really always there. For if there is a strong authoritative legal endorsement of a factual being, if they get a strong tick of legal approval, then they will be recognised by a generous conferral of rights and duties and become rich Legal Persons. They will be found to correspond with law's idea of a Person. And the cluster of rights (and duties) creating the Person will be extensive. However, if this endorsement is missing, or if it is weak, then our *potential* legal being, who is undergoing assessment, will have a poor legal existence. Their life will be pallid as far as *law* is concerned, but they will exist, as far as *they* are concerned, assuming they have consciousness. For in order to exist in law and to act in law and to use law for the advancement of their own interests, they need the endowment of rights which usually comes with duties. Without them, theirs is a reduced existence, a life of incapacities.

Dogs, for example, have little in the way of positive legal existence, though they of course have their own existence. They are not Legal Persons (though they could be) and are more accurately regarded in law as property.[23] By contrast, human babies have a considerable range of rights but no duties, and yet they are typically regarded as Legal Persons.[24] And the rational adult human, today, has most of the

(Whanganui River Claims Settlement) Act 2017 (NZ). See Patrick Barkham, 'Should Rivers Have the Same Rights as People?' *The Observer* (London, 21 July 2021).

[23] On the distinction between persons and property, see Davies and Naffine (n 4). On the legal status of animals, see Steven Wise, *Drawing the Line: Science and the Case for Animal Rights* (Cambridge, Perseus Publishing, 2002); and more recently Geeta Shyam, 'Is the Classification of Animals as Property Consistent with Modern Community Attitudes?' (2018) 41 *University of New South Wales Law Journal* 1418.

[24] On the legal status of humans of limited reason, see Naffine (n 5) ch 6.

pantheon of rights and duties – to contract, to own property, to vote, to complain of crime, to be educated and so on. Adult dogs, especially say trained guide dogs, have better cognition and decision-making ability than newborn human babies. So the law's evaluation of the relative value of the dog and the human baby does not depend on their innate qualities; rather it depends on a social/cultural/political determination of whether they should enter law as rights and perhaps duty bearers.[25]

There are therefore beings who are considered, by law, fitting subjects for rights and duties, who thus become able to act in law, once there is a legal conferral, and other beings who are not. That is, there are beings who are considered inappropriate for the conferral of rights. This is where legal existence gets tricky. For a legal view is being taken of whether a given being is the right sort of being to enter law: a legal assessment of the being occurs before the legal endowment of rights/duties creating the legal being.[26]

There is therefore a legal assessment of beings before they come into law as its subjects. They do not escape law by not being admitted as subjects; they just go somewhere else, where their lives will be impoverished by law. For some, the doors of law remain closed; they are considered (by law) ill-suited to the endowment of rights and duties, and so they are not permitted in as Persons. They can only become legally personified if law recognises them as suitable for personification. This legal assessment of a being's suitability for Legal Personhood can be linked to a political/philosophical position in law, that rights have natural subjects.

Whether legal personification is understood as the endowment of rights and duties which, once recognised, serve to create an always abstract legal being, or whether it is thought of as the determination of whether an existing being is fit for rights and duties,[27] the making of a Person in law is a way of assigning value and power, though this is only briefly alluded to by Hart. And beings or things that are made by, or endowed with, the most ample set of rights are the most powerful Persons. The concept of the Person is therefore a powerful political tool.

On either view of the Legal Person, as a pure creation of law or as pre-legal being (assessed for its natural fitness for rights) there has been one great defining consistency. The being who has ended up best equipped to act in law, the favoured subject who has always attracted the best set of rights, has been male. Men have been the most strongly personed, whether their Personhood has been understood as a legal creation or whether men have been thought of as pre-legal beings naturally attracting rights, like a magnet. And hence men, the ones most valued, have

[25] Peter Singer has pursued this point in a number of places. A useful collection of his papers advancing this argument is Helga Kuhse (ed), *Unsanctifying Human Life: Essays on Ethics* (Oxford, Blackwell Publishing, 2002).

[26] This situation is further complicated by the personality of the corporation which is not a natural being but is still brought into being by law; but again there is an evaluation being made of whether such a legal being serves social purposes.

[27] On whether law is reflective or constitutive of reality, see Maleiha Malik, 'Faith and the State of Jurisprudence' in Peter Oliver, Sionaidh Douglas Scott and Victor Tadros (eds), *Faith in Law: Essays in Legal Theory* (Oxford, Hart Publishing, 2000) 129.

been permitted to live the richest legal lives: they have been endowed with the best property rights; the best political and educational rights; they have been best protected by the offences against the person.

V. The Man as the Right Kind of Being

Historically, the Legal Person has been imagined as a man and I will be showing how, in important ways, he still is. As we will see in the next two chapters, through the nineteenth century and well into the twentieth century, when legal officials were asked to define law's 'Person', for the purpose of an endowment of fundamental rights (say the right of 'a Person' to vote, or the right of 'a Person' to receive university education), they said that 'the Person' in contemplation of law was a man, because the given right was designed for men. Thus Legal Persons and biological men were judicially conflated, and this conflation was given the force of law. Through the strong and repeated actions of legal officials, law's concept of the Person, as it arose in power-giving personifying laws, was treated as synonymous with natural men. Men of legal authority (and men were the only ones with legal authority) thus controlled and explained the definition of the concept of the Person, as it arose in power-conferring laws, and they assigned him their own sex.

The practice of eliding 'Persons' with 'men' goes back further still. Memorable and enduring are the words of William Blackstone on the elimination of women as Persons and their replacement by men, now engorged with Legal Personality. In his statement on coverture, uttered in 1765 in his *Commentaries on the Laws of England*, Blackstone articulated the vastness of male legal power over women, at the point of marriage, achieved through the concept of the Person.

> By marriage, the husband and wife are one person in law: that is, the very being or legal existence of the woman is suspended during the marriage, or at least is incorporated and consolidated into that of the husband: under whose wing, protection, and cover, she performs everything; and is therefore called in our law-french a *feme-covert*; is said to be … under the protection and influence of her husband, her baron, or lord; and her condition during her marriage is called her coverture. Upon this principle, of an union of person in husband and wife, depend almost all the legal rights, duties, and disabilities, that either of them acquire by the marriage. … For this reason, a man cannot grant any thing to his wife, or enter into covenant with her: for the grant would be to suppose her separate existence; and to covenant with her would be only to covenant with himself.[28]

As I said in *Criminal Law and the Man Problem*,

> [i]t is hard to imagine a stronger endorsement of the deliberate legal erasure of one person by another, the passing of control over one life to another. The husband was made the master of the very being, the mind, the will and the body, of his wife.[29]

[28] William Blackstone, *Commentaries on the Laws of England* vol 1 (Oxford, Clarendon Press, 1765) 430.
[29] Ngaire Naffine, *Criminal Law and the Man Problem* (Oxford, Hart Publishing, 2019) 46.

Blackstone's coverture statement was to prove hugely influential. It has been described as '[o]ne of the most quoted passages' of the *Commentaries*.[30]

Coverture, the covering of the existence of one person by another, was profoundly symbolic. It entailed the notion of a total covering, a folding over, a containment and encapsulation of a woman by a man, once she was married to him. Blackstone had no difficulty in talking of the legal extinction of married women; it was not too strong to call such women non-persons, non-existent. And, as we will see, elements of this way of thinking of married women persisted well into the twentieth century (with the lawfulness of wife rape).

Coverture was a big, broad, loose idea meant to convey the thoroughness of the domination and subordination of women by men, once married, or their 'subjection', as John Stuart Mill was to put it a century later (see chapter three). It spoke of the rightness and naturalness of male power over a woman, as soon as she became a wife. The idea of coverture as described by Blackstone was bigger, more encompassing, than the actual law, than the actual male control of women through law. However, the idea described the acceptable and the useful: a desirable system of male domination. Its woolliness, its vagueness, didn't matter. Or rather it was acceptable, even in its woolliness, because it conveyed the right message and hence proved highly durable. Certainly Blackstone's reputation was not harmed by these pronouncements about the status of women.

Sir Matthew Hale had already declared that, upon marriage, a wife gave herself up to her husband. In 1736, in his *History of the Pleas of the Crown*,[31] Hale gave this brief account of the sexual rights of the husband to the wife, thereby ousting the law of rape.[32] He said that

> the husband cannot be guilty of a rape committed by himself upon his lawful wife, for by their mutual matrimonial consent and contract the wife hath given up herself in this kind unto her husband, which she cannot retract.[33]

Hale's pronouncement on the immunity of husbands from rape prosecution was written extra-judicially and published posthumously, 60 years after his death. So these are writings from the seventeenth century and by a judge who believed in witchcraft, and who presided over a successful prosecution under the Witchcraft Act which resulted in the execution of the convicted women.[34] They are the thoughts of a legal authority who was undergoing a transition from the medieval

[30] Tim Stretton, 'Coverture and Unity of Person in Blackstone's Commentaries' in Wilfrid R Prest (ed), *Blackstone and His Commentaries: Biography, Law, History* (Oxford, Hart Publishing, 2009) 111.

[31] Matthew Hale, *Historia Placitorum Coronae* vol 1 (edited by PR Glazebrook) (London, Professional Books, 1971) 627.

[32] Hale's principle was exported to India in its Penal Code 1860, it is still in operation, and, at the time of writing, a decision of the Indian Supreme Court is pending as to whether the immunity is constitutional. Hale was treated as an important authority by the US Supreme Court in *Dobbs v Jackson Women's Health Organization* (5th Cir, No 19-1392, 24 June 2022) slip op 1.

[33] Hale (n 31) 629.

[34] See Gilbert Geis and Ivan Bunn, *A Trial of Witches: A Seventeenth-Century Witchcraft Prosecution* (London, Routledge, 1997).

to the modern, and had yet to get there. As Kos Lesses has observed, Hale thus supplied 'the original written source for what is known in English common law as the husband's "immunity" from prosecution of rape committed against his wife' and (as we will see in chapter six) the immunity persisted, century after century, by dint of the great reputation of Hale and in the absence of any effective refutation.[35]

VI. The Person and the Individual

The Legal Person, as we have seen, is a formal legal concept connoting the rights and duty bearer. The term Legal Person can thus denote law's general legal subject (the Person recognised by and in law, with their changing constellation of rights and duties, which can be richer or poorer). And the concept of the Legal Person may also be employed in a narrower, law-specific sense: it can be the critical term in a particular rights-conferring law, such as a law that confers the right of 'a person' to vote or the right of 'a person' to stand for election. The de-personification of women on a law-by law-basis is the subject of the next two chapters.

The Legal Person is strictly speaking not a natural being nor thing, something or someone you could point at or touch, but an abstraction. It is a legal idea, and a legal device, made up of the abstractions which are legal rights and duties. It is a *cluster* concept, clustering variable rights and duties which coalesce to form the concept. It shares this defining attribute with the legal idea of property which is also a cluster concept, made up of variable rights and duties.[36] These personifying legal rights and duties exist in legal relations *between* Legal Persons (who are themselves clusters of rights and duties), hence there is an inherent circularity to the concept of the Legal Person. Rights and duties make the Person, but rights and duties are always in relation to Persons and between Persons, though it is the rights and duties which make the Person. And so on. But, as we have also seen, real natural human beings, of variable valuation, are typically the subjects of these rights and duties.

Though it can sometimes be employed as a synonym for the Legal Person, the term Legal Individual is more political in nature, but nevertheless it is a concept used extensively in law and so calls for some explaining. It too has formal and abstract properties. And it is the Legal Individual who comes to assume an important linguistic and heuristic role in modern jurisprudence (as we will see in chapter 10). The concept of the Legal Individual, which derives more from political theory than jurisprudence, as the term itself suggests, connotes someone

[35] Kos Lesses, 'PGA v The Queen: Marital Rape in Australia: The Role of Repetition' (2014) 37 *Melbourne University Law Review* 786, 787.

[36] The concept of property has also been described as a cluster or bundle of rights and duties. See Davies and Naffine (n 4). For a classic statement of the various rights and duties (the sticks in the bundle) that constitute property, see AM Honoré, 'Ownership' in AG Guest (ed), *Oxford Essays in Jurisprudence* (Oxford, Oxford University Press, 1961).

who is unitary and indivisible; autonomous and discrete. Somehow it connotes a singularity rather than a plurality. Though, as we will see, it is much in use by legal thinkers, it owes a strong debt to liberal political theory, with its idea of a separate and discrete, bounded, freely contracting being, making decisions of legal significance for its own unitary self and respecting the decisions of the unitary selves of others. The Legal Individual owes much to the Lockean story of contract with its rise of the modern autonomous contracting individual. Locke conceived of the person as 'a thinking, intelligent being, that has reason and reflection, and can consider itself the same thinking thing, in different times and places'.[37]

The Individual is an idea further developed and articulated influentially by John Stuart Mill who is more fully considered in the next chapter. In this view we are rational self-governing choosers who are fitting legal subjects (who can assume the rights and duties which paradoxically make us) because of our defining capacity for the free autonomous exercise of reason, especially as those decisions determine our lives as Individuals. Because we can engage in free rational choices, we can be held to account, as Individuals, for those individual choices. Or as Lawrence Friedman put it: 'Modern law presupposes a society of free-standing, autonomous individuals.'[38] But as Mill clarified (again see the next chapter), there are moral and legal limits to our choices: we must not harm others by the decisions that we make. Thus our decisions are limited by their adverse effects on others, especially as they encroach on the physical persons of others. We cannot harm others. But over ourselves we are sovereign and this is defining of ourselves as Individuals.[39]

Like the Legal Person, the Legal Individual is both concept and abstraction. Although it typically refers to human beings, it gives those beings various defining attributes such as free choice or free will, as well as individuation and indivisibility and bodily integrity, which are all quite abstract ideas. Human beings don't really make sense as free-standing choosing autonomous Individuals, perhaps understood as separate and distinct from other like beings and the rest of the world. Instead they are porous and vulnerable biological beings, who for much of their lives actively need the intervention of others to survive, and necessarily they depend on the decisions of others. Separated they would die. We are unlike, say, tortoises that do not receive parental care after hatching but are left to their fate.

The bounded nature of human beings, understood as liberal Individuals, is a manufactured idea. In 'The Body Bag' I explained that it is an act of culture and imagination to see a human being as a bordered Individual: a being with clearly defined and non-porous borders. People are not inherently thus, and it takes a good deal of abstraction and invention to see us in this way.[40]

[37] John Locke, *An Essay Concerning Human Understanding* (London, Ward, Lock, & Co, 1689) 246.

[38] Lawrence Friedman, 'Is there a Modern Legal Culture?' (1994) 7 *Ratio Juris* 117, 125, quoted in Brian Z Tamanaha, *A General Jurisprudence of Law and Society* (Oxford, Oxford University Press, 2001) 120.

[39] The harm principle was enunciated by John Stuart Mill, *On Liberty* (London, John W Parker and Son, 1859).

[40] Ngaire Naffine, 'The Body Bag' in Ngaire Naffine and Rosemary J Owens (eds), *Sexing the Subject of Law* (London, Sweet & Maxwell, 1997). And for much more on the idea of the bounded individual, see

The attribute of 'bodily integrity' is often given to the Individual, to indicate this wholeness and distinctiveness, the bordered nature of being.[41] But again, this is not easily specified and captured as something real in the world. The Individual defined by their bodily integrity is a set of ideas rather than, say, something you could draw or take a picture of. Would they be a baby, an adult or an older person? Would they be able-bodied? Would they be male or female or something else again? What if they were eating and drinking or simply breathing or engaged in sexual activities? What if the individual were pregnant? Is she now somehow unbounded and divisible? What does bodily integrity look like?

The Legal Person and the Legal Individual both have a strong male history. The Legal Person, as we will see, has been defined explicitly as a man for many legal purposes, associated with political and legal power. And in political theory and also legal theory, the idea of the autonomous choosing Individual possessed of bodily integrity, has also had strong associations with men. He is the individual chooser, the one who decides how his life will go, asserting his personal autonomy as he keeps others at arm's length (unless they are wives).

VII. The Divided Population: Men and Women

As we will see in the ensuing analysis of the Persons Cases, for most of the period under consideration, and before, a raw basic biological determination of 'sex', by dint of the presence of male or female genitalia at birth, set one's life course. If one were 'sexed' male, law sent you off in one direction. It enabled, it preferred, it endowed, it personed and individuated. If one were 'sexed' female, the life course was dramatically different. It disabled, demoted, disendowed, unpersoned. It knocked down the borders of women. The preferences of the human about their own sexed lives made little difference.

There was a second legal moment in the life trajectory of men and women, when the courses of the two sexes both connected and diverged, by dint of law. Upon marriage, there was immediately a set of legal accruals for the husband and losses for the wife, as Blackstone articulated so graphically. The coming together of a man and a woman, by marriage, reset their legal statuses, deepening the legal differences. Though thought of as a contract, marriage had few of the indicia of a free commercial agreement, because the terms were set by the state not the parties, and the state asserted the supremacy of the man and the subordination of the woman.[42] The body of the woman was surrendered to the man, for sexual purposes as Hale made plain. Her property also passed to him. Typically she was

the works of Jennifer Nedelsky and especially Jennifer Nedelsky, 'Law, Boundaries, and the Bounded Self' (1990) 30 *Representations* 162.

[41] This is a term much used in medical law and also in the law of assault. See Ngaire Naffine, 'Hidden Presuppositions and the Problem of Paradigm Persons: Visa AJ Kurki's "A Theory of Legal Personhood"' (2021) 44 *Revus* 127.

[42] See Carole Pateman, *The Sexual Contract* (Cambridge, Polity Press, 1988).

renamed. And any children were legally controlled by the man.[43] His domicile was her domicile.[44]

Judith Butler has written about the performativity of sex or gender: she has argued that iterations or repetitions, continuing performances, bring gender into being and develop and sustain it.[45] This may well be so, but what I am talking about is in many ways cruder and more brutal than this. I am talking about a deep cut once made right through the middle of the population, so that slightly more than half was given a bad deal by law, from the moment of birth, and the other half was preferred. The course was fixed. And efforts to change it, by women and their allies, efforts to claw back to women some of the most basic rights to live a civic life, were suppressed and justified, sometimes with shows of contempt, as we will see in the next two chapters. Hard power was deployed. And we are still feeling its effects.

This bifurcation of the population, by basic biological sex, according to the presence of male or female genitalia, at birth, has been foundational for law, creating two legal populations: one endowed with a richness of rights, the other stripped of them. The division has been so basic, so fundamental, that it seems that in the modern world (where sex is no longer meant to matter, in terms of the distribution of power), it is just too big to contemplate, even by legal intellectuals whose task it is to make sense of the nature of law. And so it has been willed away, as we will see later in the book when I consider the state of current legal theory.

I am keenly aware that considerable changes have occurred very recently in the law of sex and gender. No longer are birth genitalia finally determinative of sex, for a person's lifetime; there is no longer a sharp and permanent division between members of the population according to their birth genitalia; and this is an extraordinary change.[46] The old sharp sex binary has been altered. But this does not change the foundational truth, which should confront anyone wishing to theorise and understand the nature of law, that a sharp sex binary, between men and women, has characterised law until very recently and that it has had profound effects. This problem has not gone away.

VIII. Men in, Women Out

The Legal Person and the Individual are central to liberal legal theory and men have been seen naturally to fit these concepts, with their supposed impervious borders

[43] On the early non-rights of married women, see Tim Stretton and Krista Kesselring (eds), *Married Women and the Law: Coverture in England and the Common Law World* (Montreal, McGill-Queen's University Press, 2013).

[44] 'The common law position of married women prior to 1 January 1974 was that the domicile of a married woman was that of her husband, that is, she acquired a domicile of dependence from him. Her domicile thus changed with his. This was the case throughout the UK.': HM Revenue & Customs, 'Residence, Domicile and Remittance Basis Manual' (*Gov.com*, 15 May 2024), available at www.gov.uk/hmrc-internal-manuals/residence-domicile-and-remittance-basis/rdrm22240.

[45] See Judith Butler, *Gender Trouble: Feminism and the Subversion of Identity* (New York, Routledge, 1999).

[46] Gender Recognition Act 2004.

and bodily integrity and their sovereignty over self and right to choose their relations. Women have, in important ways, been classified out of these concepts and undertheorised or rather not theorised at all as either Individuals or Persons. Women have often been implicitly missing from these concepts because they were essentially intended to denote a man. Women remain untheorised as Individuals which makes them vulnerable to arguments that they are neither Individuals nor Persons, especially when pregnant, as we will see in chapter eight.

This is not to suggest that there is such a thing as a true Person or Individual, one that we need to divine, for the very ideas of the Person and the Individual are artefacts of law and culture and of those who have had the power and influence to bring them into being. (And as Scott Gilbert the biologist has said, there is no such thing as an individual in biological life.[47]) Thus, I am not saying that there is an essential Person or Individual that law is not, yet, getting right. For I think they are cultural concepts and constructs produced by definitions and supporting explanations supplied by those with the power to advance them. Rather, I am trying to consider how the concepts of the Person and the Individual have operated in the 'language games' of law, past and present, as they apply to men and women. Men as Persons have been well considered. One could say that men have been the gold standard Persons.[48]

As we will see, even today, the idea of a female Legal Person, or Legal Person who is a woman, and the idea of the female Individual or Individual who is a woman are poorly conceptualised. This is despite the continuing operational nature of both concepts in law. Women's personhood and individualism are so untheorised that the present-day woman remains susceptible to legal analysis drawing on ancient and medieval figures, notably Aristotle, Aquinas, Blackstone and Hale, who were all opposed to women's Personhood and Individualism. Especially when a woman is pregnant, her Personhood becomes precarious. The abstraction of the Legal Person as well as the abstraction of the Legal Individual tend to import a male human form, understood as a being that is always discrete and distinct and independent of other similar types of being and who never divides. And this conceptual ambiguity is something that the legal theorist John Finnis has taken advantage of (see chapter eight).

IX. Controlling Definition and Entitling Men

Or to put it another way, men of legal authority, who have exclusively controlled the definition of the Person in law, have defined it as a concept befitting men rather than women, especially when the concept has come with a generous package of

[47] See Scott F Gilbert, 'Pseudo-Embryology and Personhood: How Embryological Pseudoscience Helps Structure the American Abortion Debate' (2023) 3(1) *Natural Sciences*, available at onlinelibrary.wiley.com/doi/epdf/10.1002/ntls.20220041.

[48] To borrow an insight from my legal friend Ian Leader-Elliott.

powers. The definition of the Person, and its justifications and explanations, have secured it as a concept for the benefit of men. Though fully aware of the artificial nature of the concept of the Person, and its potential uses to empower fairly and equitably, and indeed not to fix the concept on to any particular subject, as we will see, men of law have made the term correspond with their desired subject: people of their own sex, especially when the term has been associated with the conferral of public power. This self-serving practice will be considered in the next two chapters.

And so it is not just a being's humanity that has attracted the best rights (as compared with the legal plight of say the dog or the pig, largely reduced to the status of property and in the latter case, food). The maleness of the human being has also consistently mattered. There has been no chameleon-like movement between men and women in the legal making, or characterisation, of the most enabled Legal Person. This suggests that for much of the time there has been an operating underlying legal belief that there are the right kinds of being and the wrong kinds of being to be fully endowed with rights and duties and richly personified. Thus the Legal Person has hardly ever been a neutral, abstract, technical device designed to achieve a wide variety of legal purposes, but has much more typically been linked to an understanding of what and who already have value. The richly or thickly-conceived Legal Person has had a male persona; the more thinly-conceived person has been female.

And this male preferment, employing personification, has made an enormous difference to law as well as to men and women. It has coloured the entire legal landscape, with great consistency, over the centuries and into the present. The concept of the Legal Person has been an important means of creating and augmenting male rights by undermining female rights or refusing to assign rights to women. It has been one of the primary means of politically, legally, socially and economically incapacitating half the population and empowering the other. And in this way, society and the polity have been organised according to a divided system of the legally privileged and the legally underprivileged.

With the Persons Cases, as we will see in the next chapter, we have a legal device and technique, entailing a deeming of X as Person or non-person; a deeming explicitly employed to achieve exclusion. Recently this technique has been revived and given new applications: in modern usage the deeming tends to provide a means of inclusion. Rivers, in particular, have been the formal recipients of these benefits.[49]

X. The Moral Concept

Finally, what are we to make of the fact that law uses the word 'person' to designate its subject? Does the term itself matter? Does it import certain meanings? I suggest that it does. The concept of the Legal Person bears a close relation to the

[49] On the personification of the Jamuna River in Bangladesh, see Naveeda Khan, *River Life and the Upspring of Nature* (Durham, Duke University Press, 2023).

moral concept of the person – that is a being who counts, who is a moral subject, someone who should be respected. The Person as legal fiction, as fictional character, therefore has a strong 'family resemblance' to the moral concept.[50] To assign the term Legal Person to one class of beings (men), for the most empowering legal purposes, and to refuse to assign it to another (women) is therefore a strong statement of evaluation, positive and negative respectively.[51]

Much use has been made of these movements between the different registers of the person – from legal concept to moral being – by the men of law. To assert coverture, to assert that women were not Persons in the Persons Cases, to deny wives the thin protections of rape law, was to engage in powerful political acts, highly damaging to women, highly empowering of men, and performed with swagger and hubris, because women were seen as lesser moral beings. Blackstone did not flinch from saying that the husband extinguished the legal existence of his wife by absorbing her into his Person.

The use of the word 'person' to reduce the lives of women therefore tells us volumes about past and present understandings of the human being. It has been as direct a way as possible of saying that women were subhuman. No flinching. No resiling from it. As we will see in the Persons Cases, presiding judges relished this demeaning of women. It is truly chilling and the current way of thinking about the legal subject takes this as its unashamed history.

As we will see in the next two chapters, the concept of the Person was to prove a highly effective means of asserting and sustaining male legal power and hence male status. The Persons Cases employed a fundamental legal concept, 'the person', to declare and achieve the exclusivity of male legal entitlement to public and professional life; to say that men were the ones who mattered. The concept of the Legal Person was used by men of authority to secure and sustain men's immense legal power and importance, with the ensuing costs to the polity and to society in general. The Persons Cases declared this simply and clearly without embarrassment, as simply true.

In the ensuing chapters I ask: What did the judges in these cases take to be true when they were convinced that the Person had to be a man and made explicit this view (especially when they were in correspondence mode, matching human beings to the legal concept)? How did they understand themselves, as men endowed with exclusive public rights, and how did they understand women? Why did it seem acceptable to capacitate themselves through law and to incapacitate women? In other words, I endeavour to enter the mentality of men of legal power and work out why they took it to be right and natural that they alone should be legal subjects who were fully empowered to act in law.

[50] Again to borrow a term from Wittgenstein (n 20).

[51] In 'Who are Law's Persons?' I explain this movement between the legal fiction and the moral and vernacular concepts of the person: Naffine (n 7). See also Naffine (n 5).

3

Definitional Power in the Victorian Period: John Stuart Mill, James Fitzjames Stephen and the Persons Cases

I. Introduction

In 1859, in *On Liberty*, John Stuart Mill articulated a set of moral, political and legal precepts, now known as 'the harm principle'. Embedded in Mill's statement of liberal principle was the Individual: an autonomous, self-governing, sovereign human being, whose fundamental right was to exclude others from their body. It is a fine and rich piece of writing, worth repeating in full.

> The object of this Essay is to assert one very simple principle, as entitled to govern absolutely the dealings of society with *the individual* in the way of compulsion and control, whether the means used be physical force in the form of legal penalties, or the moral coercion of public opinion. That principle is, that the sole end for which mankind are warranted, individually or collectively, in interfering with the liberty of action of *any of their number*, is self-protection. That the only purpose for which power can be rightfully exercised over *any member* of a civilized community, against his will, is to prevent harm to others. His own good, either physical or moral, is not a sufficient warrant. He cannot rightfully be compelled to do or forbear because it will be better for him to do so, because it will make him happier, because, in the opinion of others, to do so would be wise, or even right. … The only part of the conduct *of anyone*, for which he is amenable to society, is that which concerns others. In the part which merely concerns himself, his independence is, of right, absolute. Over himself, over his own body and mind, *the individual* is sovereign (emphasis added).[1]

Though Mill spoke of *man*kind, he meant this to refer to *human*kind, for he spoke also of *any member of a civilised community* and what the state could legitimately do to this being and what it could not. And this individual should have absolute rights over the self.

Mill's statement of 'the harm principle', his declaration of the limits of legitimate state intervention in the life of 'anyone', body and mind, was taken up as a declaration of fundamental political and legal liberal principle. It has supplied a

[1] John Stuart Mill, *On Liberty* (London, John W Parkers and Son, 1859) 21–22.

liberal conception of the Individual, from then to the present day. This being still inhabits the criminal law classrooms of the twenty first century, as students are told of the supposed limits of state authority over each of us.[2]

Mill understood well the relationship between words and power: how legal power could be wielded with terms and definitions. He knew that with words and their manipulation, the exercise of power could be made to appear civil, but have harsh effects on real lives, could even be brutal. This artful legal brutality, specifically directed at women, was made the subject of a later book, *The Subjection of Women*,[3] to which we will return.

II. Mill's Endeavours to Challenge Male Power and to Get Women a Legal Life

Mill made it plain, throughout his life, that actual English law did not permit women to be Individuals and that this state constraint on their humanity did a grave disservice to women, to society in general, and also to men, who were brutalised by their legally-endorsed powers over women. And it did a disservice to law itself. In making this claim, Mill was also well aware of the opposition he would face. As the historian Christopher Harvie remarked: 'John Stuart Mill became a pillar of the mid-Victorian Liberal Party, eccentric only in his desire to extend "incorporation" to the half of the population whom politics ignored – women'.[4]

In this chapter, I consider Mill's varied endeavours to improve the legal lives of women, to bring them into law, in fact to give women a legal life. I consider the robust rejection of these endeavours by his contemporaries, notably James Fitzjames Stephen, as well as the responses of the men of the legislature and the courts to the efforts of men such as Mill (men being the only holders of public power, both its supporters and its critics) to have women thought of as Individuals and formally classified as Legal Persons who could exercise public power.

The Persons Cases of the nineteenth century reveal how the men of law responded to demands for female Personhood in the public sphere: and it was with a profound sense of male entitlement. And these cases show how legal officials sought to justify male control over the lives of women and men's exclusive rights to the exercise of public power, and how they made it law. They chose the strongest, most audacious way possible: they said that we men are Persons but you women are not Persons and, because of that, you do not have public rights; you do not have the right to be educated or to vote or to hold public office. Only

[2] See the works of Joel Feinberg, *The Moral Limits of the Criminal Law* vols 1–4 (New York, Oxford University Press, 1984–88).

[3] John Stuart Mill, *The Subjection of Women* (London, Longmans, Green, Reader and Dyer, 1869).

[4] Christopher Harvie, 'Revolution and the Rule of Law (1789–1851)' in Kenneth O Morgan (ed), *The Oxford Illustrated History of Britain* (Oxford, Oxford University Press, 1986) 461.

men do. And nor do you have sovereign rights to your person. They spoke for law, and said that they were protecting law, and their reputations were, if anything, enhanced by their advocacy of male control of law and their active exclusion of women.

Mill lived from 1806 to 1873, which makes him a mid-Victorian. He was a fine political thinker and wordsmith which is not surprising given his mastery of foreign languages as a child, acquired under the relentless tutelage of his father.[5] He employed his facility with words throughout his life, as writer, politician, political philosopher, husband, political activist and civil servant. Mill was exercised by the poor treatment of women through law, their classification as legal outsiders, and law's active preferential treatment of men. Mill objected to the absolute nature of male political and legal power and tried to change it. He set out to alter critical legislative terms so that men could no longer exercise exclusive public power and so that women could come into law. He wrote eloquently about the need for all people to have personal freedom, women too, which included sovereign rights over themselves. He condemned law for not granting these rights to women, only to men.

III. Mill as Campaigner for Women's Rights to be Persons

Mill's work for women began early. He was arrested at the age of 17 for distributing leaflets on contraception.[6] He was already aware of the need for women to have control over their capacity to reproduce, if they were to be free Individuals. As youthful pamphleteer, then as MP and later as political writer, Mill objected to the concentration, and exclusivity, of male legal power and tried to change it. According to legal historian KJ Smith, Mill was 'a strenuous platform campaigner for the cause [of women] into the early 1870s'.[7]

Three years before his death, Mill was still campaigning for women's right to bodily autonomy. The Contagious Diseases Acts of 1864, 1866 and 1869 were passed essentially to ensure the good health of military men. They permitted any woman suspected of prostitution to be arrested, internally inspected, and detained

[5] See John Stuart Mill, *Autobiography* (London, Longmans, Green, Reader and Dyer, 1873). According to his entry in the *Stanford Encyclopedia of Philosophy* by Christopher MacLeod, '[s]tarting with Greek at age three and Latin at age eight, Mill had absorbed most of the classical canon by age twelve – along with algebra, Euclid, and the major Scottish and English historians': Christopher Macleod, 'John Stuart Mill' (*The Stanford Encyclopedia of Philosophy*, Summer edn, 2020), available at plato.stanford.edu/entries/mill/.

[6] Richard Reeves, 'John Stuart Mill' (2007) 153–54 *Salmagundi* 47, 47. As Reeves observes, Mill did not separate 'thought and action' and was willing to go to prison for his beliefs and did so: 48.

[7] KJM Smith, *James Fitzjames Stephen: Portrait of a Victorian Rationalist* (Cambridge, Cambridge University Press, 1988) 186.

if found to have a contagious disease.[8] The second Act extended the time of imprisonment to a year. This state intervention and punishment did not apply to the male customers. The law was entirely one-sided. Mill was highly critical of this legislation. As Jose and McLoughlin explain,

> Mill gave evidence before a Royal Commission set up in 1870 to investigate workings of the Acts. … Mill opposed the [Contagious Diseases Acts] because they took away 'the security of personal liberty … almost entirely from a particular class of women intentionally, but incidentally and unintentionally, one may say, from all women whatever'.[9]

Mill is perhaps better known for his advocacy of the public political powers of women. In 1866, he brought before the House of Commons the Women's Suffrage Petition in the capacity of MP.[10] Emily Davies and Elizabeth Garrett brought the document to Parliament:

> The story was later told that to avoid attention on arrival in Westminster Hall, they concealed it under the stall of an apple seller, which is where Mill found it. … the House of Commons Select Committee on Public Petitions counted and logged 1521 signatures. … Mill spoke on the petition on 17 July 1866.[11]

The Petition was unsuccessful.

Mill's chance 'for bolder action' to obtain votes for women came a year later, 'when the Conservative ministry introduced its own reform bill in 1867'.[12] On his birthday, the 20th of May, he moved, 'in a powerful and eloquent speech', to replace the word 'man' used within The Representation of the People Bill with the term 'person'.[13]

The title of the Representation of the People Act 1867,[14] also known as the Second Reform Act, employed the term 'People'. But then section 3 said that '[e]very Man shall … be entitled to be registered as a voter' who is 'of full age and not subject to any legal incapacity', who is 'owner or tenant'. Then each section, up to section 6, began with '[e]very Man …'. By changing the word 'man' to 'person', Mill believed that women must be included in the franchise (for after all, weren't

[8] See Sandra Stanley Holton, 'State Pandering, Medical Policing and Prostitution: The Controversy within the Medical Profession concerning the Contagious Diseases Legislation 1864–1886' (1988) 9 *Research in Law, Deviance and Social Control* 149.

[9] Jim Jose and Kcasey McLoughlin, 'John Stuart Mill and the Contagious Diseases Acts: Whose Law? Whose Liberty? Whose Greater Good?' (2016) 34 *Law and History Review* 249.

[10] Though Mill submitted the petition, as only a man could, a small group of highly astute pioneering suffragists engineered the petition. See Theodora Bostick, 'The Press and the Launching of the Women's Suffrage Movement, 1866–1867' (1980) 13 *Victorian Periodicals Review* 125.

[11] 'Presenting the 1866 Petition' (*UK Parliament*), available at www.parliament.uk/about/living-heritage/transformingsociety/electionsvoting/womenvote/parliamentary-collections/1866-suffrage-petition/presenting-the-petition/.

[12] Kathryn Rix, '"The First Humble Beginnings of an Agitation": The Women's Suffrage Petition of 7 June 1866' (*The Victorian Commons*, 7 June 2016), available at victoriancommons.wordpress.com/2016/06/07/the-first-humble-beginnings-of-an-agitation-the-womens-suffrage-petition-of-7-june-1866/.

[13] ibid.

[14] Representation of the People Act 1867.

women persons?) Thus Mill sought to introduce voting rights for women by a change of terms. 'He tabled an amendment asking for the enfranchisement of all households, regardless of sex.'[15] (But in fact the word 'person' would not pose a problem for the men of law, for they were perfectly willing to say that women were not Persons.)

Mill later described his endeavour to alter the wording of the Second Reform Act as 'perhaps the only really important, public service I performed in the capacity as a Member of Parliament'.[16] For even though it failed (73 men in favour, 196 men against), Mill managed to attract the support of a good number of fellow parliamentarians. 'Mill was delighted by the level of support, which came from both sides of the House.'[17] According to the British historian, HCG Matthew:

> The movement for women's suffrage went back to JS Mill's attempt to amend the 1867 Reform Bill to give women the vote. Some progress was made, for some women gained the vote for local elections [etc] … But the marginal public role given to middle-class women in the 1870s and 1880s – helping the priest, the doctor, or the MP; being secretary to the charity whose chairman was almost always a man; taking university examinations but not degrees – was no longer enough. Exclusion from voting for elections of the imperial Parliament exemplified what had come to be seen as deprivation; the campaign for women's votes was a campaign for a new concept of citizenship.[18]

IV. 1868 *Chorlton v Lings*: Exclusive Male Franchise Affirmed

A year after the passage of the Representation of the People Act 1867 (or the Second Reform Act), unmodified by Mill, the Court of Common Pleas was asked to determine the meaning of the Act. Did the term 'man' in the Act include 'woman'? *Chorlton v Lings*[19] was the outcome of a large political and legal action by women, their legal grievances consolidated in the one case. The appellant was Mary Abbott but another 5,346 women were included in the appeal. All sought to be placed on the electoral register and to be permitted to vote. Counsel for Mary Abbott (and all the other women) was Thomas Chorlton (whose name went on the case), who was legal adviser to the Manchester Society for Women's Suffrage. Lings was the Revising Barrister who had removed Abbott's name from the electoral register

[15] 'John Stuart Mill Amendment' (*UK Parliament*), available at www.parliament.uk/about/living-heritage/evolutionofparliament/houseofcommons/reformacts/from-the-parliamentary-collections/collections-reform-acts/great-reform-act112/.

[16] Mill (n 5) 302.

[17] 'Presenting the 1866 Petition' (n 11).

[18] HCG Matthew, 'The Liberal Age (1851–1914)' in Kenneth O Morgan (ed), *The Oxford History of Britain* (rev edn) (Oxford, Oxford University Press, 1988) 576–77.

[19] *Chorlton v Lings* (1868) LR 4 CP 374.

'despite the fact she met the property qualification for voting'.[20] The case turned on the meaning of the word 'man'. Did this term now include women since the passage of the Interpretation Act 1850 (also known as Lord Brougham's Act) which said that the male case in a statute would now import the female case?

As Robert Sharpe explains:

> Their case was argued by John Duke Coleridge, QC, an eminent barrister and prominent Liberal member of the House of Commons, later Chief Justice, and Richard Pankhurst, a radical lawyer, who later married Emmeline Goulden, the leading figure in the suffrage movement.[21]

Coleridge was a known supporter of women's suffrage.[22] Pankhurst was husband and father of the famous Pankhurst suffragists.

John Duke Coleridge was also to become the direct successor to Chief Justice Bovill,[23] who presided over *Chorlton v Lings* and gave one of the four (unanimous) judgments against the women. Bovill died in 1873 and Coleridge immediately succeeded him as Chief Justice. One can only speculate whether the case would have gone the other way, if Coleridge had been in office at the time. One suspects that it might have, and history may have taken another course. But *Chorlton v Lings* came to be treated as the critical and inevitable authority, the case which got it right, which divined the truth of the common law about the political and legal status of women (and men). Its direct effects endured until the third decade of the twentieth century.

Coleridge QC (supported by Dr Pankhurst) advanced a number of arguments on behalf of the appellants including the terms of Lord Brougham's Act 1850.[24] He argued that the term 'man' in the Second Reform Act should cover woman. After all, section 4 of Lord Brougham's Act stated that '[i]n all Acts, Words importing the Masculine Gender shall be deemed and taken to include Females … unless the contrary … is expressly provided'. As Coleridge explained,

> [i]f the legislature had intended to exclude women from the new franchise they might have used the words 'male persons' … The legislature, however, have used the word 'man' which by the express provision of Lord Brougham's Act includes women.[25]

Women had not been intentionally excluded by the Second Reform Act, and so they were included.

[20] Serina Sandhu, 'The Court Case that Legally Denied Women the Vote – and the Women who Voted Anyway' *The iPaper* (London, 6 February 2018), available at inews.co.uk/news/uk/court-case-legally-denied-women-vote-women-voted-anyway-116375.

[21] Robert J Sharpe, 'The Persons Case and the Living Tree Theory of Constitutional Interpretation' (2013) 64 *University of New Brunswick Law Journal* 1, 4.

[22] Lydia E Becker, 'Election Intelligence' *Women's Suffrage Journal* (Manchester, 1 December 1873) 169.

[23] Who was elected a Fellow of the Royal Society in May 1867: 'List of Fellows of the Royal Society 1660–2007: A–J' (The Royal Society, 2007) 43.

[24] Otherwise known as the Interpretation Act 1850.

[25] *Chorlton v Lings* (n 19) 379.

All members of the Court disagreed. The Court put its own construction on this new legislation for interpreting words in a statute, which declared that the term 'men' in legislation now imported women. Notwithstanding Lord Brougham's Act, 'he' did not include 'she'. And so the Court, in effect, judicially reversed the meaning of this part of Lord Brougham's Act. Exclusive male franchise was affirmed.

All four judges determined that women could not vote within the borough of Manchester because of an ancient common law disability, which Lord Brougham's Act had not removed. According to Marguerite Ritchie:

> All of them reacted with shock to the idea that a mere interpretation provision could allow women to claim the right to vote as 'men'. It is clear that the Court in *Chorlton v Lings* had evidence before it that in early times women had exercised public functions. Each Judge however, rejected or explained such evidence away to his own satisfaction, and then held that women were legally incapacitated at common law to exercise such a function and were therefore still excluded as persons 'subject to legal incapacity'.[26]

Chorlton v Lings was swiftly used as precedent by the same Court in the case of *Chorlton v Kessler*[27] as authority for the proposition that women could not vote at a county level. Chief Justice Bovill now explained that

> [t]he Court in that case [*Chorlton v Lings*] purposely gave judgment on the question whether women could in any case be entitled to vote in the election of members of parliament, and did not confine themselves to the particular question of elections for boroughs.[28]

In other words, an expansive judgment was given in *Chorlton v Lings* in anticipation of women seeking further voting powers, beyond the borough, and so the judges need say nothing more but invoke the case 'just decided'. Also reported on the same day was the case of *Wilson v Town Clerk of Salford*[29] which also found against the women, here seeking the right to vote in Salford (the names of 135 women had been expunged by the revising barrister and their appeals were consolidated). The Court dealt with the claims of large numbers of women seeking public power expeditiously.

In the cases that followed *Chorlton v Lings*, the judges went further: they declared that the term 'person' did not include women. So whether the relevant legal term was 'man' or 'person', women were disqualified, with the one desired result: exclusive male political power. Mill had assumed that the term 'person' would necessarily include women, but the courts thought and found otherwise. Whether the term employed was 'man' or 'person', the legal being in question remained a man.

Chorlton v Lings relies on a strange, even bizarre, sweep of history going back to the Anglo Saxons and the Romans and to Coke's Institute's (1628–1644), and to

[26] Marguerite E Ritchie, 'Alice Through the Statutes' (1975) 21 *McGill Law Journal* 685, 694.
[27] *Chorlton v Kessler* (1868) LR 4 CP 397.
[28] ibid 398.
[29] *Wilson v Town Clerk of Salford* (1868) LR 4 CP 398.

Selden (1653).[30] It has no conventional periodisation. It is mystical, religious, and invented, rather than robust historical evidence (a method to be used again by John Finnis, see chapter eight). Though the Court was required to construe the meaning of quite recent legislation on the franchise, the 1867 Reform Act, together with Lord Brougham's Act 1850, to do so it used ancient arguments based on mysticism. That is it reached deeply into a premodern past whose legal luminaries countenanced witchcraft, for their understanding of the common law. Indeed the Court went back to the Anglo-Saxons and the Romans. The further back in time they went, the more reliable the meaning for them, rather than the more remote and the more outdated. As we will see in the next chapter, in 1922, the highest judicial official, Lord Birkenhead, did something similar. Invoking deep time, the Sex Disqualification (Removal) Act 1919 was reinterpreted so that its explicit meaning did not operate.

V. Backing the Most Anti-Woman Judge: The Rising Star of Justice Willes

The judge who became the most quoted, almost reverentially, by subsequent courts deciding on women's personhood, for decades, was not that of the Chief Justice, but rather Willes J. Justice Willes was found to be the most compelling judge, who was also the most loquacious and emphatic about the exclusive nature of male right. He was also more willing to hint at the character weaknesses of women which (it was 'sometimes … suggested') ill-suited them to the exercise of public power. He declared that:

> Women are under a legal incapacity to vote at elections. What was the cause of it, it is not necessary to go into: but, admitting that fickleness of judgment and liability to influence have sometimes been suggested as the ground of exclusion, I must protest against its being supposed to arise in this country from any underrating of the sex either in point of intellect or worth. That would be quite inconsistent with one of the glories of our civilization, – the respect and honour in which women are held.[31]

Justice Willes thus revealed his none-too-subtle prejudices against women and his probable belief in their deficiencies of character. Planted in his readers' minds was the idea of women's 'fickleness of judgment and liability to influence', as the reason for their disability. But then that unpleasant notion was dismissed. However, the slyly contemptuous tone was set. Willes then rose to the defence of English law and said there were estimable reasons for women's legal incapacities (and men's capacities). It was out of respect and honour that women had been denied the exercise of judicial and public functions, and still should be. (Pardon?) We may note that Blackstone's editor Edward Christian could not stomach this concocted reasoning,

[30] John Selden, *Ioannis Seldeni De Synedriis & Præfecturis Iuridicis Veterum Ebræorum Liber Secundus* (London, Prostant apud Cornelium Bee, 1653).

[31] *Chorlton v Lings* (n 19) 388.

when Blackstone did the very same thing, as I documented in *Criminal Law and the Man Problem*.[32]

Moreover, Willes J insisted, he was not alone in thinking this. The weight of history was on his side.

> This is not a mere fancy of my own, but will be found in Selden, *de Synedriis Veterum Ebraeorum*, in the discussion of the origin of the exclusion of women from judicial and like public functions, where the author gives preference to this reason, that the exemption was founded upon motives of decorum, and was a privilege of the sex (*honestatis privilegium*): Selden's Works, vol. 1, pp. 1083-1085. Selden refers to many systems of law in which this exclusion prevailed, including the civil law and the canon law, which the latter, as we know, excluded women from public functions in some remarkable instances. With respect to the civil law, I may add a reference to the learned and original work of Sir Patrick Colquhon [sic] on the Roman Law, vol i, p 580, where he compares the Roman system with ours, and states that a woman 'cannot vote for members of parliament, or sit in either the House of Lords or Commons'.[33]

Thus Willes J found his authorities in the far past. He drew on Selden (1584–1654), who said that it was a female privilege *not* to be permitted such exercises of power. And to strengthen this sense of things having always been so, one law for men, another for women, Willes J went back to Roman law and to the beginnings of the Western legal tradition.

The women of Ancient Rome (which was committed to slavery), the women of the early modern period (which countenanced witchcraft), and the women of the Victorian era were all treated as one. There was to be no historical sense of women and their changing lives and roles over time. It seems that women were always women, the one kind of static being.

Chorlton v Lings, and especially the judgment of Willes J, exercised their influence until 1928, when the Supreme Court of Canada relied upon it in its determination that women were debarred from the upper house of the Canadian Parliament, as we will see in chapter six. And along the way, Willes J was venerated. In this first stage of strong male entitlement and open opposition to the extension of legal power to women, the legal statements about the rightness of a two sex system, with exclusive male control, were explicitly and boldly stated.

VI. Mill's Continuing Campaign against Male Right: *The Subjection of Women*

John Stuart Mill wrote two quite different books arguing for human freedom, with different degrees of influence. *On Liberty*, with its theory of the free Individual, was met with broad acclaim and remains an important statement of liberal political

[32] See my account of Christian's extended footnote in Ngaire Naffine, *Criminal Law and the Man Problem* (Oxford, Hart Publishing, 2019).

[33] *Chorlton v Lings* (n 19) 388–89.

philosophy to this day. *The Subjection of Women*, published a year after *Chorlton v Lings*, in 1869, said that women needed freedom too, but did not have it. It was met with hostility, especially by Fitzjames Stephen, as we will see, and then became a lesser work.

In *On Liberty*, Mill had conceived of a free legal Individual, a character who would flourish and stand the test of time as an exemplar of liberty. In *The Subjection*, Mill engaged in a doomed attempt to apply these principles to women and so tackle the problem of female subjugation (and the enlarged male self). In *The Subjection*, Mill stated that:

> [T]he legal subordination of one sex to another – is wrong in itself, and now one of the chief hindrances to human improvement; and that it ought to be replaced by a system of perfect equality, admitting no power and privilege on the one side, nor disability on the other.[34]

Mill was particularly exercised by 'the law of marriage' which he saw as 'a law of despotism',[35] with 'the wife [as] the actual bond-servant of her husband'.[36]

> Above all, a female slave has (in Christian countries) an admitted right, and is considered under a moral obligation, to refuse her master the last familiarity. Not so the wife: however brutal a tyrant she may be unfortunately chained to – though she may know that he hates her, though it may be his daily pleasure to torture her, and though she may feel it impossible not to loathe him – he can claim from her and enforce the lowest degradation of a human being, that of being made the instrument of an animal function contrary to her inclinations.[37]

Here Mill spoke with unusually bold language about the wrongness of the male control of women through law (here, in effect, the husband's exemption from prosecution for the rape of his wife). Mill was explicit about the uses and misuses of male power including violence:

> It would be tiresome to repeat the commonplaces about the unfitness of men in general for power … were it not that hardly anyone thinks of applying these maxims to the case in which above all others they are applicable, that of power, not placed in the hands of a man here or there, but offered to every adult male, down to the basest and most ferocious.[38]

Mill indicted his own sex, for the uses of strong violence in the home, including sexual violence, in a manner which was unprecedented and has probably not been repeated since, in its intensity: 'Even the commonest of men', he said, 'reserve the violent, the sulky, the undisguisedly selfish side of their character for those who have no power to withstand it. The relation of superiors to dependents is the nursery of these vices of character'.[39]

[34] John Stuart Mill, *The Subjection of Women* (London, Longmans, Green, Reader and Dyer, 1869) 1.
[35] ibid 52.
[36] ibid 55.
[37] ibid 57.
[38] ibid 65–66.
[39] ibid 66. See also John Stuart Mill, *On Liberty* (edited by Stefan Collini) (Cambridge, Cambridge University Press, 1989) 153; John Stuart Mill, *On Liberty* (edited by John Gray) (Oxford, Oxford

Mill's attack on patriarchy in 1869 with *The Subjection* and its argument for 'the perfect equality' of women, was highly controversial; *On Liberty*, with its theory of the free choosing self-governing individual, published 10 years earlier, was endorsed and sustained.[40] According to David Brink,

> when viewed in historical context, Mill's defense of sexual equality is radical, courageous, and sometimes eloquent. While Mill clearly expected some aspects of his liberal principles in *On Liberty* to be controversial, their revolutionary import became especially clear when he applied them to issues of sexual equality in *The Subjection of Women*.[41]

In other words, Mill gained political purchase with his theory of the free Individual, but was vilified when he sought to secure both public and private rights of the Individual for women. Ultimately his central principle of liberty – that '[o]ver himself, over his own body and mind, the individual is sovereign'– was not applied to women. (As we will see in chapter eight, when I consider the work of John Finnis, women when pregnant were to remain under strict state control through the laws of abortion.)

A tension between the reception of Mill's two books on the needs of the Individual, the one applauded, the other treated with suspicion, tends not to be observed. And perhaps it is because the Individual of *On Liberty* was taken quite naturally to be a man. And so when Mill applied his theory of the Individual to women, there was dissent. Mill was fighting strong legal bigotry. Judicial attitudes to women expressed at the time disclosed disdain for the female populace. Some parts of the judiciary were willing to express these attitudes in court, and have their views published. To wit from an Irish judge of the time:

> That the law in recognising the distinction of the sexes assumes a greater worthiness in the male than the female, is manifest from the law of descent; that it has regard to the infirmity of bodily strength and ability in the female, by rendering her incompetent for some offices and privileges, or incapacitating her from the discharge of the duties thereto belonging, cannot be questioned. Again, that she is subject to incapacities, from a presumed inferiority of discretion and judgment, seems also certain (emphasis removed).[42]

And along the way, Mill himself was made the object of ridicule, as an insufficiently manly man. As a contemporary observed about Mill in Parliament:

> Mr. Mill seems cut out by nature not to be a parliamentary success. He has a thin, fragile, awkward frame; he has a nervous, incessant twitching of the lips and eyes; he has a weak voice and a sort of stammer; he is over sixty years of age; he had never, so far

University Press, 1991) 509. Mill's *The Subjection* precedes the passage of the Married Women's Property Acts 1870 and 1882.

[40] See David Brink, 'Mill's Moral and Political Philosophy', *The Stanford Encyclopedia of Philosophy* (edited by Edward N Zalta and Uri Nodelman) (Fall edn, 2022), available at https://plato.stanford.edu/archives/fall2022/entries/mill-moral-political/.

[41] ibid (citations omitted).

[42] Ritchie (n 26) 692, quoting *The Queen v Crosthwaite* (1867) 17 Ir Com Law Rep 463, 475.

> as I know, addressed a political meeting of any kind up to the time of the Westminster contest. Yet with all these disadvantages, Mill has, as a political leader and speaker, been an undoubted success with the country, and a sort of success in the House.[43]

Mill was a 'sort of success' in Parliament because, despite his shortcomings as an orator, 'so far as the best selection of words, the clearest style, the most coherent and convincing argument can constitute eloquence, Mill's speeches are eloquent'.[44]

One is then reminded of the modern Parliament. 'Some of the more boisterous of the Tories made many attempts to cough and laugh Mill into silence; indeed, there was obviously a deliberate plan of this kind in operation at one time.'[45] This did not deflect Mill for he

> is a man whom nothing can deter from saying or doing what he thinks right. A more absolutely fearless being does not exist. He is even free from that fear which has sometimes paralyzed the boldest spirits, the fear of becoming ridiculous.[46]

And thus,

> the Tory trick failed. Mill went on with patient, imperturbable, proud good-humor, despite all interruption – now and then paying off his Tory enemies by some keen contemptuous epigram or sarcasm, made all the more pungent by the thin, bland tone in which it was uttered. So the Tories gave up shouting, groaning and laughing.[47]

In the year of Mill's death, the man *Britannica* describes admiringly as 'English critic, man of letters, and the first editor of the Dictionary of National Biography',[48] Leslie Stephen (brother of Fitzjames Stephen), was less charitable about Mill's demeanour. Mill was too much like the lesser sex. According to Stephen in *The Nation* 1873 (the year Mill died), on witnessing Mill speak in Parliament, nothing could be 'more contrary to my preconceived notions than the slight fragile man, trembling with ill suppressed nervousness and, at times, blushing like a girl for some inappreciable cause'.[49] These scornful words about girls (to Stephen it was patently and deliberately insulting to liken a man to one) were uttered by the man who would father two girls who were ultimately to play foundational roles in the development of modern literature and modern art: Virginia Woolf and Vanessa Bell, respectively. These girls had to suffer their father's moodiness and emotional instability, his 'cacophony of contradictions'.[50]

[43] Justin McCarthy, *Modern Leaders: Being a Series of Biographical Sketches* (New York, Sheldon & Company, 1872) 113.
[44] ibid.
[45] ibid.
[46] ibid.
[47] ibid.
[48] 'Sir Leslie Stephen: British Critic' (*Britannica*, 2024), available at www.britannica.com/biography/Leslie-Stephen.
[49] Leslie Stephen, 'The Late John Stuart Mill' (*The Nation*, 5 June 1873) 382–83, quoted in GCG Moore, *Leslie Stephen and the Clubbable Men of Radical London: An Essay in Honour of John King's Retirement* (Virginia, George Mason University, 2007).
[50] Alma H Bond, 'Virginia Woolf and Leslie Stephen: A Father's Contribution to Psychosis and Genius' (1986) 14 *Journal of the American Academy of Psychoanalysis and Dynamic Psychiatry* 507, 522.

VII. James Fitzjames Stephen's Riposte to Mill: Why Male Legal Right was Necessary

To place him in a time line, James Fitzjames Stephen (Leslie's brother) was born 49 years after the death of Blackstone and 23 years after the birth of Mill.[51] Fitzjames Stephen was a prolific legal writer, expounder of the criminal law,[52] senior judge, colonial administrator, journalist and uncle of Virginia Woolf and Vanessa Bell. Stephen replied to Mill as popular writer, as treatise writer and as judge. Stephen moved across roles including the judicial function and spoke forcefully on behalf of men and against women. The enduring effects of *Clarence*,[53] a late Victorian case whose obiter affirmed the husband's immunity from rape prosecution, takes his influence into the late twentieth century.[54]

In 1873, Fitzjames Stephen published his riposte to Mill. In *Liberty, Equality and Fraternity*[55] he said, in essence, that only men were fit to be full Legal Persons. And law backed Stephen, not Mill, which is not surprising given that Stephen was ultimately making the law, and in the interests of men and against women. Stephen replied to Mill in several capacities: as popular writer, as treatise writer and then effectively as a judge. His public utterings against women, which preceded his appointment to the judiciary, did not damage his career as judge nor disqualify him from judicial office. Perhaps it even qualified him, in the patriarchal society that existed, for whom he was a spokesman in his multiple roles. Stephen became a concentration of legal power, acting against women. His opinions in *Liberty, Equality, Fraternity* on women did not undermine the credibility of his judgments on the rights of women, as with *Clarence*. And he attracted many honours and continued to be honoured. Mill called him 'brutal at his best'.[56] Stephen was strikingly different from Mill in his male physique. A contemporary described Stephen thus:

> A head of enormous proportions is planted, with nothing intervening except an inch-and-a-half neck, upon the shoulders of a giant. Force is written upon every line of his countenance, upon every square inch of his trunk. He is not a particularly engaging person, but a very impressive one. The genius of the Anglo-Saxon race is embodied in men of this stamp. He lacks geniality and play of fancy, but in their stead he has a grim and neverflagging perception of what he means and what he wants.[57]

[51] He lived from 1829 to 1894.

[52] See, eg, James Fitzjames Stephen, *A General View of the Criminal Laws of England* (London, Macmillan and Co, 1863); James Fitzjames Stephen, *Liberty, Equality and Fraternity* (New York, Holt and Williams, 1873); James Fitzjames Stephen, *A History of the Criminal Law of England* vols 1–3 (London, Macmillan and Co, 1883); James Fitzjames Stephen, *A Digest of the Criminal Law*, 4th edn (London, Macmillan and Co, 1877).

[53] *R v Clarence* (1888) 22 QBD 23.

[54] See my analysis of *Clarence*, ibid, in Naffine (n 32).

[55] Stephen, *Liberty, Equality and Fraternity* (n 52).

[56] See Kate Gleeson, 'The Problem of *Clarence*, Brutal at his Best: James Fitzjames Stephen and the Doctrine of Sexual Inequality' (2005) 14 *Nottingham Law Journal* 1.

[57] George W Smalley, *Society in London, by a Foreign Resident* (London, Chatto & Windus, 1885).

Mill's *Subjection of Women* and Stephen's *Liberty, Equality and Fraternity* both made explicit assertions about the natures of women and men. Mill wrote directly about the shortcomings of male nature, as he saw it, and said that male power over women made men and society brutal, and of course damaged women. Stephen also wrote openly about what he believed to be the natures of men and women and warned that, if men's rights over women were curtailed, men would become more brutal, not less. Their sexual passions would not be constrained within a formal legal institution (marriage) and they would cease to protect women. Stephen also portrayed vividly the physical and mental weaknesses of women, as he saw them. Mill had said that women's natures were unknown because they had always lived within a patriarchy which tightly constrained their lives. Stephen took no heed of this indubitable fact. The natures of men and women were fixed, he declared. When he became a judge, Stephen J tempered his words, and said he was only looking to the law. But he did not change his mind.

Stephen went from treatise writer (on the criminal law), to general writer about law and politics (*Liberty, Equality and Fraternity*), to judge. In fact he wore more hats than this. What was notable about Stephen was the boldness of his disdain for women. Other men of legal authority tended to cloak their views, often in chivalry. Later, as a judge, Stephen was to take more care with how he put things. But here is Stephen in reply to Mill, showing his colours about women before he went on to the bench and decided their rights. To Stephen, sex difference was the most fundamental difference, which distinguished human beings of a common age:

> I say that there are many such differences [between human beings] … and of which some are so marked and so important that unless human nature is radically changed, we cannot even imagine their removal; and of these the differences of age and sex are the most important.[58]

Then Stephen proclaimed the superiority of men, and their superior legal powers, which followed as a natural consequence of their superior natures.

> Now, if society and government ought to recognize the inequality of age as the foundation of an inequality of rights … it appears to me at least equally clear that they ought to recognize the inequality of sex for the same purpose, if it is a real inequality. Is it one? There are some propositions which it is difficult to prove, because they are so plain, and this is one of them. The physical differences between the two sexes affect every part of the human body, from the hair of the head to the soles of the feet, from the size and density of the bones to the texture of the brain and the character of the nervous system. … men are stronger than women in every shape. They have greater muscular and nervous force, greater intellectual force, greater vigour of character. … These are the facts, and the question is whether the law and public opinion ought to recognize this difference?[59]

[58] James Fitzjames Stephen, *Liberty, Equality, Fraternity* (edited by Stuart D Warner) (Indianapolis, Liberty Fund, 1993) 137.

[59] ibid 138.

Stephen clearly felt that they should. He went on to consider the nature and significance of marriage:

> Follow the matter a step further to the vital point of the whole question – marriage … whether the laws and moral rules which relate to it should regard it as a contract between equals, or as a contract between a stronger and a weaker person involving subordination … I say that a law which proceeded on the former and not on the latter … would be founded on a totally false assumption.[60]

Stephen also insisted that education was designed for the training of men not of women. This was because of 'an inequality between the sexes on which education must be founded, and which it must therefore perpetuate and perhaps increase'.[61] Here we have hard, set, impacted, consolidated patriarchy, even misogyny.

Stephen's moves against women continued in his capacity as judge. In 1888, as Stephen J, he wrote the leading judgment in the case of *Clarence*,[62] which affirmed that a man committed no crime in raping his wife. And a year later, in 1889, in *Beresford Hope v Lady Sandhurst*,[63] Stephen J affirmed the exclusivity of male rights to public office, here to election to the Brixton division of the London County Council. In the private and the public sphere, according to Stephen as judge, women were not to have fundamental rights. Thus did Stephen's anti-woman thoughts, openly expressed in *Liberty, Equality and Fraternity*, find their way into law.

VIII. The Case of *Jex-Blake*: Excluding Women from Higher Learning

In the year that Mill died, and Stephen published his riposte to Mill, the law lords of the Scottish Court of Session decided that women could not earn a degree in medicine. This case has been well documented,[64] because of its extensive and forceful judicial statements on the natures of men and women, and why only men were cut out for higher learning.[65] In *Jex-Blake v Senatus of the University of Edinburgh*,[66] the Court affirmed that higher education was a male preserve. The subject of this case, Sophia Jex-Blake, sought to obtain a degree in medicine from

[60] ibid 139.
[61] ibid 139.
[62] *Clarence* (n 53).
[63] *Beresford Hope v Lady Sandhurst* (1889) 23 QBD 79.
[64] And ultimately led to a counterfactual judgment by Lord Chloë Kennedy to be found in Sharon Cowan, Chloë Kennedy and Vanessa E Munro (eds), *Scottish Feminist Judgments: (Re)Creating Law from the Outside In* (Oxford, Hart Publishing, 2019). Kennedy explains in her reflection on her judgment that she positioned herself 'as one of the advising judges (replacing Lord Benholme)'.
[65] The writings of Sophia Jex-Blake herself have contributed to the notoriety of the decision. See for example Sophia Jex-Blake, *Medical Women* (Edinburgh, William Oliphant & Co, 1872).
[66] *Jex-Blake v Senatus of the University of Edinburgh* (1873) 11 M 784.

Edinburgh medical school. There was a long and elaborate lead up to this case in which Jex-Blake and others studied for and passed about half of the medical degree but then found that they could not attend further classes because no professors were willing to teach them. Their action was against the Chancellor, but more so the Senate, of the University. In the long lead up to the case, there was extensive and elaborate correspondence with the Senatus of the University in which a solution was sought, unsuccessfully.

Jex-Blake is the subject of a *Britannica* entry which describes her extensive education and also her sheer stamina and determination against judicial opposition to her accreditation as a doctor:

> Jex-Blake attended Queen's College, London, and then studied for three years in Boston and New York, returning to England in 1868. She was admitted to classes in medicine at the University of Edinburgh but was not allowed to take a degree. In 1877 she obtained the M.D. of the University of Bern and, through the King's and Queen's College of Physicians, Dublin, a license to practice in Great Britain.[67]

The judges in *Jex-Blake* were adamant about the unsuitability of women for the exercise of professional power and authority in the public realm, here the medical profession. They insisted that women should not be educated because of the inveterate practice of keeping women out of the universities, which was right and proper. Women should not be educated because they had never been educated. Men should be educated because they had always been educated. And to admit women to male institutions of higher education would be to change the very character of learning, for the worse.

Having been asked to consider whether women had a right to obtain medical degrees, the judges chose to expand the significance of their judgments and to consider the nature and purpose of all higher learning. According to Lord Cowan:

> I cannot hold it to be doubtful that by the original charter and Parliamentary ratification in 1621, and the other documents forming the foundation of the University of Edinburgh, the institution was framed on the footing of providing for the education of male students alone; and that any doubt suggested as to the true effect and meaning of these constitutional documents, because of the non-express exclusion of females, has been removed by the usage that has followed for three centuries.[68]

The law was unambiguous:

> I do not perceive a trace of intention on the part of the Legislature to confer any authority, or of power actually conferred, to innovate on the established constitution of the Universities of Scotland in a matter so essential and inherent as that with which these regulations have dealt, and so to change their whole character as to recognise a right in females to matriculation, – or, in the words used by the senior counsel for the pursuers

[67] 'Sophia Louisa Jex-Blake: British Physician' *Britannica* (2024), available at www.britannica.com/biography/Sophia-Louisa-Jex-Blake.

[68] *Jex-Blake* (n 66) 827.

> at the oral pleading, and not abandoned in the written argument, to make provision for boys and girls being equally eligible for matriculation in all or any of the faculties. I seek in vain for any expressions that can be held to have that import; and I see no provision empowering the Court to compel the Professors to instruct any other class of students than such as have from the institution of the University been admitted within its walls.[69]

Lord Neaves took the matter further. Higher education – 'the whole University system' – was for men:

> I am of opinion that the Universities of Scotland – and by the nature of the case I feel compelled to look incidentally to the whole University system – were instituted and maintained for the special and exclusive purpose of conferring the benefits of the higher education upon male students.[70]

And the state would suffer if women were to be admitted, for the state was made great by men:

> The … Universities, which were established in different parts of Scotland and at different periods during the fifteenth century, and that of Edinburgh, more immediately here in question, which had its origin about the time of the Reformation, and was ultimately established in the beginning of the seventeenth century, had all the same object – one which Themistocles [525–459 BC] declared to be so noble – that of converting a little state into a great one. That object was successfully attained in Scotland, and attained mainly, as I conceive, by means of those great educational arrangements which were designed to produce *able*, *learned*, and *accomplished* men.[71]

Such able men, and only men, needed to be educated, 'for the *salvation* of the state and the advancement of the public welfare'.[72] An all-male educational system ensured and secured

> learned and able divines for the service of *religion*, learned and able lawyers for the practice of the *law*, skilful and enlightened magistrates and judges for the administration of *justice*, and wise and prudent politicians and statesmen for the great purposes of national *legislation* (emphasis added).[73]

And finally, to make it absolutely clear, 'the purpose contemplated in founding these Universities was the education of young men'.[74] In short, men covered the field: in religion, and in the practice of law, as politicians and as statesmen, they rightly exercised public power because they were the right kind of being for such exalted tasks. With education, which was designed for them, they understandably became able, accomplished, skilful, enlightened, and prudent.

Men, and only men, needed to become learned in order to assume all the major functions of the secular and divine order. It had always been so, and this

[69] ibid 821.
[70] ibid 831.
[71] ibid 831.
[72] ibid.
[73] ibid.
[74] ibid.

established that it should remain so. This patriarchal ethos was perpetuated in a self-generating, institutional process:

> From the year 1411 to about the year 1860, a period of 450 years, there is no instance producible of a woman having been educated at any Scottish University. I need not dwell on the legal importance of that fact.[75]

An ought was derived from a was (a version of Hume's naturalistic fallacy of deriving an ought from an is). To Lord Neaves, 'religion' and 'skin colour' were not reasons to exclude people from higher education. But sex was a different matter altogether:

> But the material element of consideration here is, that the law does recognise the difference of sex as an established and well-known element, leading sometimes to the exemption and sometimes to the absolute exclusion, of women from a variety of duties, privileges, and powers. The Roman law, the great parent of our own system, laid this down in the clearest and strongest manner.[76]

The Romans knew it was the right thing to do, and so it was the right thing to do in the reign of Victoria and then the Queen herself was recognised as the 'one illustrious and solitary exception'.[77] Thus 'while males have a right to a University education, females have none':[78]

> This leads me to the consideration that very weighty reasons may have operated on the national mind in constituting and continuing the Universities as exclusive schools for the academical education of young men. … It is a belief, widely entertained, that there is a great difference in the mental constitution of the two sexes, just as there is in their physical conformation. The powers and susceptibilities of women are as noble as those of men; but they are thought to be different, and, in particular, it is considered that they have not the same power of intense labour as men are endowed with. If this be so, it must form a serious objection to uniting them under the same course of academical study. I confess that, to some extent, I share in this view, and should regret to see our young females subjected to the severe and incessant work which my own observation and experience have taught me to consider as indispensable to any high attainment in learning.[79]

And it was not only regard for the susceptibilities of women which animated Lord Neaves. The judge was also solicitous for education itself. Such weaker beings would weaken the system. The quality of learning would deteriorate. In fact women could sound its death knell:

> A disregard of such an inequality would be fatal to any scheme of public instruction, for, as it is certain that the general mass of an army cannot move more rapidly than its

[75] ibid.

[76] ibid 832.

[77] ibid. Queen Elizabeth II was herself home educated. Though a law degree would no doubt have been helpful in her role, it was not in question that she might acquire one. In fact her son Charles was the first in the royal line to obtain a degree.

[78] ibid.

[79] ibid 833.

> weakest and slowest portion, so a general course of study must be toned and tempered down to suit the average of all the classes of students for whom it is intended; and that average will always be lowered by the existence of any considerable numbers who cannot keep pace with the rest.[80]

Because of their lesser abilities, because they would be the 'weakest and slowest', women would 'be fatal to any scheme of public instruction', which was currently pitched at an elevated male level, and so it would weaken the preparation of men for public life in all its manifestations including for the Divine.

> Upon all these grounds I am satisfied that the non-attendance of women at the Universities in times past, which is an indisputable fact, was not a mere accident, or a mere arbitrary abstinence from the enforcement of a legal privilege, but arose from a consciousness, shared by them with the whole community, that the Universities were not instituted for them, though women would undoubtedly receive indirectly the benefits the Universities were calculated to confer, in making better men of their fathers, their brothers, their husbands, and their sons.[81]

And so the judiciary held firm on the unfitness of women for public life.

IX. The Return of Stephen, Now as Judge, and the Affirmation of Justice Willes, yet again: *Beresford Hope v Lady Sandhurst*

The belittling views of women, expressed by the Court in *Jex-Blake*, were similar to those expressed by Stephen in *Liberty, Equality and Fraternity* published in the same year. Sixteen years later, Stephen, now a judge, found himself with an opportunity to translate his views into law in *Beresford Hope v Lady Sandhurst*.[82] But now he used the more measured tones of a judge, employing statutory interpretation and drew on what he saw as the apposite case law.

Margaret (Lady) Sandhurst had stood for election for the London County Council and succeeded. A defeated conservative candidate, Beresford Hope, successfully challenged her right to be elected under the Local Government Act 1888, and so gained the seat for himself. Justice Stephen delivered the judgment in the Divisional Court, which found against Lady Sandhurst. He declared that women were not entitled to be elected because female eligibility for election 'ought to be made in perfectly plain language' and the Act contained no such

[80] ibid.
[81] ibid 835.
[82] *Beresford Hope v Lady Sandhurst* (n 63).

provision.[83] But as a contemporary commentator pointed out: 'it is equally impossible to point to any section declaring them to be disqualified'.[84]

To dispel any doubt about Lady Sandhurst's legal incapacities, Stephen J invoked *Cholton v Lings* as the clinching authority. Both Bovill CJ and Willes J were cited approvingly.[85] They had made it clear that by 'uninterrupted usage for many centuries' women had been incapacitated from voting. This is an odd double negative, but nevertheless, by invoking this tortured language and reasoning, Stephen was able to make his point, retain his prejudices and sustain his judicial loyalties. Justice Stephen's decision was affirmed on appeal and in the strongest of terms, again invoking Willes J in *Chorlton*. According to Lord Esher MR:

> I take the first proposition to be that laid down by Willes J, in the case of *Chorlton v Lings*. I take it that by neither the common law nor the constitution of this country from the beginning of the common law until now can a woman be entitled to exercise any public functions. Willes J, stated so in that case, and a more learned judge never lived.[86]

X. Controlling the Story

Through control of definition and explanation, male legal power was asserted and retained. By the artful use of words, rather than weapons, or fists, the courts made conceptual and analytical moves to assert and sustain exclusive male control of the power-wielding institutions. At each stage of the push back against women seeking some share of power, there was male manipulation of the legal narrative. In this way a distance was sustained from the complex and harsher human realities; from the actual lives of women and men. Law and its officials knowingly dealt in abstractions, with terms and concepts, which could be invested with special legal meanings, at some remove from folk or ordinary meanings and from daily life. This was the way of law and detached it from ordinary life. But law, through its definitions and human classifications, also acted with positive force on real lives, as Mill made clear. It licensed the uses of rough power. The abstractions and concepts had real effects on real people.

The determination that only men were Persons sat less easily with some and there was caution about seeming to insult women. Others were slyly contemptuous of women but attributed this attitude to distant others, disclaiming it for themselves. Whatever the approach, there was a sustained commitment to keeping the Person male, without ever conceding that legal men were acting as men for men, which was necessarily the case. There was no objective distancing; no divesting of vested interests. Nothing was said about the fact that the only people

[83] ibid 84.
[84] F Minchin Voules, 'Beresford-Hope v Sandhurst' (1889) 1 *County Council Magazine* 231, 234.
[85] *Beresford-Hope v Sandhurst* (n 63) 83.
[86] ibid 95.

deciding the rights of women vis a vis men, were men. As the historian of men and masculinity, John Tosh, observed:

> [M]en have seldom advertised the ways in which authority over women has sustained their sense of themselves as men. … One explanation for John Stuart Mill's intense unpopularity in conservative circles is that he voiced unpalatable truths in precisely this area – like his assertion in *The Subjection of Women* that 'the generality of the male sex cannot yet tolerate the idea of living with an equal'.[87]

XI. The 'Sure Instinct' of Pollock and Maitland that Women should not be Persons

By the end of the nineteenth century, despite Mill's interventions, little had changed by way of legal attitude, including within the academy. In 1895 (and again in 1898) the distinguished legal historians Pollock[88] and Maitland[89] made clear, with neither apology nor discomfort, that for the purposes of public law, women had neither rights nor duties. They were not 'persons' in law and this was so obvious that text writers did not need to spell it out:

> We have been rapidly diminishing the number of 'normal persons', of free and lawful men. We have yet to speak of half the inhabitants of England. No text-writer, no statute, ever makes any general statements as to the position of women. This is treated as obvious, and we believe that it can be defined with some accuracy by one brief phrase: – private law with few exceptions puts women on a par with men; public law gives a woman no rights and exacts from her no duties save that of paying taxes and performing such services as can be performed by deputy.[90]

And to leave us in no doubt:

> On the whole we may say that, though it has no formulated theory about the position of women, a sure instinct has already guided the law to a general rule which will endure until our own time. … public functions they have none. In the camp, at the council board, on the bench, in the jury box there is no place for them.[91]

These explanatory statements about women's lot in the history of English law are to be found within a chapter entitled 'The Sorts and Conditions of Men' and come directly after a section on 'Lepers, Lunatics and Idiots'.

[87] John Tosh, 'What Should Historians do with Masculinity? Reflections on Nineteenth-century Britain' (1994) 38 *History Workshop* 179, 184.

[88] Frederick Pollock was Professor of Jurisprudence at Oxford.

[89] Frederic Maitland was Professor of the Laws of England at Cambridge.

[90] Frederick Pollock and Frederic William Maitland, *History of English Law* vol 1 (Cambridge, Cambridge University Press, 1895) 465.

[91] ibid 468.

It is worth reflecting on what Pollock and Maitland, as university law professors, were not saying, but instead taking as a given, and taking to be right. In fact they said it (it being the ousting of half the population from the public realm) did not need to be gone into. The authors described an all-male legal system which had secured an exclusively male public realm. Its most defining feature was its maleness and the fact that it thereby secured the maleness of the rest of the public world. Pollock and Maitland were themselves the products of an education system designed for men, as the case of *Jex-Blake* made clear. The law they were analysing and describing was made by men, because only men were permitted to make it. Law's basic terms and concepts were defined and explained by men. This iron male control of legal power was of almost no interest to Pollock and Maitland, whose 'classic' text on the early history of English law continues to be described as a classic. As products of the system, they did not take a critical view of the system that had made them, nor did they take a scholarly interest in its tight demography and their place within it. Indeed they failed the basic tests of scholarliness: open mindedness, genuine curiosity, and no vested interests in the outcome of the inquiry. Thus are the foundations of law weakened.

4

Definitional Power in the Early Twentieth Century: The Persons Cases and the Role of the Lord Chancellors

I. Introduction

Behind the courtliness of Blackstone, as he spelled out the components of coverture, was supreme confidence in the breadth and depth of male power. England was the great protector of women and it fulfilled its duties to women by making the husband cover the existence of his wife, her very person. Fitzjames Stephen later made clear that if women were not thus protected as dependent subordinates in marriage, over time men would grow weary of these pathetic and increasingly unattractive creatures, as they aged, and would treat them badly; chivalry would go and with it would go civility. 'The result would be that women would become men's slaves and drudges'.[1] In 1914, the distinguished scientist William Sedgwick issued a warning to women:

> [L]et the feminist programme of greater sex liberty for women, with its demolition of wifehood and the home, be carried through; then will women indeed find that the knightliness and chivalry of gentlemen have vanished, and in their stead will arise a rough male power that will place women where it chooses.[2]

Well of course it already had, as John Stuart Mill spelled out. And Mill faced it himself in Parliament as he quietly uttered his liberal sentiments. In this chapter, I consider how the Lord High Chancellors, the highest legal officials, deployed the concept of the Legal Person in the first quarter of the twentieth century, to sustain male public power.

[1] James Fitzjames Stephen, *Liberty Equality Fraternity* (edited by Stuart Warner) (Indianapolis, Liberty Fund, 1993) 153.

[2] Sedgwick quoted by George MacAdam, 'Feminist Revolutionary Principle is Biological Bosh: Prof William T Sedgwick, Noted Biologist, Riddles the Pretensions of Supporters of the New Doctrine for Women and Says if the Movement Succeeds it Will Throw the World Back a Thousand Years' *New York Times* (Online, January 1914), available at www.nytimes.com/1914/01/18/archives/feminist-revolutionary-principle-is-biological-bosh-prof-william-t.html?searchResultPosition=275. See also Cordelia Fine, *Delusions of Gender: How our Minds, Society, and Neurosexism Create Difference* (New York, WW Norton, 2010) 67.

II. Introducing the Lord High Chancellor

It is first worth taking a few moments to consider the nature of the office of the Lord Chancellor and its remarkable array of powers. In 1867, in *The English Constitution*, Walter Bagehot described '[t]he whole office of the Lord Chancellor' as 'a heap of anomalies'.[3] He said of the Lord Chancellor:

> He is a judge, and it is contrary to obvious principle that any part of administration should be entrusted to a judge; it is of very grave moment that the administration of justice should be kept clear of any sinister temptations. Yet the Lord Chancellor, our chief judge, sits in the Cabinet, and makes party speeches in the Lords.[4]

This highest of legal positions put both legal and political power into the hands of the one man. The office commenced at the time of Edward the Confessor (in the 11th century) and it was held by an uninterrupted line of men until 2016.[5] RFV Heuston said in his *Lives of the Lord Chancellors 1885–1940* that

> the Lord Chancellor combines within himself the three functions of government, executive, legislative, and judicial. On the executive side he is a member of Cabinet and one of the chief government spokesmen in the House of Lords.[6]

Thus, in actuality and effect, power was unseparated (ie there was no separation of powers) so the same man could hold all roles and slip from one to another within the same day.

As Lord Chancellor Buckland observed in 2021, about the once capacious role of the Lord High Chancellor:

> In the days when the Lord Chancellor was not only a Parliamentarian and a Cabinet Minister, but also sat on the bench and appointed all their judicial colleagues, the role was often described as a 'linchpin' that linked all three branches of the state and managed the relationships between them.[7]

Gilbert and Sullivan produced witty satirical accounts of the office in the 'Mikado' and 'Iolanthe'.[8] A more circumspect description of the office is to be found in the *Oxford Dictionary of Law*. The Lord Chancellor was:

> Historically, the head of the judiciary, a government minister (in charge of the Lord Chancellor's Department), and Speaker of the House of Lords. … He was entitled to preside over the House when it sat as a final court of appeal; he appointed magistrates

[3] Walter Bagehot, *The English Constitution* (London, Chapman and Hall, 1867) 256.

[4] ibid.

[5] See 'Lord Chancellor: British Official' (*Britannica*, 16 November 2024), available at www.britannica.com/topic/lord-chancellor.

[6] RFV Heuston, *Lives of the Lord Chancellors 1885–1940* (Oxford, Clarendon Press, 1964) xvi.

[7] Robert Buckland, 'Lord Chancellor's Speech: Law and Politics – the Nightmare and the Noble Dream' (Queen Mary University Conference, 25 March 2021).

[8] WS Gilbert and Arthur Sullivan, 'Mikado' (London, Savoy Theatre, 14 March 1885); WS Gilbert and Arthur Sullivan, 'Iolanthe' (London, Savoy Theatre, 25 November 1882).

and higher judicial officials; and he oversaw such matters as the administration of the courts, the Community Legal Service, law reform, data protection, and human rights.[9]

With his immense powers, the Lord Chancellor could pursue a cause, close to his heart, with great effectiveness. He could set, control and reinforce the framing of a preferred argument in at least two capacities: the one legal, the other political. And so if he had a cause to advance, this gave him at least two bites of the cherry.

The Lord Chancellors I consider here did just that, openly, in the interests of men and against the interests of women. They moved easily between legal and political roles, to achieve their desired goal. They exercised their vast legal and political authority to control and shape the definition of the Legal Person, in order to retain male public power. They did this within the office of Lord Chancellor, which fully countenanced this mix of powers. And they did this from legal and political positions assumed either before or after assuming this high office, typically with an eye to preferment and the acquisition of greater status and power. While keeping women down, they advanced themselves.

In 1908, in *Nairn v University of St Andrews*,[10] Lord Loreburn, as Lord Chancellor, and head of the House of (Law) Lords, upheld the exclusion of women from voting for parliamentary representatives for the University of St Andrews and the University of Edinburgh. He expressed strongly his views about the need for men to be the sole bearers of such power. In 1918, now as parliamentarian, Lord Loreburn attempted to derail the Representation Bill which conferred the franchise on women over 30 years of age. (He was unsuccessful.)

Four years later, in 1922, Lord Birkenhead, as Lord Chancellor, in *Viscountess Rhondda's Claim*,[11] resorted to more elaborate practices to exclude women from the House of Lords. (He was successful.) Within this period, Gwyneth Bebb in *Bebb v Law Society*[12] sought to be declared a Person for the purposes of the Solicitors Act and was refused by the Court of Appeal.

Both Lord Chancellors proceeded with braggadocio to advance the cause of men, while invoking the formal constraints of inveterate legal practice. And as Sachs and Wilson observe of what they term 'the male monopoly cases', 'the judges serenely ignored not only the natural meaning of the word "person" but also factual and historical evidence which demonstrated that the legal status of women was one of subordination rather than elevation'.[13] In truth, the exercise of male legal power, through the manipulation and explanation of terms, was directly responsible for the legal suppression of women, the cramping of female life, and the enlarging of male life. But none of this was said. Dubious legal and political

[9] See the definition of 'Lord Chancellor' in Jonathan Law and Elizabeth A Martin, *A Dictionary of Law*, 7th edn (Oxford, Oxford University Press, 2009).

[10] *Nairn v University of St Andrews* [1909] AC 147.

[11] *Viscountess Rhondda's Claim* [1922] 2 AC 339.

[12] *Bebb v Law Society* [1914] 1 Ch 286.

[13] Albie Sachs and Joan Hoff Wilson, *Sexism and the Law: A Study of Male Beliefs and Legal Bias in Britain and the United States* (Oxford, Martin Robertson, 1978) 50.

practices were employed at the highest level to retain exclusive male power by declaring women not to be persons.

The cases at the heart of this chapter consider women's right to vote, to be lawyers, and to sit in the upper House of Parliament or to put it another way, they deal with men's exclusive right to vote, to be lawyers, and to be lawmakers. Each case endorsed exclusive male public power by saying that women did not satisfy the definition of 'Persons' who could exercise these rights. The term Person was reserved for men.

III. Lord Loreburn (Robert Threshie Reid) and *Nairn v University of St Andrews*: Women should have not Even 'the Smallest Foothold'[14]

The first Law Lord of interest is Lord Loreburn, Lord High Chancellor of Great Britain from 1905 to 1912. He was to play more than one role in the advancement of exclusive male right through law. In *Nairn* (10 December 1908), he was the highest judicial official possible in a court of complete agreement (the House of Lords) to say that female graduates were not Persons for the purpose of a university franchise. Later, as a Member of the Parliamentary Lords, he endeavoured to stop the inclusion of women in the General Franchise. Thus, he shifted from judicial to parliamentary role, retaining the one goal: to stop women having the vote.

The appellants appearing before Lord Loreburn in the House of Lords[15] in *Nairn* were five female graduates of the University of Edinburgh: Margret Nairn, MA, Frances Simson, MA, Jessie Macmillan, B SC,[16] Frances Melville, MA and Elsie Inglis, MB, CM. Their claim was that, as graduates and so registered members of the General Council of the University, they were entitled to vote for its parliamentary representatives. The Representation of the People (Scotland) Act 1868 had created this franchise. Section 27 stated that

> every person whose name is for the time being on the register … of the general council of such university, shall, if of full age, and not subject to any legal incapacity, be entitled to vote in the election of a member to serve in any future Parliament for such university in terms of this Act.

When this legislation was passed, women were permitted to study, but not to graduate, as we saw in the case of *Jex-Blake*. But by the time of the *Nairn* case, in 1908, women could graduate.[17] (Cambridge did not award degrees to women until 1948.) The question was whether they could vote as graduates.

[14] From the judgment of Lord Loreburn. See below n 21 and accompanying text.

[15] This was the first time a woman had argued a case before the House of Lords.

[16] Jessie McMillan was called to the Bar in 1924. See the entry on McMillan in Jennifer Uglow (ed), *The Macmillan Dictionary of Women's Biography*, 2nd edn (London, Macmillan, 1989) 346. The Lord Advocate of Scotland is now a woman, only the second in the very long history of the office.

[17] By dint of an Ordinance of 1892 made under the Universities (Scotland) Act 1858.

In 1906, these women asked for voting papers but were refused by the university registrar and so they brought an action against the university courts, and the vice chancellors and the chancellors and the registrars. They did not do things by halves. In 1906, The Lord Ordinary and then the Extra Division of the Court of Session in 1907 held that they were not Persons entitled to vote.

In 1908, their case was heard on appeal to the House of Lords. The same result. The word 'Person' meant a 'man'. (And of course every judge was a man and every appellant was a woman.) Lord Loreburn, as Lord High Chancellor, said that his exclusive task was to find what the law was. Implicitly, his determination had nothing to do with the rights or wrongs of it. He was adamant, throughout, that this female right did not exist and probably had never existed:[18]

> It is *incomprehensible* to me that *any one* acquainted with our laws or the methods by which they are ascertained can think, *if, indeed, any one does think*, there is room for argument on such a point. It is *notorious* that this right of voting has, in fact, been confined to men (emphasis added).[19]

There was no room for doubt. Lord Loreburn reached back into the distant past to see if there were instances of women voting, casting back to Lord Coke (1552–1634). He found what he seemed to be looking for: that it was a legal given that women did not have this capacity.

> A few *equivocal* cases were referred to. I was *surprised how few*. And it is the same in regard to judicial precedents. Two passages may be found in which Judges are reported as saying that women may vote at Parliamentary elections. These are *dicta derived from an ancient manuscript of no weight. Old authorities are almost silent* on the subject, except that *Lord Coke at one place incidentally alludes to women as being under a disqualification, not dwelling upon it as upon a thing disputable*, but alluding to it for the purpose of illustration as a matter certain. This disability of women has been *taken for granted* (emphasis added).[20]

Loreburn was determined to remove any suggestion that women may have ever possessed such public power. The 'ancient manuscript' that suggested that women might have voted was 'of no weight'. However the ancient authority of Lord Coke which 'alludes to women' being under a disqualification was compelling, according to Loreburn.

Thus Lord Loreburn sifted and winnowed the long legal past to arrive at absolute legal certainty. There was no legal basis for such a right, whichever way you looked at it.

> If the word 'persons' in s 27 of the Act of 1868 is wide enough to comprise women, then they are shut out by the exception of those subject to a legal incapacity. If the word 'persons' is not wide enough to include women, then there is nothing in any Act of Parliament that gives the smallest foothold for the appellants' contention.[21]

[18] Australia had granted the vote to women six years earlier.
[19] *Nairn* (n 10) 160.
[20] ibid.
[21] ibid 161.

Again, *Chorlton v Lings* was found to be definitive about the status of women in the common law: 'I will not linger upon this subject, which, indeed, was fully discussed in *Chorlton v Lings*. If this legal disability is to be removed, it must be done by Act of Parliament.'[22]

Having said that it was up to Parliament to confer the franchise on women (thus washing his hands of the matter as a judge), ten years later, now as a Member of the Parliamentary House of Lords, Loreburn proposed an amendment to the Representation of the People Act 1918 (the Reform Act) to stop this happening, for the purpose of the general franchise. Loreburn's first stated concern was that women would have the numbers to control public decision making and this was not in the public interest. Because of Britain's imperial powers, it would put women in charge of 'over one quarter of the human race'.[23]

> This Bill gives this enormous number of voters, who in a little time will become a majority of the entire electorate, the power over Imperial policy, the power over questions hereafter of peace or war, the most solemn questions that can affect the destinies of the nation.[24]

Too much was at stake:

> It is needless to argue upon a subject of this kind, because it is a question of experience and opinion. I think that it is inexpedient that these things should be in feminine rather than in masculine hands. No great State has ever done anything like this, even after deliberation. … This Bill is to hand over the control of the House of Commons – varying in different parts of the world, but always able, to affect the destinies more or less of all the British Empire.[25]

Hence Loreburn's concern about 'handing over the present powers to feminine instead of masculine hands. It is the same thing with the Army and the Navy as with foreign policy'.[26] And then he combined chivalry and apparent concern for women, while ousting them from public power. It was not that he was against women, he insisted:

> I yield to no one in my admiration of what women have done during this war. I am not in the least surprised at it. It is just what I should have expected of them. … I think myself that women share with men to the full – perhaps a little more – the bereavements and the privations caused by war, and the plague, pestilence, and famine that may come from it.[27]

But men made war and faced war. And simply they were the right kinds of being to make weighty decisions about the fate of the country.

[22] ibid 160.
[23] *Hansard*, HL Deb 9 January 1918, vol 27, col 416.
[24] ibid 415.
[25] ibid 415–16.
[26] ibid 416.
[27] ibid 416–17.

> Is it wise to say that the judgment of women may prevail upon these things – although I do not doubt for a moment that the desire to do right would be as strong with women as it is with men – when upon the whole men are safer than women as judges upon such solemn matters? It is impossible to adduce arguments. It comes from our knowledge and from what insight we may possess, but it looks to me a very dangerous leap in the dark to take all this volume of business and duty and to transfer it to what may be a majority of women.[28]

And so Loreburn openly appealed to male common sense, to men's implicitly superior knowledge and insight, rather than evidence, about the dangers that women would pose to the proper running of the country and Empire. These assertions and these legal findings did not hamper his reputation. For if we now turn to the entry on Lord Loreburn in the *Oxford Dictionary of National Biography*, we learn that he was 'a vigorous, [and] reforming lord chancellor', a man of 'impartiality and discernment'. He possessed 'staunch independence of mind'.[29]

Loreburn's colleague on the bench in *Nairn*, Lord Robertson, came to the same conclusion via a different route. He said that '[i]n truth the case of the appellants rests on a very narrow and slender basis, and that is the word "person"'.[30] And further that 'the case of the appellants is entirely one of words'.[31] (As if his predecessors had not been engaged in a similar exercise.) And then he employed some creative reasoning. He said that as Lord Brougham's Act had determined some time earlier that the word 'man' in a statute should thenceforth import the female case, the word 'Person' in a statute now had 'the smaller significance in the direction of including women'.[32] That is, because the term 'man' now included woman, the term 'person' must have contracted with respect to women. Multiple readings of this passage by this author have not rendered its meaning entirely clear, which may well have been intended. But this seems to be the gist of it.

IV. Women's Political Protests and the Forceful Response of the State

Were women quiescent during the time of *Nairn*? Not at all, though you might think so from Loreburn's words. As Millicent Garrett Fawcett reported:

> In February 1907, 3000 women marched in procession in London, from Hyde Park to Exeter Hall. In October 1907, 1500 women marched in procession through Edinburgh. In October 1907, 2000 women marched in procession through Manchester. In June 1908,

[28] ibid 417.
[29] A Lentin, 'Reid, Robert Threshie, Earl Loreburn', *Oxford Dictionary of National Biography* (May 2006) 25, available at www.oxforddnb.com/display/10.1093/ref:odnb/9780198614128.001.0001/odnb-9780198614128-e-35719?rskey=VtoQ5a&result=2.
[30] *Nairn* (n 10) 164.
[31] ibid 165.
[32] ibid.

> 15,000 women marched in procession in London to the Albert Hall. In June 1911 more than 40,000 women, representing all the suffrage societies, walked in a procession four miles long to the Albert Hall.[33]

In June of 1908 the Women's Social and Political Union organised the Women's Sunday demonstration in Hyde Park, London. It was attended by great numbers of people from around the country. As *The Guardian* reported:

> The women made London their own. They gathered in their thousands on the Embankment. Motor-cars, brakes and cabs drove up every moment laden with women who wanted to demonstrate. … The procession was a new thing to London. The crowd was half bewildered – but entirely convinced – by the number of women wearing academic regalia. Some feeble jokes were attempted as medical sections passed, but the women doctors, wearing their scarlet gowns and hoods, looked so completely indifferent that the ridicule changed to admiration. … Miss Emily Davies LLD, frail but determined, set the pace bravely along the streets. She was one of the women who presented the first women's suffrage petition to John Stuart Mill many years ago.[34]

A year later, in 1909, AV Dicey published his short treatise opposing the female franchise *Letters to a Friend*[35] (Dicey is the subject of the next chapter), explaining why it would ruin the country. Also in 1909 suffragist Marion Wallace Dunlop[36] became the first woman to hunger strike in prison, after being refused status as a political prisoner, setting a model of political protest which was adopted by Mahatma Gandhi.[37] With a rubber stamp, made for the purpose, she had stamped a section of the 1689 *Bill of Rights* on the wall of St Stephen's Hall of the House of Commons, the furthest a woman was permitted to enter.[38] She was charged with wilful damage to property, convicted, refused to pay the fine and so imprisoned. She asked to be granted the status of a political prisoner.

> I claim the right recognized by all civilized nations that a person imprisoned for a political offence should have first-division treatment; and as a matter of principle, not only for my own sake but for the sake of others who may come after me, I am now refusing all food until this matter is settled to my satisfaction.[39]

[33] Millicent Garrett Fawcett, *Women's Suffrage: A Short History of a Great Movement* (London, TC & EC Jack, 1912) 86.

[34] 'From the Observer Archive, 14 June 1908: 10,000 Women March for Suffrage' *The Guardian* (Online, 17 June 2012), available at www.theguardian.com/news/2012/jun/17/archive-1908-suffragette-march. See also Diane Atkinson, *Rise Up Women! The Remarkable Lives of the Suffragettes* (London, Bloomsbury, 2019); Sandra Stanley Holton, *Feminism and Democracy: Women's Suffrage and Reform Politics in Britain, 1900–1918* (Cambridge, Cambridge University Press, 1986).

[35] AV Dicey, *Letters to a Friend on Votes for Women* (London, John Murray, 1909).

[36] Wallace Dunlop was trained in art at the Slade and was a fine artist – witness her portrait of her sister which can be found online.

[37] June Purvis, 'Suffragette Hunger Strikes, 100 Years On' *The Guardian* (Online, 6 July 2009), available at www.theguardian.com/commentisfree/libertycentral/2009/jul/06/suffragette-hunger-strike-protest.

[38] ibid. The words stamped on the wall by Wallace Dunlop were these: 'It is the Right of the subjects to petition the King and all commitments and prosecutions for such petitioning are illegal'.

[39] 'Marion Wallace-Dunlop' (*Spartacus Educational*), available at spartacus-educational.com/Wwallace-Dunlop.htm.

She was refused political status and so she refused food. There followed the practice of forcibly feeding hunger strikers. As June Purvis explains:

> Forcible feeding became particularly cruel and dangerous after the notorious Cat and Mouse Act of 1913 which allowed a hunger striking suffragette who became ill to be released into the community, in order to regain her health, only to be re-arrested when she was well enough to complete her sentence. The process often extended the period of the sentence. Many women, such as Grace Roe and Kitty Marion, were force fed more than 200 times.[40]

V. Preserving the Legal Profession for Men: *Bebb v Law Society*

In 1914 in *Bebb v Law Society*[41] the meaning of the term 'Person' was again placed under judicial scrutiny, now for the purpose of determining women's right to enter the legal profession, a right open to qualified 'Persons'. Did this mean men or people?

Gwyneth Bebb was a first class student of jurisprudence at Oxford. In 1911, she

> passed her law finals with first-class honours, the first woman at Oxford to do so. According to Nancy Nettlefold, Miss Bebb's examination performance was so brilliant that, had the candidates' names been placed in order of merit (which was not the custom at Oxford), she would have been joint top of the list with one of the men.[42]

However, Oxford did not award degrees to women until 1920. Women could study but not qualify. This notwithstanding, along with three other women, Gwyneth Bebb applied to the Law Society to sit the preliminary exams which would ultimately allow her to become a solicitor and enter the legal profession. The Law Society refused.

Bebb brought an action against the Law Society in the High Court 'asking for a declaration that she was a "person" within the meaning of the Solicitors Act, 1843'.[43] Section 2 of the Solicitors Act 1843 stated that:

> No person shall act as an Attorney or Solicitor … unless such Person shall after the passing of this Act be admitted and enrolled and otherwise duly qualified as an Attorney or Solicitor, pursuant to the Directions and Regulations of this Act.

Section 48 of the Act then stated that 'every Word importing the Masculine Gender only shall extend and be applied to a Female as well as a Male … unless it

[40] Purvis (n 37). The official title of the Cat and Mouse Act was the Prisoners (Temporary Discharge for Ill Health) Act 1913.

[41] *Bebb* (n 12).

[42] Rosemary Auchmuty, 'Whatever happened to Miss Bebb? *Bebb v The Law Society* and Women's Legal History' (2001) 31 *Legal Studies* 199, 211.

[43] *Bebb* (n 12) 286.

be otherwise specially provided or there be something in the Subject or Context repugnant to such Construction'.

Bebb failed in the High Court, which decided that she was not 'a Person' for the purposes of the Act. The Court of Appeal affirmed the decision of the High Court. It reasoned that, as women had never been attorneys, they were not to be considered 'Persons' for the purposes of the Solicitors Act and so were rightfully excluded from sitting the solicitors' exams. Thus the Court of Appeal endorsed the refusal of the Law Society to enrol women and so become solicitors.

Swinfen Eady LJ[44] looked to ancient practice 'from the earliest times':

> Not only has it been the constant tradition, alike of all the three kingdoms, but it has also been the constant practice, so far as we have knowledge of what has happened from the earliest times down to this day. Only the clearest proof that a different state of things prevailed in ancient times could be entertained by a Court of law in probing the origin of so inveterate a usage.[45]

Swinfen Eady LJ clarified that it had never been a job for a woman from which he drew the inference that it was still not a job for a woman.

> In my opinion, it is sufficient to rest this case upon the inveterate practice of the centuries that, ever since attorneys as a profession have existed, women have never been admitted to the office, and, in my opinion, that shews what the law is and has been. For these reasons, I am of opinion that the present applicant is not entitled to insist that she has a right to be examined by the Law Society with a view to her entering the profession of solicitors.[46]

Philipmore LJ indicated the unsuitability of women for the job of attorney, in the view of his profession, while dissociating himself from this view:

> I do not say that this may not be an office suitable to women; what I say is it has never been, in the view of the Courts, suitable to women, and in all the discussions in those cases, in all the quotations with respect to hereditary offices that a woman may hold or her husband may hold in her right, there has never been a suggestion that the office of attorney was one which was open to a woman.[47]

VI. FE Smith (Future Lord Birkenhead): Preserving the Franchise and the House of Lords for Men

The second Lord Chancellor of interest is Lord Birkenhead. As Frederick Edwin (FE) Smith, he was educated in law at Oxford, he became a successful and highly

[44] Who in 1 November 1919 was raised to the peerage as Baron Swinfen, of Chertsey. Ms Bebb died from complications after giving birth: see Auchmuty (n 42).

[45] *Bebb* (n 12) 296–97.

[46] ibid 297.

[47] ibid 299.

remunerated barrister, and was made King's Counsel in 1908 by Lord Loreburn (of the *Nairn* case). He was a Conservative Member of Parliament (1906–18), Solicitor General for England (1915) and Attorney General for England (1915–19). In 1919, he transmogrified into Lord Birkenhead, the Lord High Chancellor of Great Britain, who sat on the woolsack.[48] As Lord Chancellor he was also a parliamentary member of the House of Lords, sat in Cabinet and was 'a key member of the government'.[49] In 1921 he went from Baron to Viscount; the next year he became an Earl. He was also to become Secretary of State for India.

Smith/Birkenhead had 'the glittering prizes'.[50] Smith/Birkenhead moved between legal and political roles, including the highest judicial position.[51] As a politician he gave searingly eloquent speeches and was known for his wit and daring and admired for this.[52] His biographer John Campbell tells us in his entry on Birkenhead in the *Oxford Dictionary of National Biography* that he was '[t]all, darkly handsome, unashamedly ambitious, endowed with a scathing wit and an inexhaustible appetite for life and pleasure'. To Campbell, 'he made himself the epitome of the Oxford Union "Swell"' and this was during 'a golden age' of his college 'in the 1890s'.[53] That golden age was a golden age for men only (not said by Campbell).

In multiple capacities, Smith/Birkenhead acted vigorously and effectively, for much of his career, to keep women out of positions of public power: to ensure that those positions remained exclusively for men. Women shouldn't vote. They shouldn't sit in Parliament. And he went out of his way to ensure that this was the case, slipping from role to role, and drawing on a range of political and legal arguments to arrive at the one conclusion: women should keep out. He was adept at playing with words and rhetoric to achieve this feat.

According to Campbell, Birkenhead's 'belief that force ultimately rules underlay his opposition to women's suffrage'. As Campbell elaborates:

> At one level his attitude was simply the protection of male privilege. Characteristically however he rationalized his case on a more philosophical basis, arguing that 'votes are to swords exactly what bank notes are to gold – the one is effective only because the other is believed to be behind it'.[54]

[48] To an Australian this conjures up a bale of wool in a sheep shearing shed, but from long tradition this was the dignifying furniture for this great office bearer and it still is.

[49] John Campbell, 'Smith, Frederick Edwin, First Earl of Birkenhead', *Oxford Dictionary of National Biography* (17 September 2015), available at www.oxforddnb.com/display/10.1093/ref:odnb/9780198614128.001.0001/odnb-9780198614128-e-36137?rskey=UuDw8o&result=4.

[50] As FE Smith he was famous for saying that '[t]he world continues to offer glittering prizes to those who have stout hearts and sharp swords': see Frederick Edwin Smith, *America Revisited* (London, Cassell, 1924) 200. One assumes he thought he had both, hence the prizes.

[51] His remarkable variety of powerful roles brings to mind the Lord High Chancellor of the Mikado.

[52] See John Campbell, *FE Smith: First Earl of Birkenhead* (London, Jonathan Cape, 1983).

[53] Campbell (n 49) 2.

[54] ibid 5.

Women essentially should not have what he had and enjoyed. Birkenhead lived in an all-male social, political and legal world, which he revelled in. With Churchill he established The Other Club which attracted an all-male influential membership, and still seems to be going today.[55] Another glamourous and influential club, The Garrick Club, admitted women for the first time in 2024, its membership having been revealed by *The Guardian*. (It included judges, the head of the Civil Service, and the head of MI6, the latter two quitting from the Club after this revelation.)[56] The Garrick Club, at the time of writing, has two women members (Dame Judi Dench and Dame Sian Phillips) and 1,500 men; the head of the Civil Service has returned to its fold.[57]

VII. As FE Smith and MP for Liverpool Walton in 1910: The Female Franchise Bill and Black Friday

In 1910, as Member for Liverpool Walton, FE Smith opposed the Parliamentary Franchise (Women) HC Bill at its second reading (a Bill that failed). He spoke at length on why women could not be trusted with the exercise of public power. In essence they were the wrong kinds of being. He noted 'the frequently used' argument that 'man, actually or potentially, is a fighting animal … women are, actually or potentially against fighting' and gave this opinion his support, saying that 'the differentiation of the sexes grows more acute, and not less, with every day of civilisation'.[58]

Smith set his mind to the task of denouncing women. He quoted at length the thoughts on women of the 'fascinating writer HG Wells' who thought much like he did:

> The trend of evolutionary forces through long centuries of human development has been on the whole towards differentiation. An adult white woman differs far more from a white man than a negress or pigmy woman from her equivalent male. The education, the mental disposition of a white or Asiatic woman reeks of sex; her modesty, her decorum, is not to ignore sex but to refine and put a point to it; her costume is clamorous with the distinctive elements of her form. The white woman in the materially prosperous nations is more of a sexual specialist then her sister of the poor and austere peoples, of the prosperous classes more so than the peasant woman.[59]

[55] ibid 4; Fred Glueckstein, 'The Other Club: Founded by Churchill and FE Smith' (*The Churchill Project*, 12 September 2016), available at winstonchurchill.hillsdale.edu/club-founded-churchill-f-e-smith/.

[56] See the extensive writings of Amelia Gentleman in *The Guardian* including Amelia Gentleman, 'Head of Civil Service Simon Case Rejoins Garrick Club Six Months after Quitting it' *The Guardian* (Online, 3 October 2024), available at www.theguardian.com/uk-news/2024/oct/02/head-of-civil-service-simon-case-rejoins-garrick-club-six-months-after-quitting-it.

[57] ibid.

[58] *Hansard*, HC Deb 11 July 1910, vol 19, cols 67–68.

[59] ibid 68.

Smith then endorsed this characterisation of women, saying that this was why they should not exercise state power. He explained:

> The most characteristic quality in the conception of law is its sanction, or the means by which it is made effective. In making it effective no woman can play the slightest part. … It is an elemental disqualification, and one which is periodical in its source of weakness, even before maternity, and during and after maternity it can generally be pronounced chronic.[60]

He added: 'We are the legatees of the most nicely adjusted political fabric which the world has ever known.'[61]

Many women were not of this view. In the same year, 1910, on what came to be known as 'Black Friday', women publicly protested against their exclusion from the franchise. Sylvia Pankhurst gave an account of the event:

> As, one after the other, small deputations of twelve women appeared in sight they were set upon by the police and hurled aside. Mrs Cobden Sanderson, who had been in the first deputation, was rudely seized and pressed against the wall by the police, who held her there by both arms for a considerable time, sneering and jeering at her meanwhile … Just as this had been done, I saw Miss Ada Wright close to the entrance. Several police seized her, lifted her from the ground and flung her back into the crowd. A moment afterwards she appeared again, and I saw her running as fast as she could towards the House of Commons. A policeman struck her with all his force and she fell to the ground. For a moment there was a group of struggling men round the place where she lay, then she rose up, only to be flung down again immediately. Then a tall, grey-headed man with a silk hat was seen fighting to protect her; but three or four police seized hold of him and bundled him away. Then again, I saw Miss Ada Wright's tall, grey-clad figure, but over and over again she was flung to the ground, how often I cannot say. It was a painful and degrading sight. At last, she was lying against the wall of the House of Lords, close to the Strangers' Entrance, and a number of women, with pale and distressed faces were kneeling down round her. She was in a state of collapse.[62]

VIII. Excluding Women from the Full Franchise: Birkenhead as Lord Chancellor in 1919

In January of 1919, FE Smith was appointed Lord Chancellor of Great Britain, and received a hereditary peerage, becoming Lord Birkenhead. At the same time, by dint of office, he became a member of the parliamentary House of Lords. Thus he inhabited the highest legal role and was a member of Cabinet, advising the Prime Minister. Now as Lord Birkenhead, he secured the failure of the Labour party's

[60] ibid.
[61] ibid 70.
[62] Sylvia Pankhurst, *Votes for Women* (London, 25 November 1910) 121.

Women's Emancipation HC Bill (1919) ('Emancipation Bill') by supporting a more conservative bill which was the Sex Disqualification (Removal) Act of 1919.[63]

As Mari Takayanagi explains, the Emancipation Bill 'contained three clauses: to remove the disqualification of women from holding civil and judicial appointments; to include women on the franchise on the same terms as men; and to allow women to sit and vote in the House of Lords'.[64] Initially it looked as if the Bill would go through: 'The Women's Emancipation Bill successfully passed all stages in the House of Commons including a division at third reading against whipped government opposition.'[65] But the coalition Government introduced its own Bill in the House of Lords: the misleadingly named Sex Disqualification (Removal) HL Bill (1919).[66] Again Takayanagi explains:

> The Women's Emancipation Bill stood no chance against the government bill, was 'torn to pieces' by the Lord Chancellor and inevitably fell. Only the substance of the first clause (on civil and judicial appointments) eventually made it through to become law in the Sex Disqualification (Removal) Act. The clauses about the franchise and women peers were lost.[67]

Lord Birkenhead made plain his feelings about women having equal franchise to men and also sitting in his House. He said this in his second reading speech about the Sex Disqualification Removal Bill:

> To give women the same parliamentary franchise as men at this moment would involve the addition of some 5,000,000 new voters to the electorate, and a General Election certainly ought, if we adhere to constitutional precedent, to follow closely upon the passing of a measure which had produced so great a change in the existing constituencies.[68]

Hence the Government had good reason to continue to exclude women from the full franchise and also from membership of the House of Lords. Birkenhead seemed to be saying that Parliament, within the context of a general election, would simply be far too busy to deal with all these new women voters. And when it came to women sitting in the House of Lords, he turned to the niceties of the royal prerogative, which he insisted must be respected.

[63] Mari Takayanagi, 'The Significance of the Sex Disqualification (Removal) Act 1919' (First Women Lawyers Series, More House, 25 January 2019), available at www.innertemple.org.uk/women-in-law/the-significance-of-the-sex-disqualification-removal-act-1919/. See also Mari Takayanagi, 'A Changing House: The Life Peerages Act 1958' (2008) 27 *Parliamentary History* 380.

[64] Mari Takayanagi, 'Sacred Year or Broken Reed? The Sex Disqualification (Removal) Act 1919' (2020) 29 *Women's History Review* 563, 565.

[65] ibid.

[66] Sex Disqualification (Removal) Act 1919 s 1: 'A person shall not be disqualified by sex or marriage from the exercise of any public function, or from being appointed to or holding any civil or judicial office or post, or from entering or assuming or carrying on any civil profession or vocation, or for admission to any incorporated society (whether incorporated by Royal Charter or otherwise), and a person shall not be exempted by sex or marriage from the liability to serve as a juror'.

[67] Takayanagi (n 64) 565. See also John Garahy, 'First Lady of the Law' (*Law Society of Scotland*, 19 August 2019), available at www.lawscot.org.uk/members/journal/issues/vol-64-issue-08/first-lady-of-the-law/.

[68] *Hansard*, HL Deb 22 July 1919, vol 35, col 894.

> The creation of Peers having a seat in Parliament is, of course, a matter of Royal Prerogative, and both on constitutional and other grounds it is improper, in my judgement, that the ladies who at present possess Peerages in their own right should be seated in the House automatically without the King on the advice of his responsible Ministers having considered the matter in each case.[69]

IX. Keeping Women Out of the House of Lords: Lord Chancellor Birkenhead in *Viscountess Rhondda's Claim* 1922

Three years later, Birkenhead got his chance to block women, more securely, from the House of Lords, using the (ill named) Sex Disqualification (Removal) Act. The timing of this matter was crucial because much happened swiftly, with critical changes of personnel, which made all the difference to the result. Margaret Haig, Viscountess Rhondda, a hereditary peer in her own right, petitioned the King for a writ to summon her to Parliament to sit in the House of Lords. No woman had been admitted to the House of Lords before. Haig was a strong political activist and suffragist, prominent business woman, and literary editor. As her entry in the *Dictionary of Welsh Biography* tells us:

> She attended London demonstrations, wrote in the suffrage and local press, spoke at meetings countrywide and even jumped onto the running board of Prime Minister Asquith's car in St Andrews. In 1913 she was briefly imprisoned in Usk Gaol and went on hunger strike after setting a letterbox alight in Newport … By 1919 she sat on 33 boards and chaired 7. In the 1920s she held more directorships than any other woman in the UK … She was the first president of the Women's Press Club and an assiduous editor.[70]

So the title 'Viscountess' is deceptive.[71]

Haig's petition was referred to the House of Lords Committee of Privileges. It was heard on 2 March 1922. The then Attorney General, Sir Gordon Hewitt, was a Liberal appointment. (His immediate predecessor was FE Smith, a Conservative appointment.) Hewitt offered no opposition to Haig's petition and it was granted by the Committee of Privileges, which agreed that the Sex Disqualification (Removal) Act 1919[72] had removed any obstacles.

[69] ibid 895–96.

[70] Angela V John, 'Thomas, Margaret Haig, 2nd Viscountess Rhondda (1883–1958), Suffragette, Editor, Author and Businesswoman', *Dictionary of Welsh Biography* (11 June 2021), available at biography.wales/article/s12-THOM-HAI-1883.

[71] 'Suffragette Viscountess Rhondda's Newport Bomb Attack Remembered' (*BBC News*, online, 2 June 2013), available at www.bbc.com/news/uk-wales-22740340. Lady Rhondda dies just before female enduring peers sit in the House of Lords.

[72] Recall that Smith helped to install this Act in order to oust the more emancipatory Female Emancipation Act.

Hewitt ceased as Attorney General on 6 March[73] and on the same day a conservative Attorney General was appointed, Sir Ernest Pollock, a known opponent of female suffrage. On 30 March, on the motion of the Lord Chancellor, Lord Birkenhead (the former Conservative Attorney General FE Smith), the report of the Committee was referred back to the Committee for reconsideration and set down for reargument on 18 May. The Attorney General, now Pollock, acted for the Crown and opposed the claim.[74]

On June 27 the decision of the Second Committee was delivered: it now refused the petition under the Lord Chancellorship of Birkenhead. The Committee – now a 'lay tribunal' because a number of its members had no legal training – decided 20 to 4 that the claim had not been made out. However Viscount Haldane, in dissent, explicitly regretted the haste with which the matter was brought on: 'I regret much that the desire of the Committee to give an immediate decision precluded us from having the benefit of the fully considered examination of the law'.[75] Lord Wrenbury also expressed his concern about the process:

> [I]n no Court of Justice from the lowest to the highest, including your Lordships' House, can this case hereafter be cited as an authority upon any construction of the statute [the Sex Disqualification (Removal) Act]. This Committee is a mixed tribunal of laymen and of those generally styled as 'learned in the law'. The former did not, before giving their vote, even wait to receive such assistance as their legal colleagues could give them in applying the law to that which is purely a legal question. … no judge will be bound to follow the present case as any authority upon the true construction of the Sex Disqualification (Removal) Act, 1919.[76]

Meanwhile Lord Birkenhead, who was rushing the matter through, still found time to prepare and issue a lengthy decision designed to persuade his colleagues, many of whom he knew to have no legal training and to be ill-prepared and so heavily reliant on him.

In *Viscountess Rhondda's Claim*, Birkenhead reasoned thus:

> The case is not one of suspension of a right or abeyance of an activity. The holder of a peerage dignity who is a minor is not entitled to receive a writ, but he may grow up and will then become so entitled. A felon or a bankrupt is not entitled to receive the writ, but a felon may receive a pardon and a bankrupt his discharge. These things are possible in nature and permissible in law; but a person who is a female must remain a female till she dies. Apart from a change in the law, she could not before 1919 both be a woman and participate in the legislative proceedings of the House of Lords. By her sex she is not … disqualified from the exercise of this right. In respect of her dignity she is a subject of rights which ex vi termini [by definition; by force of the term] cannot include this right. The judgment of Willes J, in *Chorlton v Lings*, is express authority to this effect. No authority was cited to the contrary, and I believe the true view to be that

[73] Gordon Hewitt went off to become Lord Chief Justice of England from 1922–40.
[74] His brother was Frederick Pollock of Pollock and Maitland.
[75] *Viscountess Rhondda's Claim* (n 11) 389.
[76] ibid 400–01.

> the practice of drawing the patents with remainders to females in the form which is now many generations old, and which is exemplified in this case, shows how long it has been the unanimous view of the profession.[77]

In other words, minors, felons and bankrupts could acquire the writ (to sit in the House of Lords I presume) because their status could change, 'but a person who is a female must remain a female till she dies' and this had always been the case and it had been 'the unanimous view of the profession'. So women's non-personhood for this purpose could not change.

Birkenhead continued that

> a peeress in her own right is not a person who has an incident of peerage but is disqualified from exercising it by her sex. She is a person who for her life holds a dignity which does not include the right of a female to exercise that function at all.[78]

Does this make sense? Is it meant to make sense? Is it a cruel joke? Clearly its purpose was to circumnavigate the Sex Disqualification (Removal) Act by asserting that the Committee was not considering disqualification and hence the Act did not apply. She was not disqualified because she had never been qualified and couldn't be because she was female. She had never had the right and couldn't have the right. Sex disbarred her. This was nasty sophistry and pedantry demonstrated at length. It was dismissive of, and entirely uninterested in, the ethics of this situation or its accord or disaccord with fundamental legal principle concerning equality. As Sachs and Wilson summarise:

> [T]he Lord Chancellor remained obdurate in his opposition [to admission of women to the House of Lords]. His special position as leader of the House of Lords and head of the judiciary enabled him to have the recommendation of the Committee [approving women's admission] referred back to a larger committee which was substantially weighted against the admission of women to the House of Lords. It appears that against the strong objection of members of the original committee, he quickly pressed the matter to a vote, with the result that what had originally been an unopposed report in Lady Rhondda's favour was converted into a decision against her by 20 votes to 4, with 5 abstentions.[79]

Birkenhead, aka Smith, took pride in the fact that he almost singlehandedly kept women out of the Upper House of Parliament. But, of course, he was not operating alone. His moves worked because he could find ample support. And, subsequently, he was not criticised or denounced for these actions because they were not regarded as deeply unacceptable. Birkenhead was treated as a man's man, and his promotion of the cause of men did him no harm. By contrast the promotion of the cause of women by John Stuart Mill provoked opposition and hostility.

[77] ibid 362 (citations omitted).
[78] ibid 363.
[79] Sachs and Wilson (n 13) 33.

A significant number of the members of the House of Lords (unsuccessfully) opposed the admission of women in 1958, when life time peers were created by Harold Macmillan.[80] Four female life peers (and 10 men) were admitted that year.[81] Haig died just before the first women were admitted to the House.[82] Female hereditary peers were admitted in 1963[83] (the same year that the Beatles released 'Love me Do' to put the timing in perspective). If Birkenhead had been swimming against the tide of male opinion, his 1922 move would not have lasted for over 40 years. In 1999 Tony Blair greatly reduced the numbers of hereditary peers, from over 600 to 92.[84] The very small number of female hereditary peers was thereby removed and so at the time of writing, all hereditary peers are again male. (Also at the time of writing Prime Minister Starmer has plans to remove such peers altogether.)[85]

X. Birkenhead's Legacy Despite the Misuses of Male Legal Power

So why spend so much time looking at the many anti-woman manoeuvres of Birkenhead in political and legal office? Because he did so from the highest legal office, he took full advantage of the great powers of the Lord Chancellor, his moves against women were bold, unprincipled, sustained, shrewd and conniving; they demonstrated open bigotry, they were hugely successful, and none of this seemed to matter to the legal establishment or to the theorists of law. Law could be openly manipulated for male advantage and yet this was of little interest. It was not condemned; it barely registered. Birkenhead continued to be excused as an eloquent quick-footed glamourous 'bounder',[86] the man who loved giving offence.[87] And he was also remembered as a sage judge. The maleness of law and

[80] Life Peerages Act 1958. See 'Life Peerages Act 1958' (*UK Parliament*), available at www.parliament.uk/about/living-heritage/evolutionofparliament/houseoflords/parliamentacts/overview/lifepeerages-act/: 'An amendment to exclude women from the House was defeated at committee stage by 134 votes to 30.'

[81] They included the criminologist Barbara Wootton. See Ann Oakley, *A Critical Woman: Barbara Wootton, Social Science and Public Policy in the Twentieth Century* (London, Bloomsbury Academic, 2011).

[82] 'Suffragette Viscountess Rhondda's Newport Bomb Attack Remembered' (n 71).

[83] Peerage Act 1963.

[84] This was achieved by the House of Lords Act 1999.

[85] See Harriett Sherwood, 'The Last of the Hereditary Peers in the House of Lords' *The Guardian* (Online, 20 July 2024), available at www.theguardian.com/politics/article/2024/jul/20/hereditary-peers-house-of-lords-end. And on why the House of Lords is a wholly undemocratic but nevertheless functional chamber, see Ian Dunt, *How Westminster Works … and Why it Doesn't* (London, Orion Publishing, 2023).

[86] David Cannadine, 'Lord Bounder' (*London Review of Books*, (London, 19 January 1984), available at www.lrb.co.uk/the-paper/v06/n01/david-cannadine/lord-bounder.

[87] See Robert French, 'The Fine Art of Giving and Taking Offence' (Birkenhead Lecture, London, 18 November 2015).

its institutions, to which he was so deeply committed, was too commonplace to raise concern.

In 1935 David Lloyd George had this to say about Birkenhead (in the foreword to the biography of Birkenhead written by Birkenhead's son):

> Judged by the essentials of manhood, intellect, courage, kindliness, loyalty, Lord Birkenhead was a great man. It is one of the tragedies of public life that the country he loved never got the best and highest of which he was capable, for he was cut off when he had only reached an age when most statesmen attain the height of their opportunity.[88]

In 1984 David Cannadine offered another assessment of Birkenhead. In his review of Campbell's biography of Birkenhead, he described the subject thus: 'Driven by remorseless ambition, and aided by a first-rate brain of quicksilver speed, he amassed a remarkable tally of gongs, baubles and glittering prizes, at Oxford, in the law, and in politics.'[89]

Birkenhead's sustained moves against women, in different capacities, over years, generally have not featured in his record. Birkenhead's long-term effects on the constitution of the UK Parliament are hardly mentioned,[90] or they are quietly noted but not disapproved. He did much to shape public power and to ensure that only men could wield it. But his role in achieving a treaty with Ireland was seen as his legacy and also the reform of the law of property.

Smith was praised for his wisdom and dignity as a judge. According to his biographer John Campbell:

> The major constitutional and judicial responsibilities of his position he would discharge with a dignity beyond all criticism. … Above all he intended to enjoy himself, to indulge the glory and the grandeur of simply being Lord Chancellor in his forty-seventh year, to point the contrast with his elderly predecessors, to make the Lord Chancellorship an active and conspicuous, as well as an honoured and historic office.[91]

Smith's open insistence on an all-male franchise and his leading role in ensuring an all-male House of Lords, for decades, was neither memorable nor remarkable and do not even feature in modern accounts of his professional life. The *Britannica* entry on Birkenhead still speaks glowingly of his law reform efforts in relation to property law and the judiciary and then explains his role in the making of Irish independence, but there is nothing on *Viscountess Rhondda's Claim*. So too with the *Oxford Dictionary of National Biography* entry.

As FE Smith and as MP he actively opposed the female franchise and articulated his disdainful views of women (to male acclaim). His active opposition to female rights did not disqualify him from becoming the highest judicial officer.

[88] Frederick Winston Furneaux Smith Earl, *Frederick Edwin, Earl of Birkenhead: The Last Phase, by His Son, the Earl of Birkenhead* (London, Thornton Butterworth, 1935) 13.

[89] Cannadine (n 86).

[90] Campbell's *Oxford Dictionary of National Biography* entry on Birkenhead does not mention *Lady Rhondda's Claim*.

[91] Campbell (n 52) 469.

In government, now as Lord Chancellor, he supported the Sex Disqualification (Removal) Act because it tactically wiped out a more emancipatory act. Then his very political work, against women, as Lord Chancellor in *Lady Rhondda's Claim* did not become part of his legacy. RVW Heuston refers to

> the true weight of his [Birkenhead's] achievement on the Woolsack … The learning and wisdom of his judgments, the vigour and good sense of his efforts at law reform, and the essential rightness and wisdom of his public opinions on all public issues.[92]

Heuston praises Birkenhead in all his capacities, for his wisdom and intelligence:

> As Lord Chancellor Birkenhead takes a very high place in the list of holders of that office. From the very start he devoted his great talents to excelling in all three of the aspects of the work of Lord chancellor, in Cabinet, as head of the judicial system, and as speaker in the House of Lords.[93]

This is despite the fact that, in every role, Birkenhead spoke against women and highly effectively, so that the consequences were felt until late in the twentieth century. David Cannadine once dubbed Lord Birkenhead 'Lord Bounder', which carries an amused tone. But Cannadine also said this:

> His attitude to women was chauvinist in the extreme: they were conveniences, 'mere conduit pipes', ordained for men's use as relaxation and entertainment, to bolster their morale and massage their egos. They were not intelligent, should not be given the vote, and must be kept out of the Lords at all costs.[94]

XI. The Persons Cases and the Male Mentality of Law

Through the Persons Cases, and the deployment of the concept of the Legal Person, legal men at the highest levels gave to themselves almost exclusive control of the public sphere. They said women were not Persons which was akin to saying that women were not human beings and they did not flinch from this implication and this continued right up to the last Persons Case (which I will consider in chapter six). As Sachs and Wilson remark,

> [o]ne of the characteristics of judicial pronouncement in England, particularly noticeable in these cases, was its lack of selfconsciousness or strain. The judges asserted the law with what Karl Mannheim in another context has called a 'somnambulistic certainty with regard to truth'.[95]

The term Person was used in defiance of its natural meaning and in a highly offensive manner. Some people got to be Persons, others did not. Rather than the

[92] Heuston (n 6) 391.
[93] ibid 382.
[94] Cannadine (n 6).
[95] Sachs and Wilson (n 13) 50 (citations omitted).

concept of the 'Person' providing a means of including and recognising all human beings, it was used to establish in groups and out groups. So when judges came upon the word in an empowering statute, one which at first blush would appear to recognise all people/humans/persons who could do X, they used the term to achieve the very opposite. They said the term could not possibly have been meant to include all. The assemblage of the unfortunate – women, lunatics, children, animals – was an assemblage of the unpersoned, to varying degrees.

The Persons Cases show how deep-seated this shared legal belief in male legal right was. It went to the very definition of a Person and it was acceptable to make this manifest in law. When it really mattered, women were not Persons. This thinking was embedded within the male culture of law. It was a male legal mentality. As Sachs and Wilson observed, again drawing on the insights of Karl Mannheim:

> [W]hen a conceptual apparatus is the same for all the members of the group, the presuppositions underlying the individual concepts never become perceptible; human beings do not theorise about the actual situations in which they live as long as they are well adjusted to them. The judges were accordingly content to adopt modes of classification without questioning the assumptions about power, property and sex that underlay them.[96]

And yet the facts are simple, indisputable, ugly and obvious when looked at. Until well into the twentieth century, women were positively excluded by men of legal authority from the institutions of legal and political and economic power, from education, from property, from the commercial world. Once married, women's bodies were made legally available to their husbands for sexual purposes, with or without their consent. Thus force and coercion were licensed. And this was all done through law and with the active support of lawmakers. There remains remarkably little intellectual curiosity about how these bald facts have shaped law and its scholarship. Moreover, leading legal figures who spoke for men and against women, and who insisted that male right should be clearly reflected in law, have retained their reputations and are still revered. They are still admired, their achievements celebrated.

Men, simply because they were men, had access to the perquisites of public power, including legal knowledge formation. Women, because they were women, were precluded from education in law (and the other disciplines) and so they could not act in any official capacity in law, they could not interpret the law and they could not explain the law. Only men could engage in legal knowledge formation, because only men were permitted the education that could make them legal experts. Crude biological classifications, based on genitalia and reproductive capacity, meant that women could not become authorities in law (could not enter educational or public roles which would let them become such). They could not participate in the formation of law's basic concepts, because they were denied the education and the exercise of public power, which could allow them to do so.

[96] ibid.

In other words, men of law exclusively controlled what Gerda Lerner has called the 'explanatory systems': how sense was made of law, and who were to be deemed its most authoritative interpreters, who would be deferred to and quoted, and invoked for their wisdom and deep learning. In her extended anthropological analysis of patriarchy, and its origins, Lerner avows that women were 'systematically excluded from the enterprise of creating symbol systems' including those of law.[97] Moreover, male control of definition was 'deliberate and pervasive'.[98]

The men of law who advocated strongly for men, legal men such as Loreburn and Birkenhead, were not making outlier statements. Rather they were speaking openly from within the shared legal mentality which found male legal rule to be natural and inevitable and appropriate. That acceptance and enforcement of male legal rule has yet to be considered seriously for its significance for the formation and nature of law.

All of this is on the public record. It should not call for argument and proof, though it feels that argument and proof are called for. The reason it feels that argument and proof are needed is that these basic facts about law still do not feature in law's main explanations and justifications, as I will show in the last two chapters, when I bring the story up to the present.

XII. Coda: Lord Hailsham and *DPP v Morgan*

Before leaving the Lord Chancellors, and their deployment of concentrated legal power in the interests of men, it is worth bringing the story up to date. A third Lord Chancellor, Lord Hailsham, was the longest serving man in this office in the twentieth century, under two conservative Prime Ministers.[99] Hailsham is of interest because he effectively diminished the Personhood of women, through his legal decision-making, but in a different way from his predecessors. He did not belittle women, in order to deny them public power, as Persons. Rather he defined central criminal law, concerned with forceful sexual intrusions, from the perspective of the male defendant doing the intruding, while shrinking the legal significance of the wishes of the woman victim, who was being intruded upon.

To explain. In 1975, Hailsham was the leading majority judge in the rape case of *DPP v Morgan*.[100] The case concerned the rapes, by three men, of Daphne Morgan, the wife of William Morgan. William Morgan as husband orchestrated

[97] Gerda Lerner, *The Creation of Patriarchy* (Oxford, Oxford University Press, 1986) 5.

[98] ibid 220.

[99] He was Lord High Chancellor from 20 June 1970 to 4 March 1974 under Edward Heath, and from 4 May 1979 to 13 June 1987 under Margaret Thatcher.

[100] *DPP v Morgan* [1976] AC 182. Hailsham's judgment is the most cited. At the time of *Morgan* he had only recently been replaced on the woolsack by labour appointment Baron Elwyn Jones, but was still sitting as a Law Lord. Hailsam was returned to the woolsack five years later by Margaret Thatcher. He therefore cast a long shadow.

the rape of his wife by his three friends and then raped her himself. Morgan was not charged as a principal offender for the rape of Daphne Morgan,[101] because of the husband's immunity from rape prosecution, which was accepted by Hailsham, and drew little comment from him. The case had adverse effects on women, well into the twenty-first century, because of Lord Hailsham's formulation of the mental element of rape. He said that if the defendants believed, however unreasonably, that the victim was consenting, then they did not have the requisite guilty mind and so there was no rape.[102] An honest but unreasonable belief in consent meant that they did not have the mental element of a rapist. Hailsham was fully aware of the significance of his determination. He said it was 'of great academic importance in the theory of English criminal law'.[103]

Hailsham's anticipation of his legacy was appropriate. His formulation of the subjective test of the mental element of rape, his framing of the crime in terms of what was actually thought by the defendants, however unreasonable that belief, endured. It was not until 2004 that the law changed,[104] so that the reasonableness of the belief that the victim consented became legally relevant and part of the test of the guilty mind.

To many lawyers, Hailsham's determination made good legal sense and meshed well with legal principle. For as Hailsham put it, a person should not be guilty of a serious crime if he did not intend all the elements of the crime.[105] However, this framing of the law meant that a rape that had occurred from the point of view of the victim (she did not consent to sexual intercourse and she had made this as plain as she could) did not determine whether a rape had occurred in law. The crime turned on what the defendant honestly believed, no matter how unreasonable that belief, not on what the woman wanted, nor what she went through, which was in fact a rape. The fact that law and society educated men poorly in the meaning of female sexual autonomy, and had for centuries doubted its very existence, made this a hazardous law for women.

The same case is also notable for its silences about the experiences of wives living with sadistic husbands. (John Stuart Mill would have been alert to them.)

[101] Morgan was charged with aiding and abetting the other men to commit rape. The case was therefore, in law, not a marital rape case because the husband's rape of his wife was not considered to be rape.

[102] The defendants in this case were not believed when they said that they thought the victim was consenting, but then this was a brutal group rape, with a pinned down and struggling, manifestly terrified victim. Had the defendants been led to believe, albeit unreasonably, that Morgan's wife was consenting, no one would have been responsible for rape, in any capacity, including Morgan himself, for he would no longer be aiding and abetting rape. This necessary implication of Hailsham's reasoning was pointed out to me by my colleague Ian Leader-Elliott.

[103] *Morgan* (n 100) 204.

[104] Sexual Offences Act 2003. It is rape if the prosecution can establish that the accused (A) intends penetration, the victim (B) 'does not consent to the penetration' and the accused 'does not reasonably believe' that the victim consents. Then '[w]hether a belief is reasonable is to be determined having regard to all the circumstances, including any steps A has taken to ascertain whether B consents'.

[105] Hailsham's formulation became the gold standard on subjective intent in that he linked the wrong of the crime to the accused's understanding of the wrong, no matter how misguided. See Ngaire Naffine, *Criminal Law and the Man Problem* (Oxford, Hart Publishing, 2019).

Lord Hailsham did little to censure the husband for the rape of his wife, even though he vehemently condemned the actions of the other defendants, and the husband's role in them. Lord Hailsham permitted the husband to recede from the case as a (lawful) rapist in his own right and, for decades, Lord Hailsham's framing of the case meant that *Morgan* did not come to be seen as a marital rape case, with the husband exempted from prosecution for a very nasty brutal rape, because of ancient law about male sex right, a right which extinguished the sexual autonomy of the wife. Instead *Morgan* came to stand for another legal principle: that the *mens rea* of serious offences should depend on what the accused subjectively thought to be the case, no matter how misguided and unreasonable that belief, because criminal culpability resided in the mind of the accused. Meanwhile, a law going back to Hale, and congealed by Stephen in *R v Clarence*,[106] immunising the husband from rape prosecution, was quietly affirmed by Hailsham in *Morgan* and persisted until the last decade of the twentieth century.[107]

[106] *R v Clarence* (1888) 22 QBD 23.
[107] See my extended analysis of *Morgan* (n 100) in Naffine, n 105.

5

Case Study 1: AV Dicey's Argument for Male Rule

I. Introduction

With his bracing honesty, the long-lived Albert Venn Dicey[1] comes almost as a breath of fresh air in the authoritative discussions of the Legal Person and why the concept was, and should be, aligned with men. He did not beat around the bush. To Dicey, the legal and political world was controlled and peopled exclusively by men (his descriptive statement, which was accurate) and this was a healthy state of affairs and should be retained (his normative statement, which was questionable). To Dicey, the legal subject was patently, manifestly, a man *and* should stay that way.

Dicey articulated and endorsed a powerful, self-serving male mythology. There was the strong protecting man, of good character, who would safeguard the state and the woman of weak character who would necessarily weaken the institutions of Britain, if she were herself endowed with public power. After all, '[t]he State has been built up by men; its welfare depends on the encouragement of manly qualities'.[2] As we will see, Dicey's interpreters, decades on, wished neither to acknowledge nor engage with his boldly stated male supremacism. Dicey was not to be seen in this manner. Dicey's honest description of the maleness of the institutions of the state was simply ignored. And a veil was drawn over Dicey's strong partiality for this state of affairs.

In the previous two chapters, we saw judges sometimes being delicate about the problem of women wanting power, thereby threatening to dilute the male state and its male officialdom. When asked to define the concept of the Legal Person, and explain why it was fitting for men but not for women, many judges said, 'well we have the greatest respect for women, but this is just how things have always been, and it is not of our making'. The Legal Person, they declared, was a man, of course (a descriptive statement). And further, there was nothing wrong with it. They said, in essence, that this distribution of legal power was what women really wanted, that it was in their interests and men were only being solicitous when they garnered power to themselves, given women's physical and character

[1] Dicey was born on 4 February 1835 and died on 7 April 1922 at the age of 89.
[2] AV Dicey, *Letters to a Friend on Votes for Women* (London, John Murray, 1909) 49.

weaknesses (all normative statements). James Fitzjames Stephen as a writer, but not on the bench, spoke more plainly than some about the need to keep law and state male. Lord Birkenhead as a politician, but again less so on the bench, also spoke his mind. Dicey spoke on behalf of the male state and against women, without qualification.

II. Dicey's Advocacy of Male Public Power and the Rule of Law

Dicey positively advocated for male public power, and its exclusive exercise, and openly opposed the rights of women in two works. The first was a short treatise, published in 1909, *Letters to a Friend*,[3] dedicated to the argument that women should not be permitted the franchise. The second was his introduction to the eighth edition of his most celebrated work, *Introduction to the Study of Law and the Constitution*,[4] published in 1915. Here Dicey did much the same thing. He insisted, now with some urgency, that for the purposes of the franchise, women should not be classified as 'Persons'. And women certainly should not be considered Persons who could exercise more extensive powers, which was, for Dicey, the worrying further development. Indeed, in both works Dicey spoke of women's unfitness for the exercise of pretty well all public power. He was explicit and adamant.

Dicey's statements of 1915 were in nervous anticipation of the female franchise which succeeded, in part, three years later, despite Dicey's interventions. In 1918, notwithstanding Dicey's profound misgivings, some women obtained the franchise. (Four years later, Lord Birkenhead came in to stop further erosion of male power by blocking women from the House of Lords.)

Dicey's fierce endorsement of male power, and his equally fierce opposition to female power, may seem odd, given his association with the idea of the rule of law: the idea that both ruler and ruled should equally be subject to law. No-one should be above the law, in this view. Dicey, as scholar, is said to have articulated the basic constitutional principles of England based on equality before the law, legality and the rule of law. According to Martin Loughlin, 'AV Dicey … is widely regarded as the high priest of orthodox constitutional thought in Britain'.[5]

As Kristen Rundle elucidates Dicey's central idea: the 'core political demand' animating the idea of the rule of law is 'mutual subordination to law'.[6] That is, ruler and ruled, official and subject, government and governed, should all be subordinate to the demands of law. If certain parts of the population are

[3] ibid.

[4] AV Dicey, *Introduction to the Study of the Law and the Constitution*, 8th edn (London, MacMillan, 1915).

[5] Martin Loughlin, 'Dicey, Albert Venn (1835–1922)', *Routledge Encyclopedia of Philosophy* (1998), available at www.rep.routledge.com/articles/biographical/dicey-albert-venn-1835-1922/v-1.

[6] Kristen Rundle, *Revisiting the Rule of Law* (Cambridge University Press, 2022) 61.

treated differently, if they are systematically demoted, if their 'legal agency',[7] as Rundle calls it, is diminished, if there are arbitrary exclusions from the principle of 'mutual subordination', then the integrity of the rule of law suffers accordingly. Dicey seemed not to see that his advocacy of exclusive male public power had these damaging implications for his theory of the rule of law. Nor did his successors.

In his expansive statements about the rule of law, Dicey declared that '*no* man' should be punishable unless there was a breach of law, established by the courts, and all should have access to the ordinary courts of law. Dicey put it in this way:

> [N]o man is punishable or can be lawfully made to suffer in body or goods except for a distinct breach of law established in the ordinary legal manner before the ordinary courts of the land. In this sense the rule of law is contrasted with every system of government based on the exercise of persons in authority of wide, arbitrary, or discretionary powers of constraint.[8]

As Kristen Rundle spells out the ingredients of Dicey's rule of law:

> Three elements, or demands, are associated with it. The first is the demand that government proceed through a framework of legal norms and procedures rather than through unconstrained discretion. The second is the demand of equality between government officials and private individuals before the same ordinary law and the same ordinary courts. The third is the establishment and protection of individual rights through the development of the judge-made common law.[9]

So, to Dicey, everyone should have equal access to the ordinary courts of law and within those courts, all people should be placed on the same footing, officials and ordinary persons alike. But as we will see, Dicey did not regard women as the main agents or recipients of these legal protections, when he set down his demands for the rule of law. He was actively opposed to women acquiring the capacity to act as legal officials (who might themselves go to law and be subjected to law) and he believed that the ordinary courts should be run by men, and that only men should develop the common law. Women should not exercise such sovereign power. Male privilege was therefore woven into the very fabric of Dicey's rule of law, whose ostensible purpose was to secure the equality of all before the law and to remove the uses of arbitrary authority.

Dicey was mid Victorian,[10] but his long life carried him through to the 1920s. Dicey spans two centuries in his writing and three centuries in his reputation. He advanced fundamental legal principles: parliamentary sovereignty, equality and the rule of law and legality. To Loughlin, he 'presented constitutional law as a system resting on three basic precepts: parliamentary sovereignty, the rule of law

[7] ibid 61.
[8] AV Dicey, *Introduction to the Study of the Law of the Constitution*, 5th edn (London, Macmillan, 1897) 188.
[9] Rundle (n 6) 17.
[10] Victoria reigned from 1837 to 1901.

and a set of rules not directly enforced by courts which he labelled "constitutional conventions".[11]

Dicey is still regarded as an important figurehead of English constitutional law.[12] And yet in the first and second decades of the twentieth century, Dicey was interceding to prevent women from acquiring the sort of public power he was theorising about. He hoped to stop women getting the vote and then from acquiring the more extended power which he thought was its natural corollary. To Dicey, the rule of law should be a rule by men. Dicey conjured up a legal world of male officials and the law with which they operated secured their own entitlement and interests. The law that ruled in Dicey's understanding of the rule of law was the law of male power. Men were the rulers and they ruled through the law that invested them with political and legal power and at the same time ensured that women could not hold such power.

Dicey did not openly consider what this shutting out of women from his idea of the rule of law did to his rule of law. And nor did his later followers and interpreters. Was the rule of law therefore 'knocked off balance', to borrow Rundle's words, by this open preference for the one-sided allocation of legal power?[13] It seems that Dicey himself did not see that his advocacy of men, as officials, might pose a problem for his theory and its internal logic. The maleness of the officials of the rule of law was noted, accepted, supported, even regarded as necessary to the effectiveness of English law. This exposes a contradiction within Dicey's basic thinking. And then there was a deafening silence about this central contradiction in his thinking from those who came after Dicey, from those who sought to explain and defend his constitutional thought.

III. The Makings of Dicey

Dicey was an accomplished man of legal authority, who had a fine education and career, during which he helped to articulate a constitution for England. As Dylon Lino observes, Dicey 'was writing during the height of the "age of empire", [and] the rule of law was also bound up with the rule of empire: the British Empire in particular, at whose metropolitan centre he resided'.[14] Dicey had the blessings of the life of a well-connected Englishman, which allowed him to cultivate the people and circumstances in which he could flourish. Dicey had the right kin and connections. He was a part of 'the Victorian intellectual aristocracy'.[15] As his biographer Mark Walters informs us:

[11] Martin Loughlin, 'AV Dicey and the Making of Common Law Constitutionalism' (2022) 42 *OJLS* 366, 367.

[12] Kristen Rundle says this in Rundle (n 6).

[13] ibid 61.

[14] Dylan Lino, 'The Rule of Law and the Law of Empire: AV Dicey in Imperial Context' (2018) 81 *MLR* 739, 742.

[15] As he was so described in Roger Michener's foreword to AV Dicey, *Introduction to the Study of the Law of the Constitution* (Indianapolis, Liberty Classics, 1982) xii.

Dicey's mother's brother was Sir James Stephen (1789–1859), an influential lawyer in the Colonial Office whose children included Sir James Fitzjames Stephen (1829–94), author, lawyer, and judge, and Sir Leslie Stephen (1832–1904), author and literary critic, and father of author Virginia Woolf (1882–1941).[16]

Dicey went to the right universities, then on to the Bar and then on to the esteemed professorship, that he so strongly desired, which enabled him to mix in the best intellectual, legal and political circles, on both sides of the Atlantic. In 1882, Dicey was appointed Vinerian Professor of English Law at Oxford. As Walters continues:

> Dicey had (according to [his wife] Elinor Dicey) 'for years' wanted the Vinerian chair, Blackstone's chair, for unlike other chairs, including the Corpus chair in Jurisprudence, which he had also eyed for a time, it was in 'his own particular subject' and so was something of which he could 'make a great deal'.[17]

'Only in England', quips Martin Loughlin, in light-hearted mode.[18] 'A mid-Victorian Whig professor of law steeped in "old morality" publishes his undergraduate lecture notes on constitutional law and sets the hegemonic framework of the British constitution that, for good or ill, prevails to this day'.[19] Dicey had the very things that he came to consider vital for the development of an intelligent, knowing outlook on life, which equipped him to comment on what was needed in a good working constitutional state. And these were precisely the things from which women, rightly in his view, were actively precluded.[20]

Dicey benefited from the (all male) Oxbridge system. As Walters observes in his biography of Dicey (of which more later), 'Oxford offered to the young Dicey the opportunity to engage in political discourse … Dicey was active in the Oxford Union serving as its president in 1859. Here Dicey refined his abilities to articulate political ideas'.[21] Dicey was at the intellectual and social centres of the right universities. Cambridge had its scholarly men's club, The Apostles. Oxford, which was Dicey's intellectual home, had the Old Mortality which held 'a small but secure place in the history of mid-Victorian letters and thought'.[22] According to Martin Loughlin, in a review of Mark Walters' biography of Dicey,

> we should also not overlook his lineage and his connections. Dicey was the grandson of James Stephen, the legal brains behind John Venn's Clapham Sect of Evangelical Whigs who had supported Wilberforce's campaign to end slavery. Through intermarriage, the Wilberforces, Venns and Stephens formed a tightly bound Victorian intellectual aristocracy who also campaigned for Catholic emancipation, parliamentary reform and the extension of the franchise. Their tenacious advocacy of liberal causes passed on through the generations: Dicey's cousins included John Venn of Venn diagram fame,

[16] Mark D Walters, 'Dicey's Law of the Constitution' (2012) 32 *OJLS* 21, 26, fn 35.
[17] ibid 28.
[18] Loughlin (n 11) 366.
[19] ibid.
[20] Eloquently described by Virginia Woolf in *A Room of One's Own* (London, Hogarth Press, 1935).
[21] Mark D Walters, *AV Dicey and the Common Law Constitutional Tradition: A Legal Turn of Mind* (Cambridge University Press, 2020) 38.
[22] ibid, quoting Melvin Richter, *The Politics of Conscience: TH Green and his Age* (London, Weidenfeld and Nicolson, 1964) 80.

> James Fitzjames Stephen, the prominent lawyer and judge who sought to codify the English criminal law, and the essayist Leslie Stephen, father of Virginia Woolf.[23]

But this patrilineage is not a cause for concern about the narrowness of its world, its privileges, its possibly shrinking effects on intellectual range.

Dicey was made a founding Fellow of the British Academy in 1902, along with Sir Frederick Pollock, Frederick Maitland, Thomas Holland and cousin Leslie Stephen. (It was nearly 30 years until the first woman, Beatrice Webb, was made a Fellow.)

IV. Dicey's 1909 *Letters to a Friend*

In 1909, Dicey published *Letters to a Friend* as Vinerian Professor of English Law in the University of Oxford. This book was not a private side interest. Dicey employed his postnominals: KC, Hon DCL, LLD. His full professorial title appeared on the title page, lending it authority. William Blackstone was the first Vinerian Professor, holding the Chair from 1758–66. No woman has held the Chair.[24] *Letters* appeared one year after Gwyneth Bebb was refused admission to the Law Society. It was therefore impossible for a woman to acquire Dicey's great distinction.

This short book takes an epistolary form, to an unnamed recipient.[25] It is conversational in style, and not constrained by the usual academic impedimenta (such as evidence). In it, Dicey reflected on why women should not have the vote, and why they should be kept out of the public sphere. Here Dicey openly condemned John Stuart Mill's reasoning in *The Subjection of Women*[26] and also explained why Mill's *On Liberty* did not really make the case for *all* people being legal Individuals, but rather supported the continuing disempowerment of women. The reason was, according to Dicey, that Mill's *On Liberty* was about free Individuals serving the public interest, but as women's participation in the political realm would harm rather than help the state, they were necessarily not included in Mill's concept of the liberal Individual. The public interest would not be served by the female exercise of public power. Ipso facto, Mill's concept of the free Individual did not apply to women. As Dicey explained, for Mill:

> Later reflection has, indeed, shown me that, whilst his [Mill's] 'Subjection of Women' contains, side by side with much noble sentiment, some singularly fallacious reasoning,

[23] Loughlin (n 11) 369. And Loughlin repeats the idea that here we have 'intellectual aristocracy'. The best of the best?

[24] Dicey established the *Law Quarterly Review*. Contributors to the first issue in 1885 are an interesting line-up, including Pollock and Maitland, Dicey, Oliver Wendell Holmes and James Fitzjames Stephen.

[25] Compare with the epistolary form also adopted by Woolf some three decades later in Virginia Woolf, *Three Guineas* (London, Hogarth, 1938).

[26] John Stuart Mill, *The Subjection of Women* (London, Longmans, Green, Reader and Dyer, 1869).

> the treatise 'On Liberty,' so far from supporting the claim of women to political authority, really supplies an argument against the moral claim either of woman or of any other class of the community to share in political power if such participation is opposed to the welfare of the State. It was a great relief, at any rate to myself, to discover that I could reconcile my enthusiasm for everything which promotes the personal freedom and the education of women with the strenuous denial to them of any share in sovereign power.[27]

Dicey's interpretation of Mill's work *On Liberty* might have surprised Mill, though Mill was familiar with opposition and was rarely, if ever, deflected. But now he was in no position to reply.[28]

The enforced impoverishment of women's professional and public lives was the very thing that made Dicey decide that women were unfit for public power and public decision-making: indeed they were so poorly equipped for public office that they would pose a positive threat to the safety and welfare of the nation, were they to be given 'sovereign power'. Women lacked his own, far richer, experiences, because they were not permitted to acquire them. Women therefore lacked the necessary experience and training for public power and so should not have it. This was the Catch 22 for women.[29]

To Dicey, it was not a matter of whether women wanted to vote – strangely perhaps for a constitutional lawyer, participatory democracy was not the issue – but whether England would benefit from the women's vote, an analysis which seems to say that the women of England were not quite part of England. Because he was not convinced that English women voting would benefit England, he declared that he had become 'of necessity an opponent of woman suffrage'.[30] Such a change 'cannot be attempted without the greatest peril to England'.[31]

> Who can contemplate without dread a state of things under which democratic passion, intensified by feminine emotion, may deprive the country both of the calmness which foresees and the resolution which repels the onslaught of foreign enemies? There is, we venture to say, no man, and no woman either, who at moments of calm reflection can believe that, at a time of threatened invasion, the safety of the country would be increased by the possibility that British policy might be determined by the votes and the influence of the fighting suffragists.[32]

Women were, and were not, a class to Dicey. Sex difference was a natural difference, a natural classification, he believed, which somehow meant that the interests of women and men naturally did not conflict. It also meant that women, as a class

[27] Dicey (n 2) 6.

[28] Mill died in 1873 in the same year that Stephen published his riposte to Mill: James Fitzjames Stephen, *Liberty, Equality and Fraternity* (New York, Holt and Williams, 1873). Dicey's objections to Mill came 36 years later, well into the twentieth century.

[29] See Joseph Heller, *Catch-22* (London, Jonathan Cape, 1967).

[30] Dicey (n 2) 8.

[31] ibid 10.

[32] ibid 61–62.

of persons, lost little by being denied the exercise of political power and having men exercise it for them. Men would do the right thing by women, 'at any rate in a civilized country like England'.[33] True, there were a few problems to be ironed out, a few inequalities arising from the different classifications of men and women. However Dicey sought to diminish and dismiss them. He declared, unconvincingly, that '[p]rimogeniture itself, as a rule governing descent of land, does not in reality afford such an instance'.[34] Then there was the matter of women's unequal access to education and accreditation. Again, this was waved aside: 'the refusal of degrees to women at Oxford and Cambridge might be got rid of to-morrow by half the exertion used for obtaining votes for women'.[35]

Dicey's principal concern was the public sphere and what the granting of the franchise to women might do to England. He warned of the slippery slope: 'woman suffrage must with us finally lead to its logical result – that is, the complete political equality of men and women'.[36] And this carried dangers. Dicey was concerned that, perhaps unfortunately, there were simply too many English women. In the Fourth Letter he said:

> Woman suffrage, then, I repeat, assuredly means, if not to-day, yet within a short time, the introduction of adult suffrage, and, independently of the new electors being women, must add to the defects of manhood suffrage. … Authority passes into the hands of persons who possess neither the independence due to the possession of property nor the intelligence due to education.[37]

Dicey then did the numbers. And they were dreadful.

> Our electorate now consists of some 7,000,000 men. Adult suffrage would create an electorate of, say roundly, at least 20,000,000 individuals, of whom considerably over 10,000,000 would be women. This mere increase in numbers is no slight evil. That more than half the new electors should be absolutely devoid of political training and traditions creates of itself a national peril; but common sense forbids any fair reasoner to stop at this point. This uneducated majority of the electorate would be women.[38]

Women were an unknown (but worryingly large) number of the untrained and the uninitiated:

> The very advocates of woman suffrage make it part of their case that the civic virtues of women have never as yet been fully developed. Assuredly the most ordinary prudence warns us against admitting to a full share of sovereignty persons who have lacked all experience of its exercise.[39]

[33] ibid 24.
[34] ibid 24–25.
[35] ibid 25.
[36] ibid 10.
[37] ibid 58–59.
[38] ibid 59.
[39] ibid.

To Dicey it would be madness, indeed 'the height of folly to entrust the guidance of the State, at a time when the country is surrounded by perils of all kinds, to unskilled apprentices who have no experience in piloting the commonwealth through pressing dangers'.[40]

Dicey spelled out just what was wrong with women, and why experience, training and education would only get you so far with them. The implicit question perhaps, posed by Professor Henry Higgins in *My Fair Lady*,[41] was 'why can't a woman be more like a man?' After all, as the song continues in Diceyan vein: 'Men are so honest, so thoroughly square, Eternally Noble, historically fair.' And Dicey answered Higgins' question. The sad truth was that women did not have it in them. Women were a sorry lot.

> We hear, as I have pointed out to you, much of the keenness of women's personal sympathies, of their capacity for passionate and often generous emotion; we are told that either nature or training, or both in combination, may lead women to see more readily than men the minute details on which depends the transaction of business. Yet it would not be unfair to say that, while women often perceive more readily than men the actual facts before them, they have a less firm grasp on principles; that a woman, in short, compared with a man of equal ability, may have a better eye for the circumstances around her, but has less of foresight. She has assuredly also less of tenacity. From differences, upon some of which, in whatever form they ought to be expressed, no man has insisted more strongly than Mill, it follows that the participation of women in sovereign power must introduce into English politics a new and incalculable element which will not work wholly for good.[42]

Dicey warned of 'the danger which lurked under the concession of sovereign power to women, who as a body are more readily influenced than men by the emotions of the moment'.[43]

V. Law is a Man

Law, government, authority and force are combined in this analysis, and force was something only men had, in Dicey's view. Men also had reason and firmness of character and apparently 'judicial serenity' when placed on the bench. The very institution of law, even the idea of law which Dicey expounded, was bound up with the perceived nature of men. Reason, integrity, strength of character, impartiality,

[40] ibid 60.

[41] Song by Frederick Loewe and Alan J Lerner, 'Why Can't a Woman be More like a Man?' performed in the film musical directed by George Cukor, *My Fair Lady* (1964). Film and play plot adapted by Lerner and Loewe from George Bernard Shaw's play *Pygmalion* (1912). See Patricia Bauer, 'My Fair Lady' (*Britannica*, 17 January 2024), available at www.britannica.com/topic/My-Fair-Lady-film-by-Cukor.

[42] Dicey (n 2) 60–61.

[43] ibid 4.

firmness, measured use of force and resolve were ascribed to law and ascribed to men. Men were in law's DNA. Men's DNA was in law.

This might seem to be anthropomorphising law and it probably is. But it seems to flow from Dicey's analysis, and it also comes out in the Persons Cases, which not only said what sort of person was the Legal Person but often spoke of the character of the institution itself, or rather law itself. Dicey listed the requirements of equality and legality and justice and found these qualities in men, but not women. Women would wreck the institutions of the state, carefully built up by men, was the message of Dicey and of the Persons Cases. And never mind the internal logic of the reasoning which went like this: Women were uneducated and inexperienced, because educational institutions could and did lawfully exclude them, and so women were not fit for public office because they were uneducated. This circular reasoning became a self-fulfilling prophecy. Dicey was fed up with men being polite. Of course, the Legal Person was a man because law was so bound up with manhood.

Men had what the country needed, especially those from the upper echelons and even the middle ones:

> Now, every student of British history can see that … the statesmanlike foresight, and still more certainly the intense tenacity or obstinacy of purpose, which have marked the British aristocracy and the British middle classes, have been the salvation of the country.[44]

Even 'Englishmen … of an ordinary type'[45] had what it took to make public decisions, but not so women. Thus, 'the belief, entertained by nearly every man' (men are his entire reference group here) was that even 'women of pre-eminent goodness are often lacking in the virtues, such as active courage, firmness of judgment, self-control, steadiness of conduct, and, above all, a certain sense of justice'.[46] The unfortunate truth was that women were 'unskilled apprentices who have no experience in piloting the commonwealth through pressing dangers'.[47]

Dicey was convinced of the innate inferiority of women and the innate superiority of men which law was right to recognise and endorse because it was in 'the nature of things', almost laying the ground for the natural law thinking embedded in the work of John Finnis discussed in chapter eight:

> Distinctions of rights founded upon sex have often given rise to injustice, but they have this in their favour – they rest upon a difference not created by social conventions or by human prejudice and selfishness, or by accidental circumstances (such as riches and poverty), which split society into classes, but upon the nature of things. This difference is as far-reaching as it is natural and immutable. It is one which, just because it is permanent and unchangeable, every honest thinker must take into account.[48]

[44] ibid 61.
[45] ibid 82.
[46] ibid 82.
[47] ibid 60.
[48] ibid 75.

Dicey turned to 'an obvious platitude': 'That men are men and women are women.'[49] The thing is, it was true:

> [I]t contains an undeniable truth which, like some other unwelcome facts, rhetoric, even when, as with Mill, it masquerades as strict reasoning, cannot conceal. This is a matter worth insisting upon, for there is nothing which hinders the calm discussion of a political problem requiring for its solution something like judicial serenity so much as the difficulty, inseparable from all discussions involving reference to sex, of putting plain facts into plain language.[50]

Dicey here is referring to women's 'weaker nature', about which he demands plain speaking. And because of women's weaker nature, they should not have the powers afforded to men. On this Dicey was clear:

> The comparative weakness of women inevitably means loss of power. Nor can it be forgotten not only that women are physically, and probably mentally, weaker than men, but that they are inevitably, as a class, burdened with duties of the utmost national importance, and of an absorbing and exhausting nature, from which men are free. In any case, the close connection between government and force tells against the claim made on behalf of women to the possession of as much political authority as is conceded to men.[51]

Women made the babies; men were not so encumbered, and they had the physical force to do what needed to be done; to act forcefully for the state and to enforce its man-made laws. And law, in its male wisdom, had to reflect these biological truths.

VI. Style and Genre of *Letters to a Friend*

The genre, style and addressee of Dicey's *Letters to a Friend* are all illuminating. As author, Dicey is titled Vinerian Professor of English Law in the University of Oxford, a distinguished academic post. His letters are all there after his name. This is a proper publishing house, John Murray. *Letters* continues to be published as a book. At the time that he was writing *Letters*, Dicey was a highly recognised, even revered, constitutional lawyer and he invoked his scholarly credentials. But this publication does not look like a conventional piece of academic writing. It is styled *Letters to a Friend* and the addressee, the friend, remains anonymous. It starts 'My Dear C' and proceeds in a conversational style, as if indeed he is talking to a friend, which is the conceit and the device. The chapters are called Letters.

But *Letters to a Friend* are not really letters. There is no real addressee and hence no letters in reply. They are short essays in which Dicey said what he really thought about men and women and the respective roles they should play in public

[49] ibid.
[50] ibid 75–76.
[51] ibid 76.

life. This freed him from the demands of a scholarly publication, allowing him to issue unsubstantiated (unevidenced and unfootnoted) statements about the natures of men and women and why the former were suited to the exercise of public power and office and the latter were not.

By styling them *Letters to a Friend*, Dicey was casting them as private correspondence and private thoughts, but publishing them as a public book under his own name and as Vinerian Professor. He did not adopt a formal academic style. He let himself off the leash, saying what he actually thought about women, as if he were speaking in a private capacity, but this was a publication, intended for public consumption. Dicey was having his cake and eating it too.

VII. Contemporary Responses

As expected, there were public responses at the time, including from Bertrand Russell and *The Spectator*. *Letters* were not really private musings, but a public statement by a public intellectual about the importance of male rule. First from *The Spectator* there was a ringing endorsement:

> Professor Dicey's arguments against woman suffrage take the form of private letters to a friend, but we have felt after reading them rather as though we had listened to a trial in Court, with statements for the plaintiff and the defendant, and the Judge's charge to the jury. Professor Dicey's method and manner are in fact judicial, as one might expect; and if his summing up is a tremendous condemnation of the case for the plaintiff (or woman suffragist), that is because it is sometimes a Judge's duty to leave the jury in no sort of doubt as to what the verdict should be. Some Judges in this case might even have dropped a hint to the jury that they would do well to 'stop the case.' To those who want a brief statement of all that there is to be said for and against woman suffrage, and to have that statement set forth in clear English and fortified with wide legal and political learning, we cannot do better than recommend this little book.[52]

Bertrand Russell was more critical but still sought to neutralise Dicey's scare tactics. When women get the franchise, he explained:

> [T]hey will find a political system established which has been made by men, where the parties are divided according to the divisions of opinion among men, where all the candidates are men, and all the questions mainly discussed at elections will be such as have been considered important by men.[53]

Thus, the political system was male and would stay male for some time. Dicey and his acolytes did not need to worry. Men had defined, classified and explained the public world. They wouldn't be ousted quickly, if at all. 'The inertia of this state of

[52] 'Professor Dicey's Letters on Woman Suffrage' *The Spectator* (19 June 1909) 23.

[53] Bertrand Russell, 'On AntiSuffragist Arguments' in Jeff McLaughlin (ed), *The Originals: Classic Readings in Western Philosophy* (Yukon, British Columbia, Press Books, 2017) 319.

things will make it impossible to change it suddenly. There will not be any sudden emergence of a large women's party, advocating the supposed special interests of women.'[54]

Dicey was by no means a lone voice, though he has tended to be characterised as a legal outlier in his later thinking on women. As social historian Sandra Stanley Holton reveals about the 'masculinism' of the time and its treatment of the British suffragists: 'in the tabloid press of the day; in magazines like *Punch*; in the Hansard record of debates in parliament; and in old but still influential work by male historians', leading figures of the movement were demeaned through ridicule.[55] '[M]asculinist history', Holton maintains, 'rests upon the use of stereotypes of women that, when they do not mock, either marginalise or altogether refuse them a place in the larger narratives of community, state and nation'.[56]

Dicey was with the men of his time. Thus accounts of the suffragists included 'lofty denial of women's capacity for reasoning, political debate and any adequate understanding of affairs beyond the purely domestic'.[57] Holton also points to the popular context, with its 'scurrilous innuendo, clubroom chatter and music-hall and pantomime representations of women'.[58] There was 'active resort to sexual stereotyping' so that women were infantilised or assigned 'roles drawn from farce, the comic postcard and the clinic'.[59] There was also 'an enormous degree of generalisation'[60] and this was certainly present in the work of Dicey.

In *Letters to a Friend*, Dicey adopted a literary form which located his analysis of women, and the threat they posed to the state, outside of his formal constitutional scholarship. He adopted an informal style and addressed an anonymous correspondent, who never replied, which was no doubt convenient. But one senses silent agreement with every word. In 1915 Dicey placed his analysis of women squarely within his primary scholarship.

VIII. Dicey's 1915 *Law of the Constitution*

As Dicey explained in his Introduction to the eighth edition of his *Introduction to the Study of the Law of the Constitution*,

> [t]he rule of law, as described in this treatise, remains to this day a distinctive characteristic of the English constitution. In England … every man's legal rights or liabilities are almost invariably determined by the ordinary Courts of the realm, and each man's

[54] ibid.

[55] Sandra Stanley Holton, 'Challenging Masculinism: Personal History and Microhistory in Feminist Studies of the Women's Suffrage Movement' (2011) 20 *Women's History Review* 829, 832.

[56] ibid 829.

[57] ibid 832.

[58] ibid.

[59] ibid.

[60] ibid.

> individual rights are far less the result of our constitution than the basis on which that constitution is founded.[61]

Is Dicey referring here to men, when he talks of man and his individual rights? From *Letters* we know that Dicey understood the polity to be a male polity, and that he thought it should stay that way. Men were, rightly, making the laws which set the limits of their conduct. Men, like him, were exclusively making, defining, explaining and enforcing the law.

In his Introduction to *Law and the Constitution*, Dicey said this about British subjects, which leaves us in little doubt that his subject *was* thought of as a man. Here he was discussing the relative rights of natural-born versus other country-born British subjects and declaring that they had equal rights. But his idea of a British subject was of a male subject. He tells us that:

> The kind of equality among British subjects which Englishmen, whether wisely or not, hoped to establish throughout the whole Empire is best seen by considering the sort of equality which actually exists and has for many years existed in England. Speaking broadly, every British subject has in England at the present day the same political rights as every natural born Englishman, e.g. an Englishman born in England and the son of English parents settled in England. Thus a British subject … [has] the same right to settle or to trade in England which is possessed by a natural-born Englishman. He has further exactly the same political rights. He can … vote for a member of Parliament; he can … take his seat as a member of Parliament. There is no law which forbids any British subject, wherever he be born, or to whatever race he belongs, to become a member of the English Cabinet or a Prime Minister.[62]

This was true for men but not for women. Thus in *Law and the Constitution*, Dicey was again explicit about the necessary maleness of England's political and legal institutions (and who should man them), which would be ill served by women becoming involved: the participation of women would not '*conduce to the* welfare of England' (emphasis added).[63] This is why women should not be given the franchise (repeating the argument advanced in *Letters*). The rule of law was, and should stay, a rule by and of men.

> The claim of parliamentary votes for women as now put forward in England is in reality a claim for the absolute political equality of the two sexes. Whether its advocates are conscious of the fact or not, it is a demand on behalf of women for seats in Parliament and in the Cabinet. It means that Englishwomen should share the jury box and should sit on the judicial bench.[64]

Again we learn how ill-suited are women for the exercise of such powers, and how well suited are men. In fact the 'difference of sex … is one of the most fundamental and far-reaching differences which can distinguish one body of human

[61] Dicey (n 4) xxxvii.
[62] ibid xxxvii, fn 1.
[63] ibid lxv.
[64] ibid.

beings from another'.[65] The differences between men and women are indelible. Here quoting Burke: 'they are not of our devising, but moulded "into the nature and the essence of things, [and so] will endure with the sun and moon …"'.[66]

Though considered a scholar of the Victorian period, Dicey's long life gave him a long reach, which did not serve women well. Well into the first quarter of the twentieth century Dicey was writing against female public power, especially the franchise, but also against any sort of significant role for women in government or as any sort of public or legal official. He spoke as a man, for men, against women, with almost no sense that he spoke from a position of tremendous advantage, which enabled him to say what he did, and little appreciation of what it was like to be locked out of public life, nor the implications of this misogyny for his own theory. To Dicey, the concept of the Person was not a formal legal device, designed to empower all humans, but was necessarily a reference to a biological man, especially when it was connected to the exercise of any sort of public power, and in his view it was vital that this be recognised by law. Dicey shaped constitutional thought while pressing explicitly for women to be kept out of the constitutive power.

IX. Ignoring Clever Women and the Patriarchal Dividend

Simply put, Dicey considered women to be unfit for public power. Indeed women were so poorly equipped for public offices, for want of experience, that, in his view, they posed a positive threat to the security and welfare of the nation, were they to be given 'sovereign power'. Women lacked his own capabilities, because they were not permitted to acquire them; and because women were not familiar with the workings of public power, they should not be permitted to acquire such knowledge. Such was the logic.

In view of Dicey's beneficial marriage to a well-connected, highly intelligent woman, Elinor Bonham Carter, these declarations about the hopeless ineptitude of women seem odd. Dicey's wife Elinor was an intellectual aid and collaborator. She was also a translator from French to English, and translated a book on comparative constitutional law (by Emile Boutmy)[67] which greatly influenced Dicey. (Walters refers to Elinor briefly but takes his inquiry no further.) Dicey's mother and his female cousins were thinkers and writers, who in other contexts, Dicey admired. His cousin once removed was Virginia Woolf, herself no slouch when it came to thinking and writing.

[65] ibid.

[66] ibid lxvi, quoting Edmund Burke, *Correspondence of the Right Honourable Edmund Burke* (London, Rivington, 1844) 332–33.

[67] Emile Gaston Boutmy, *Etudes de droit Constitutionnel: France, Angleterre, États-Unis* (Paris, Plon, 1885); Emile Gaston Boutmy, *Studies of Constitutional Law: France, England, United States* (translated by EM Dicey) (London, Macmillan, 1891).

Notwithstanding the intellectual abilities of his mother, his wife, his cousins, and his intellectual debts to them, in 1909 Dicey affirmed the natural unfitness of women for public power because of their deficient underlying natures and he did so again in 1915. Perhaps the women in his life were set aside in his own thinking as rare exceptions or he just couldn't factor them into his thinking. There were the women of his circle and then there were the men and their law. And of course he was not alone in this intellectual habit.

Virginia Woolf wrote of the 'patriarchal machine' which turned men into the holders of position and power. In *A Room of One's Own*[68] and also in *Three Guineas*[69] she said that male power had been very important to men as a sex, to the point that it entailed exalted posts, public commendation, display and ornamentation. The men of her circle and beyond wanted such power and recognition and kept if for themselves. This is because of what Raewyn Connell has called 'the patriarchal dividend'. This is

> the advantage to men as a group from maintaining an unequal gender order. Money income is not the only kind of benefit. Others are authority, respect, service, safety, housing, access to institutional power, emotional support, and control over one's own life. The patriarchal dividend, of course, is reduced as overall gender equality grows.[70]

As Dion Kagan explains, '[a]lthough sexuality, race and socioeconomic status may place men in positions of subordination to other men, as Connell's concept of the "patriarchal dividend" suggests, all men are rewarded for their participation in gender orders'.[71]

Why would you want to give this up? Dicey had the advantages of his sex, but not the awareness of the effects of those advantages on himself and on other men of his class: 'the patriarchal dividend'. He seemed not to appreciate how all these privileged men inhabiting the most senior positions of law and state experienced and thought of themselves, as they enhanced their abilities as a sex class, and enjoyed those enhancements.

Nor did Dicey see that women were thus hampered, and diminished by those very male advantages, even when the women thus hampered were highly intelligent and wished to do more. Many were living with the men of advantage. Women were shut out of sovereign power. They were aware that they were shut out. And perhaps the greater their abilities, the greater the sense of exclusion, as Woolf revealed. Dicey seemed insensible to this.

[68] Woolf (n 20).
[69] Woolf (n 25).
[70] Raewyn Connell, *Gender: In World Perspective*, 2nd edn (Cambridge, Polity, 2009) 142.
[71] Dion Kagan, 'Diminished Patriarchal Dividend' (*Meanjin*, 18 July 2022), available at meanjin.com.au/books/diminished-patriarchal-dividend/.

X. Reputation

Dicey's thoughts and interventions on behalf of the male state did him little damage. Nor did they stimulate inquiry into the maleness of law, which Dicey openly recognised, and also endorsed. He brought it squarely into the discussion. Dicey's interpreters have tended to set aside the difficulty of a rule of law with only one sex permitted to be its rulers and to enjoy the fullest benefits and protections of the law that rules. A rule of law with only male rulers, was openly acknowledged and defended by Dicey. Does this render his rule of law an oxymoron and false as he proposes it?

Dicey had other political preoccupations for which he is better known. He opposed Home Rule in Ireland, while Lord Birkenhead helped to achieve Home Rule. And the Irish Question became much more prominent in the records of both men, much more so than the Woman Question, which sadly disappeared from view. Both men are remembered for their thoughts on Irish partition, not for their thoughts on women, nor on men, as men. Dicey's thoughts on the deficiencies of women were strongly stated, repeated, and yet did not become part of his reputation even though they should have had a bearing on it, in view of his general subject matter. (Birkenhead did not endure in the same manner, though he was active during his lifetime.)[72]

Despite this, or rather without this being considered, Dicey's reputation as a constitutional scholar and theorist of law persists to the present. His writings on constitutional law secured his reputation as part of the legal canon. His writings in favour of men and against women are mentioned only very briefly in his recent biography by Mark D Walters, to which I will return.[73] They are not considered alongside his other writings or to inform his constitutional theory in general. His thoughts on women are set aside, though Dicey himself was explicit and vehement about the need for law to be run by men. As Kristen Rundle has commented: 'It is relatively rare for theorists of the rule of law to pay explicit attention to the people to whom its claimed offerings are denied'.[74] Dicey did in fact consider the people denied, women, and considered their exclusion to be right. His successors and interpreters preferred not to attend to the exclusion at all.

To modern writers on Dicey, his thinking about the necessary maleness of the state – which, as we have seen, he declared openly and boldly – is not part of his constitutional writing, on legality, equality and the rule of law. Men and women, and their respective roles, as Dicey saw them, go missing. Modern analysts of Dicey seem to shy away from what they see as his other persona, in which he said, anticipating George Orwell, that all humans were equal, but some were more equal than others.[75] Men were made to rule; women were made to be ruled. And Dicey

[72] See their respective *Oxford Dictionary of National Biography* entries.
[73] Walters (n 21).
[74] Rundle (n 6) 62.
[75] To borrow from George Orwell, *Animal Farm* (London, Secker & Warburg, 1945).

implored other men to join him to ensure that the (male) opportunities of politics and law were never extended to women. It is Dicey's work on the constitution and the rule of law which has endured, generally denuded of his thoughts about women. There seems to be, still, a silent pact about Dicey, as his thoughts have moved into the twenty-first century: that whatever he said about the deficiencies of women, as potential political participants, played no real part in what he had to say about the rule of law.

XI. 85 Years on, Mark D Walters on Dicey in 2020

Dicey remains a major figure and a considerable influence on the understanding of English constitutional law. In 2020 his work on the constitution was made the subject of a substantial biography by Mark D Walters.[76] In Peter Cane's review essay on Walters' book, we are left in no doubt about Dicey's continuing eminence:

> The publication in 2020 of Mark Walters' marvellous book, *Dicey and the Common Law Constitutional Tradition: A Legal Turn of Mind* … amply justifies the view that AV Dicey's *The Law of the Constitution*, first published in 1885, continues, into the twenty-first century, to be the most influential single volume ever written on what … Dicey called 'English constitutionalism'. None of the illustrious predecessors of *The Law of the Constitution*, such as Coke's *Institutes of the Laws of England*, Montesquieu's *The Spirit of the Laws* and Blackstone's *Commentaries on the Laws of England*, nor any other work written since 1885, looms as large.[77]

Walters himself almost reveres his subject. He offers an admiring account of his achievements as student and eventually as professor. Dicey is described as 'the biggest legal mind we have'.[78] But to sustain this favourable view of his subject, Walters selectively edits Dicey's work on constitutional law and he edits his life. We know that Walters is familiar with *Letters*, because he refers to its racism, but *Letters* is not to be found in the index. He notes Dicey's opposition to the female suffrage, but we are left with the impression that this was the only thing Dicey said against women. Walters does not refer to Dicey's extended denunciation of women (and positive characterisation of men) over the entire course of the *Letters* book and Dicey's advocacy of women's exclusion from sovereign power, not just from the vote.

Dicey did not confine his anti-woman thoughts to the *Letters* book. By putting these thoughts in his Introduction to *Law of the Constitution*, Dicey openly linked them to his work on Constitutional law. Walters implicitly separates them, which is not what Dicey did himself. Walters also separates them in his bibliography.

[76] Walters (n 21).

[77] Peter Cane, 'AV Dicey as Legal Theorist' (2022) 85 *MLR* 247, 247.

[78] This is the title of chapter 2 of Walters' biography and Walters is here employing, approvingly, Lord Chancellor Haldane's words about Dicey. See Walters (n 21) 13.

There are Dicey's constitutional works and then there are 'other books', where we find *Letters*. So *Letters* is not about the constitution, according to Walters, though clearly it was, in Dicey's mind.

What is to be made, if anything, of the fact that Dicey advocated forcefully for the total control of the institutions of public power by men whom he regarded as inherently more capable than women? Walters himself does not appear to see the significance of Dicey's anti-woman opinions for his general work on the constitution, even though Dicey puts them into the Introduction to the book which forms the subject of Walters' intellectual biography. A few times Walters notes that Dicey came to oppose the female franchise. Walters maintains, for example, that '[o]n certain points, Dicey changed his opinions in indefensible ways'.[79] He is referring here, inter alia, to Dicey's opposition to female suffrage. We are told that these 'later writings create some challenges for our understanding of his legacy'.[80] But Walters does not rise to this challenge. There is no analysis of the implications of these anti-woman views for Dicey's general theory of the constitution.

Consequently, Walters contracts the significance of Dicey's antipathy towards women, and refers only to his views on the female franchise. And then Walters does not consider what bearing this might have on Dicey's general theory of the constitution, with its strong themes of equality and legality. Instead, Walters notes it and sets it aside.[81] Loughlin, in his essay on Walters' book, gives Dicey's views against women half a sentence.[82]

Is Walters deciding on behalf of Dicey that what Dicey was saying in *Letters* did not have a bearing on his general work on the Constitution, even though it was an extended opposition to women and strongly made? Is he judging Dicey to be aberrant here, an older man having a fit of pique? Or is he entering a gentlemen's agreement with Dicey that Dicey can say these 'unforgiveable' things and they will not tarnish his reputation? Is he deciding that it would not be in Dicey's posthumous interests to consider the place of *Letters* in his writings? Is he protecting Dicey?

It is said, repeatedly, by Walters and others that Dicey started his intellectual life as a liberal sympathetic to the rights of women but later became an opponent of the female vote.[83] This is where the recognition of Dicey's views on women tends to start and stop. The idea is that the true Dicey is the early Dicey and that it is regrettable that Dicey came to form these views, but that they did not typify his intellectual life and implicitly had no bearing on his theories of the constitution. (More interesting was his opposition to Irish Home Rule which is given vastly more attention, as was Frederick Edwin Smith's support for Home Rule.

[79] ibid 378.

[80] ibid.

[81] In Walters' Appendix we see his slight treatment of *Letters*, which is not indexed, and his extended treatment of the Irish Question.

[82] See Loughlin (n 11) 370.

[83] Walters (n 21) 378; Michener's foreword to Dicey (n 15) xviii.

Their open vigorous opposition to the public rights of women was permitted to disappear from their legacy.)

Not said is that at the time that Dicey was writing, public power was entirely in male hands, and so was the ability to define and explain it. This is commonplace knowledge. Dicey's colleagues were all highly-achieving men and this is noted and even celebrated, but its relevance to the nature and understanding of law is not seen. It is known but it is not of interest and discussion moves on.

For Dicey, the legal officials who manned and operated his constitution were men and the fully-endowed legal subject was also a man, and was rightly a man. Men and women were not, and should not be, equally and mutually subordinated to law, nor mutually empowered to exercise legal power as legal officials, within his own thinking. Dicey was against men *and* women having what he termed 'sovereign power', equally, similarly or mutually. Such power was for men.

XII. Dicey Alerting Us to the Maleness of Law

Dicey was keenly aware that legal power was held by men. He supported this exclusive possession of power. What are the implications of this knowledge for his theory of the rule of law? As Kristen Rundle explains: 'AV Dicey argued for a strong association between the rule of law and equality' and he meant 'the equality of all before the same law'.[84] At the same time, as we have seen he made clear that women should not share equally in the 'offerings'[85] of the rule of law. It looks very much as if Dicey had in mind a rule of men.

Vanessa Munro has observed:

> [i]t is a liberal truism that to live as a citizen in a society governed by 'the rule of law' means both to be ruled *by* law and to be the ruler *of* law, at least insofar as submission is the consequence of a quasi-contractual or reciprocal exchange of chaos for order.[86]

But as we have seen, Dicey himself did not believe that these principles applied to both women and men, and so he did not adhere to his own requirements and demands for the rule of law. Dicey said, forcefully, that only men should be the rulers of law. He did not just oppose the female franchise. In *Letters*, a book-length work, he opposed the exercise of public power by women. He was adamant that only men had the temperament, the resolve, the emotional steadfastness, the reason and the wisdom to rule England and to rule the Empire. And Dicey was not swimming against a strong tide of public opinion.

[84] Rundle (n 6) 61.

[85] ibid 62.

[86] Vanessa E Munro, 'Feminist Critiques of the Rule of Law' in Jens Meierhenrich and Martin Loughlin (eds), *The Cambridge Companion to the Rule of Law* (Cambridge, Cambridge University Press, 2021) 340.

There are prompts for Walters to place Dicey in his patriarchal setting and to consider how and why men alone controlled the state and its constitutive powers and what bearing this might have on his theory. Walters refers explicitly to 'the great patriarchal machine' (Virginia Woolf's term) that produced Dicey; he mentions the small, aristocratic, intellectual and social elite of which he was a part, and the fact that only men could vote. But male control is so mundane, so accepted, so unremarkable (and yet so antithetical to the principle of equality) that it is barely noticed, and it is certainly not up for discussion. Walters' two reviewers do the same thing.

Walters does not explain his selective treatment of Dicey's oeuvre, with its careful omissions. We are told that his views on women were 'indefensible'.[87] But there is no attempt to explain them or to reflect on their broader significance for his theories. There is no sense that the part omitted (Dicey's insistence on male sovereign power) might affect the part that is considered (sovereign power and the rule of law). Rather the anti-woman statements are dismissed as the unfortunate views of an older man who should have known better. But this is a highly paternalistic attitude to Dicey. Why don't all his published words count?

Dicey made an important point when he wrote about the need for public power *to stay* in male hands. His point was that power was held by men and, in his view, was defining of the nation and its law. Dicey thought this mattered. His subsequent interpreters edited out these views, probably in a protective move. But as a consequence they did not consider the significance of the maleness of law and the state which Dicey brought to our attention, strongly. They did not consider its bearing on constitutional theory.

Dicey's opposition to Irish Home Rule (with its necessary diminution of the reach of the British Parliament), which formed part of his later politics, was strongly noted and criticised. Apparently 'most commentators condemn Dicey in harsh terms for abandoning principle in the face of partisan political preference'.[88] There is simply no equivalent analysis of Dicey and his strong and explicit advocacy of exclusive male public power. There is a deafening silence.[89] But why isn't it important and fundamental? Dicey wanted the law to be seen for its maleness. His analysts treat these thoughts as unfortunate eccentricities, despite their obvious truth.

Open neutral inquiry lies at the heart of academic scholarship. Holding truth to power really means this. As David Cannadine has observed, 'there needs to be a greater degree of respect for evidence-based learning, for truth, reason and ideas'.[90] Our task is to consider the evidence with an open mind and to deal with

[87] Walters (n 21) 378.

[88] ibid 388–89.

[89] See WEH Stanner's reference to 'The Great Australian Silence' in his 1968 Boyer lectures *After the Dreaming*, referring here to the silence about Australia's white origins: 'WEH Stanner and the Great Australian Silence' (*ABS Radio National*, 26 March 2009), available at www.abc.net.au/listen/programs/latenightlive/weh-stanner-and-the-great-australian-silence/3143396.

[90] David Cannadine, 'David Cannadine: Interview' (2017) 31 *British Academy Review* 4, 14.

the inhospitable evidence, that is evidence which does not confirm what we expect to find or want to find. Facing such evidence might then reveal something more interesting than we expected to find: a basic human injustice.

XIII. Current Significance

It seems that Dicey is not to be seen as an advocate of legal patriarchy even though he clearly was and considered it important. Dicey's patriarchal world and world view are therefore unexamined. *Letters* does not loom large in his record, despite their clear (and quite fascinating) male supremacism and the case they made for a rule of law, with only men as the rulers. The *Letters* book was let drop, effectively treated as private musings. Dicey saw himself as a mid-Victorian but his occupancy of a Chair at Oxford was well into the twentieth century and then remarkably he was off to the London School of Economics.

The current writers on Dicey do not turn their minds to his male world view, with its political and intellectual world of men, and what it all means for legal thought. On certain matters they consider Dicey's politics: the Irish question, what sort of constitutional law he is outlining, whether he ends up departing from his principle of parliamentary sovereignty. But the cultural male world which Dicey inhabited, and also proselytised for, as a sound one, was taken out of consideration. It was a given, normal, unproblematic and certainly not intellectually interesting.

Dicey thought it vital that the male preserve of the public domain of England and her Empire be acknowledged and protected from women: that women were less able beings whose moves to acquire power, to rule through law, represented a threat to this healthy ecosystem. Dicey advocated for patriarchy but his analysts did not look at this. In fact they preferred to set it aside, and the way of dealing with it was to say that it was of limited significance and did not really count in terms of his broader constitutional thought. The patriarchal Dicey did not call for comment: he was quietly ushered out of the room and so the world of powerful legal men that he described, and brought to the fore, was left unconsidered and so perpetuated.

6

The Reform Stories: The Last Persons Case and the Abolition of the Husband's Rape Immunity

I. Introduction

In this chapter I examine the legal change of mind about the Personhood of women, and the correlative Personhood of men, and how this 'reform' of the law was presented, justified and explained. I consider two main Reform Stories, one from the 1920s, the other from the 1990s. The First Reform Story was told at the formal end of the Persons Cases when it was decided, by the new Lord High Chancellor in the Privy Council, that Canadian women were 'Persons' who could be admitted to the Canadian Senate. The Second Reform Story was told with the abolition of the husband's rape immunity in a series of cases, which followed swiftly upon each other. Each of these cases produced cursory narratives of change.

With both Reform Stories, there was a sustained history of subjugation of women through law, then a removal of that subjugation, by changing the meaning of a critical legal term. Then there was a need to give an account of these changes, and why they had come about, and with both Stories, the governing idea was of enlightened reform, and a dissociation from past legal practices. The change of legal mind was explained so as to downplay the active legal suppression of women, before the change, to excuse those who had denied rights to women, and then to cast a warm glow over those who had finally agreed to implement reforming change. There was barely any inquiry into what had changed, why it had changed and what the change meant for the rest of the law.

In the First Reform Story, told in the so-called last Persons Case, there was a change to the meaning of the term 'Person': who was one and who was not. There was a decision to include women in the concept of the Person, after so much resistance by male legal authorities to the exercise of public power by women. And then legal attention was allowed to move on to other more pressing matters. It seemed that nothing more needed to be done to change the sex of the Legal Person, who had been so rigidly male for so long. The explanation of legal change was minimal. There were more important things to get on with and so the line of Persons Cases was set aside and receded from memory. As Stephen Sedley observed, poignantly and accurately:

> One of the episodes now largely forgotten by legal history is the line of so-called 'persons cases' by which the courts of this country consistently obstructed the extension to women of university education, entry into the professions, the electoral franchise and access to elected office.[1]

In the Second Reform Story, there was a change to the meaning of the term 'rape' as an offence against 'the Person'. Here, I examine the legal 'reform' decisions to bring wives into the population of women who could be raped, with husbands included as potential offenders. These are the cases that abolished the husband's immunity from rape prosecution and so changed the scope and definition of the term 'rape', one of the most serious crimes in the criminal calendar. This changed the population of Persons who could commit the crime, and it changed the population of Persons who could be raped (and complain of it). It shrank the powers of the husband, but only down to the status of a Person, understood as an Individual; and in equal measure, it expanded the powers of the wife, so that she became a Person herself, for the purposes of this law. She became someone who could exclude all others from her person, her husband included. John Stuart Mill had expressed his disgust with this male right, well over a century earlier. The courts were slow to respond to Mill's grave concerns.

Perhaps it is unorthodox to think of rape law as law about Legal Persons and Legal Personhood. But because rape is one of the most serious Offences *against* the Person, and necessarily committed *by* Persons, it warrants consideration here. The husband's rape immunity placed *both* husbands and wives outside of this central offence, and in so doing it unpersoned both. The husband (as husband) could not be held responsible, as a Person, for this crime in relation to his wife, for she was legally considered an extension of him, in this respect. He was a sort of bloated legal being, and therefore no longer an Individual, and no longer a Person, who could be held responsible for this offence. Therefore, the immunity morally shrank the husband, as Mill explained. And because the wife (as wife) was not considered an eligible victim of this offence against the Person (because she, as wife, was not one of the Persons in contemplation of this Offence against the Person),[2] she too was unpersoned by her husband's immunity from prosecution. The husband thereby gained a great benefit from the immunity (almost unfettered sexual access to another) and the woman had all the disadvantage (no right to exclude him). But, conceptually, both were legally unpersoned, for the purposes of this crime, in that both husband and wife were taken out of this most serious offence by a Person[3] against a Person.

[1] Stephen Sedley, 'Persons Aggrieved' (*London Review of Books*, 22 May 1997), available at www.lrb.co.uk/the-paper/v19/n10/stephen-sedley/persons-aggrieved.

[2] Rape was proscribed by the Offences Against the Person Act UK 1861, s 48 under the heading 'Rape, Abduction and Defilement of Women'. Rape is now to be found in the Sexual Offences Act 2003.

[3] Some explanation is really needed here. Only men could commit the crime of rape, at law, and so it was only husbands as persons who were removed from this offence.

II. The First Reform Story: The Canadian Women who Claimed to be Persons

The First Reform Story begins with the actions of five distinguished Canadian women – Emily Murphy, Nellie McClung, Irene Parlby, Louise McKinney and Henrietta Muir Edwards – who sought a declaration from the Canadian Supreme Court that they were Persons who could sit in the Upper House of the Canadian Parliament.[4] They were informed by the Supreme Court that they were not and so they appealed this decision, taking it to the Privy Council in England. Their appeal in the case of *Edwards v A-G of Canada*[5] was successful. The English Lord Chancellor (now a Chancellor of a different hue) declared women to be Persons, for the purposes of the British North America Act of 1867 ('BNA Act').

The background to this case is illuminating. For at least the first quarter of the twentieth century, Canadian women had pressed for the right to enter the political realm, to exercise public power, and were consistently refused it by the governing men of politics and law who asserted men's exclusive entitlement. We are now in Canada because the Privy Council decision of *Edwards v A-G of Canada* is thought of as the final Persons Case. It arose in Canada, it concerned the powers of Canadian women to sit in the Upper House of the Canadian Parliament, but it was ultimately decided offshore by the Judicial Committee of the Privy Council in England (by England's new Lord Chancellor, Lord Sankey), because that was the final court of appeal for Canada, as it was for Australia, another outpost of Empire, as I learned in law school. Britain thus exercised its imperial power, exporting its thoughts about men, women and their respective roles in law, this time in reforming mode.

There was a long lead up to the petition and to the legal decision about the nature of male and female public power. According to Sharpe and McMahon, in their book-length treatment of *Edwards v A-G of Canada*,

> the case began not in the courts, but in the political arena. Emily Murphy, the woman behind the petition and the push to appoint a woman to the Senate of Canada, was indefatigable in her attempts to persuade one prime minister after another to appoint a woman, especially her, to the Senate. She met with great resistance.[6]

The petition, eventually signed by Murphy and her four 'fellow' activists,[7] sought a determination of the meaning of the term 'Person' within the BNA Act. The goal was to have women admitted to the Senate, as Persons.

[4] *In the Matter of a Reference as to the Meaning of the Word 'Persons' in Section 24 of the British North America Act, 1867* [1928] SCR 276 ('*Reference re Meaning of "Persons"*').

[5] *Edwards v A-G of Canada* [1930] AC 124.

[6] Robert J Sharpe and Patricia I McMahon, *The Persons Case: The Origins and Legacy of the Fight for Legal Personhood* (Toronto, University of Toronto Press, 2007) ix.

[7] Five signatories were needed for such a petition.

The reasoning of the Canadian Supreme Court on why women were not such Persons failed to recognise the long and sustained, and no doubt exhausting and disillusioning, campaign by Canadian women against exclusive male exercise of power. The case seemed to entail a mere clarification of a term: 'Person'. Did the word only mean men? This was the question. It is an objectionable question. It should not be a dry question, as it is about half of humanity and whether they are Persons in law. But that is how the case reads. Adding to the insult, and the horrible logic, the question was whether women should have the right to exercise legislative power within the Upper House of the Canadian Parliament. It was necessarily an all-male judicial determination about legislative meaning, and that legislative meaning was about whether women should participate in the making of legislation and its meaning. Should women have the power to scrutinise and review law in this House, or only men?

The BNA Act is an Act of the United Kingdom (UK), in the reign of Queen Victoria. I am stating this perhaps obvious fact for the benefit of non-Canadians. The Act united the provinces of Canada, Nova Scotia and New Brunswick into the British Dominion of Canada: 'under the Crown of the United Kingdom of Great Britain and Ireland, with a Constitution similar in Principle to that of the United Kingdom'. As the preamble to the Act continues, 'such a Union would conduce to the Welfare of the Provinces and promote the Interests of the British Empire'.[8] So the judges of the Canadian Supreme Court were effectively deciding who should decide how these interests of Empire were to be promoted.

To give the BNA Act, and the ensuing case about its meaning, some near and far context: it was enacted between the publication of Mill's *On Liberty*[9] and his *The Subjection of Women*.[10] In 1895, the author's home state of South Australia granted women the right to vote and the right to stand for Parliament, making them 'the most enfranchised [women] in the world'.[11] Canadian women, like the women of England, were politically active, demanding the right to be legal and political actors. 'In 1902 Henrietta Muir Edwards … urged women to enter the political world to make their "written and unwritten" laws capable of being enforced outside the home.'[12] In that same year the (Australian) Commonwealth Franchise Act 1920 (Cth) 'granted most Australian men and women the right to vote and to stand in federal elections'[13] making Australia 'the first nation in the world to grant [white] women these dual rights'.[14] Indigenous Australian women and men had to wait until 1962 before being granted the right to enrol and vote.[15]

[8] British North America Act, 1867.
[9] John Stuart Mill, *On Liberty* (London, John W Parkers and Son, 1859).
[10] John Stuart Mill, *The Subjection of Women* (London, Longmans, Green, Reader and Dyer, 1869).
[11] 'Women's Suffrage in Australia' (*Parliament of Australia*), available at aph.gov.au/Visit_Parliament/Art/Stories_and_Histories/Womens_Suffrage_in_Australia.
[12] Sharpe and McMahon (n 6) 9.
[13] 'Women's Suffrage in Australia' (n 11).
[14] ibid.
[15] ibid.

In 1915, another signatory to the Canadian petition, Nellie McClung, 'expressed similar frustration when she campaigned for female suffrage' saying that: 'One very contemptible bit of "dope" handed to women to keep them quiet was the hoary old lie "that the hand that rocks the cradle rules the world"'.[16] That same year, English constitutional theorist AV Dicey was still pushing back against Mill, in his *Introduction to the Study of Law and the Constitution*.[17] He was hugely concerned about the possibility that British women might exercise such vast imperial power, through the vote and other public powers, thereby extending themselves into the far reaches of Empire such as Canada, Australia and India, with its huge population. Canada was holding firm and so was England. (Australia had thrown in the towel within its own domain of power and ceded political power to women and the sky had not fallen and the rule of law had not been dismantled.) In Canada, according to Sheryl Hamilton: 'Between 1917 and 1927, five consecutive governments indicated that they wanted to appoint a woman to the Senate, but could not do so because of Section 24 [of the BNA Act]'.[18]

In August 1927 Emily Murphy, herself a magistrate, called her meeting of prominent women to sign a petition to challenge the meaning of the word Person in section 24. It was an impressive group. Nellie McClung was 'a novelist, reformer, teacher, journalist, and suffragist'.[19] Louise McKenny was 'the first woman elected to serve as member of any legislative assembly in the Commonwealth'.[20] Henrietta Muir Edwards (whose name went on the case based on alphabetical order) 'was well known for two law handbooks entitled *Legal Status of Women in Canada* (1917) and *Legal Status of Women in Alberta* (1921)'.[21] Irene Parlby 'was appointed the first female cabinet minister in 1921 (the second in the British Commonwealth)'.[22]

Murphy formed a group of five women in order to satisfy section 60 of the Supreme Court Act, which said that five persons could petition the Government to direct the Supreme Court to interpret a point of law in the BNA Act. Murphy's petition asked the Supreme Court to rule on the following two questions:

> Is power vested in the Governor-General in Council of Canada, or the Parliament of Canada, or either of them, to appoint a female to the Senate of Canada?
>
> Is it constitutionally possible for the Parliament of Canada under the provisions of the British North America Act, or otherwise, to make provision for the appointment of a female to the Senate of Canada?

[16] Sharpe and McMahon (n 6) 9.

[17] AV Dicey, *Introduction to the Study of the Law and the Constitution*, 8th edn (London, MacMillan, 1915).

[18] Sheryl N Hamilton, *Impersonations: Troubling the Person in Law and Culture* (Toronto, University of Toronto Press, 2009) 77.

[19] ibid 78.

[20] ibid.

[21] ibid 79.

[22] ibid.

According to Hamilton, Murphy had avoided using the word 'Person' in the petition because that word 'had been the basis upon which the Crown had repeatedly declared publicly that women were not eligible for appointment'.[23] But in the Government's referral of the matter to the Supreme Court, the question became: 'Does the word "Person" in s 24 of the British North America Act 1867 include female persons?'

III. The Response of the Supreme Court of Canada: Women are not Persons

In 1928, the Supreme Court of Canada was asked by Cabinet to decide whether women were 'Persons' within the terms of section 24 of the BNA Act.[24] This section stated that:

> The Governor General shall from Time to Time in the Queens Name by Instrument under the Great Seal of Canada summon qualified Persons to the Senate and subject to the Provisions of this Act every Person so summoned shall become and be a Member of the Senate and a Senator.

The Act did not say whether the term 'Person' included women. For that matter, nor did it say whether it included men. In essence, the question was whether women were 'Persons' who could sit in the Upper House of the Canadian Parliament.

By way of response, the Supreme Court of Canada invoked the wisdom of Willes J (yet again) in *Chorlton v Lings*, Lord Loreburn in *Nairn* and Lord Birkenhead in *Lady Rhondda* to decide in the negative. The members of the Supreme Court insisted, from the outset, that their decision had nothing to do with their own inclinations, nor the politics of the matter. They were only dealing in law. (They doth protest too much?) 'In considering this matter we are, of course, in no wise concerned with the desirability or the undesirability of the presence of women in the Senate, nor with any political aspect of the question submitted.'[25] The Supreme Court avowed that:

> The decision in *Chorlton v Lings* is of the highest authority, as was recognized in the House of Lords by Earl Loreburn, LC, in *Nairn v University of St Andrews*, and again by Viscount Birkenhead, LC, in rejecting the claim of Viscountess Rhondda to sit in the House of Lords.[26]

Justice Willes was quoted and endorsed. The Canadian Court agreed with Willes J's specious reasoning that

[23] ibid 81.
[24] *Reference re Meaning of 'Persons'* (n 4).
[25] ibid 281.
[26] ibid 290.

> in modern times, chiefly out of respect to women, and sense of decorum, and not from their want of intellect, or their being for any other such reason unfit to take part in the government of the country, they have been excused from taking any share in this department of public affairs.[27]

The Supreme Court homed in on Willes J's doubts about women's character and their fitness for public office. It repeated his admission

> that fickleness of judgment and liability to influence have sometimes been suggested as the ground of exclusion, I must protest against its being supposed to arise in this country from any underrating of the sex either in point of intellect or worth. That would be quite inconsistent with one of the glories of our civilization, the respect and honour in which women are held.[28]

Then Selden and the Romans were again invoked as important authorities. Thus in the Court's opinion,

> Chorlton v Lings is conclusive against the petitioners alike on the question of the common law incapacity of women to exercise such public functions as those of a member of the Senate of Canada and on that of their being expressly excluded from the class of 'qualified persons' within s 24 of the BNA Act.[29]

And so the Court concluded that

> We are, for these reasons, of the opinion that women are not eligible for appointment by the Governor General to the Senate of Canada under Section 24 of the British North America Act, 1867, because they are not 'qualified persons' within the meaning of that section. The question submitted, understood as above indicated, will, accordingly, be answered in the negative.[30]

IV. The Last Persons Case: The Decision of the Privy Council in *Edwards v A-G of Canada*

Emily Murphy and her compatriots then appealed the matter to the Judicial Committee of the Privy Council which decided that women were 'Persons' for the purpose of the right to be nominated to the Canadian Senate.[31] The Privy Council thus reversed the decision of the Canadian Supreme Court, with the paradoxical effect that women became Persons for the purposes of admission to the Upper House of the Canadian Parliament, while England stayed with Lord Birkenhead,

[27] ibid 283, quoting *Chorlton v Lings* (1868) LR 4 CP 374, 392.
[28] *Reference re Meaning of 'Persons'* (n 4) 283, quoting *Chorlton v Lings*, ibid 388.
[29] *Reference re Meaning of 'Persons'* (n 4) 290.
[30] ibid.
[31] The final Persons case is often said to be *Edwards v A-G of Canada* (n 5). See Albie Sachs and Joan Hoff-Wilson, *Sexism and the Law: A Study of Male Beliefs and Legal Bias in Britain and the United States* (Oxford, Martin Robertson, 1978).

and continued to exclude women from its Upper House. These effects were felt in England until 1963.

The decision of the Privy Council was delivered by Lord Sankey, as Lord Chancellor (7 June 1929–7 June 1935). He had only recently been appointed by the newly elected first Labour Prime Minister Ramsay McDonald (5 June 1929–7 June 1935). Sankey delivered the judgment of the Court on 18 October 1929, about four months into his time in office. Whereas Lord Birkenhead, as Lord Chancellor, had been emphatic, some seven years earlier, that the women of England were not Persons who could sit in the Upper House of Parliament, Lord Sankey arrived at the opposite conclusion for the women of Canada. Birkenhead relied on *Chorlton v Lings*. The majority of the Supreme Court of Canada relied on *Chorlton v Lings*. The brand new labour appointed Lord Chancellor Sankey came to an entirely different conclusion. Who was right? Had patriarchy abated? Had the winds changed? Had a move from a conservative to a labour Lord Chancellor made the difference?

Lord Sankey was feted as the reforming judge, in *Edwards v A-G of Canada*, the so-called last Persons Case.[32] According to Sankey, the 'exclusion of women from all public offices is a relic of days more barbarous than ours',[33] going on to say that 'to those who ask why the word [Persons] should include females the obvious answer is why should it not?'[34] This might seem a glib reply to the question he posed himself. But Lord Sankey did go through several legally-recognised steps, drawing on the conventions of common law and statutory interpretation. And with these legal moves he was able to achieve the desired result, without condemning his legal forbears and his legal contemporaries.

Lord Sankey did not even have to say they got it wrong. Certainly he did not say they were a phalanx of entitled men, who couldn't abide the thought of women exercising similar public power and didn't mind manipulating legal terms to keep women out and down. Rather, he proceeded on the basis that there were other perfectly acceptable legal ways of looking at the matter, which he planned to adopt.

Sankey did not say that it was eccentric analysis to go back into deep time, to the ways of 'the ancient tribes' and then the ways of the Romans to find out whether women were now Legal Persons, as *Chorlton v Lings* and its successor cases had done, including the Supreme Court of Canada. He did say that 'their Lordships think that the appeal to Roman Law and to early English decisions is not itself a secure foundation on which to build the interpretation of the British North America Act of 1867'.[35] Perhaps the implication was that it did not supply a secure foundation for the English law of Persons either, but this was not his remit. He did

[32] This is how it is celebrated in Canada on Persons Day.
[33] *Edwards v A-G of Canada* (n 5) 128.
[34] ibid 138.
[35] ibid 135.

say that '[c]ustoms are apt to develop into traditions which are stronger than law and remain unchallenged long after the reason for them has disappeared'.[36]

Lord Sankey proceeded diplomatically. Their Lordships were permitted to take a larger view of the nature of Modern Canada which should be freed from its ancient (patriarchal?) past. It was not

> right to apply rigidly to Canada of to-day the decisions and the reasons therefor which commended themselves, *probably rightly*, to those who had to apply the law in different circumstances, in different centuries, to countries in different stages of development (emphasis added).[37]

Thus, much was excused.

Sankey employed a biological metaphor to depict the constituting law of Canada and its healthy development. The BNA Act 'planted in Canada a living tree capable of growth and expansion within its natural limits. The object of the Act was to grant a Constitution to Canada'.[38] He sustained the metaphor of plant growth and flourishing.

> Their Lordships do not conceive it to be [their] duty … it is certainly not their desire – to cut down the provisions of the Act by a narrow and technical construction, but rather to give it a large and liberal interpretation so that the Dominion [of Canada] … may be mistress in her own house.[39]

In view of the male domination of the institution whose perpetuation was the very thing under consideration, the term 'mistress' was remarkably ill-conceived.

But then Sankey explained that their Lordships' task was one of constitutional interpretation, that they were not 'deciding any question as to the rights of women but only a question as to their eligibility for a particular position'.[40] This begins to sound like 'a narrow and technical construction' of the task at hand, the very thing he deplored. And it washed the hands of Sankey and their Lordships of any extrajudicial and so improper interest in the human rights of women. This was not what the case was about. And yet there was a brief political moment in the judgment:

> Neither is it without interest to record that when upon May 20, 1867, the Representation of the People Bill came before a Committee of the House of commons, John Stuart Mill moved an amendment to secure women's suffrage, and the amendment proposed was to leave out the word 'man' in order to insert the word 'person' instead thereof.[41]

Mill had thought that the use of the term 'Person' would necessarily enfranchise women, who were surely persons. The subsequent case law on the meaning of

[36] ibid 134.
[37] ibid 134–35.
[38] ibid 136.
[39] ibid.
[40] ibid 137.
[41] ibid 143.

the term 'Person', as we have seen, simply said that this was not so, as Sankey was well aware. But now Sankey grasped and implemented Mill's strategic thinking, some 60 years on, this time for Canada, not for the UK, where Lord Birkenhead's decision in *Viscountess Rhondda's Claim*[42] held firm (until 1963). In a modern Canada, women were now Persons.

Lord Sankey proceeded carefully. There was to be no disrespect to past decision-makers. And Sankey even conceded that the statutory word 'Person' was ambiguous, because of its various uses within the BNA Act. Sometimes the term was used in a manner that necessarily included women; other times the relevant section excluded women with the qualifier 'male persons'. But the general 'object of the Act' helped to clarify matters: it was 'to provide a constitution for Canada' which was 'a responsible and developing State'[43] and this was to be thought of as a 'living tree'.[44] Even if there was ancient growth, this living tree had now put out female shoots, to sustain Sankey's metaphor. By 1929 Canada and its women had matured and blossomed.

With this first Reform Story, which I have dated from *Edwards v A-G of Canada* 1929, the prevailing talk was of modernisation and reform, a celebratory mode was adopted and the injustice of the immediate past ignored. When the Persons Cases supposedly came to an end, through Lord Sankey, reputations were retained. The state remained the same in its priorities and values. Women were added to the male order, but the male order stayed male. A male legal actor and his role and priorities remained in place, in the sense that law that was found to have been explicitly male was not re-evaluated. (After all it was explicitly male the day before the *Edwards A-G of Canada* judgment.) What happened the following day? Were law reform commissions set up to work out what to do? No, in fact little happened by way of deep reflection. There was no rupture in legal thought; no paradigm shift; and so the same Reform Stories could be repeated decades later and to the present day. According to Baroness Hale, the legal past

> was all blithely swept aside with the assertion that their lordships 'did not think it right to apply rigidly to Canada of today the decisions and the reasons therefore which commended themselves, probably rightly, to those who had to apply the law in different circumstances, in different centuries in different stages of development …'.[45]

As Sachs and Hoff-Wilson observed, this was how the Persons Cases notionally ended, with celebration and congratulations for the 'legal statesmanship' of the judges and for the trailblazing women.[46] There was nothing about the political

[42] *Viscountess Rhondda's Claim* [1922] 2 AC 339.
[43] *Edwards v A-G of Canada* (n 5) 143.
[44] ibid 136.
[45] Baroness Brenda Hale, 'Beanstalk or Living Instrument? How Tall can the European Convention on Human Rights Grow?' (Gray's Inn Reading, 16 June 2011) 1.
[46] Sachs and Hoff-Wilson (n 31) 40.

realities of women's lives, let alone their legal protests, the imprisonment of women who engaged in political protest, the denial of the status of political prisoners and forcible-feeding. Nor was anything said about the exclusion of women from the Upper House of the UK Parliament, effected by Lord Birkenhead, some seven years earlier. The last Persons Case for Canada was not the last Persons Case for the UK. Perhaps it was easier to recognise female Personhood offshore.[47]

According to the UK Government Legal Department (GLD),

> [t]he rights of some women to vote (the centenary of which we celebrated last year), and the rights of women to become civil servants and lawyers, which we're celebrating this year, marked fundamental stepping stones towards building the society, and the GLD, we see today.[48]

In 2019 this was still the tone adopted by legal officialdom, that is the legal advisors to the UK Government, about the removal of women's legal incapacities. It was a matter of celebration, 'stepping stones', and 'building the society … we see today'. There was silence about the nature and scale of the past oppression of women by the men of law. And there was silence about the scale and significance of change.

In truth, the adding of women to the concept of the Person, which is so recent in historical terms, was according to Stephen, Dicey and Birkenhead statistically hugely significant and potentially of great import. Birkenhead called it a 'momentous … revolution'.[49] It deeply worried these men that women might outnumber men for the purpose of the franchise, for example, which is why the concession made in 1918 required a woman to be 30 years of age to vote, while men aged 21 were enfranchised. Meanwhile, in England, men continued to exercise exclusive power in the Upper House of Parliament.

The First Reform Story of the admission of women to (Canadian) Parliamentary Personhood by the Privy Council in *Edwards v A-G of Canada* is often referred to as the end of the Persons Cases but so much was left in place. True, after ferocious opposition, professional and political powers were ceded to women. But that is not the whole of Personhood. Though power was ceded to women in much of the male public sphere, in the so-called private sphere of sex and reproduction, powers were ceded very differently. In fact, much stayed the same. In the most fundamental ways, law continued to stunt women's autonomy and bodily integrity and hence their Personhood.

[47] And as we know this remained so in the UK until the late 1950s (with the recognition of life peers of both sexes) and until the 1960s (with the admission of women as hereditary peers).

[48] Government Legal Department, 'The Sex Disqualification (Removal) Act 1919: 100 Years ago the Sex Disqualification (Removal) Act was Given Royal Assent' (*Gov.UK*, online, 24 December 2019), available at www.gov.uk/government/news/the-sex-disqualification-removal-act-1919. And who is the GLD? In its own words: '17 Jan 2023 – We are the government's principal legal advisers. Our core purpose is to help the government to govern well, within the rule of law.'

[49] *Viscountess Rhondda's Claim* (n 42) 375.

V. The Second Reform Story: The Removal of the Husband's Immunity from Rape Prosecution

While many of the standard rights of Persons in the public sphere were extended to women by the first quarter of the twentieth century, a wife's right to exclude all others from her physical person was not granted until the end of the twentieth century. With the husband's immunity from rape prosecution (which I documented in *Criminal Law and the Man Problem*),[50] wives were denied perhaps the most fundamental protection of criminal law. Criminal law denied women a central legal norm: the right to one's own body or personal sovereignty, as Mill put it. Sir Matthew Hale and coverture persisted in this respect. (And as we saw in chapter four, the immunity was fully deployed by Lord Hailsham in the landmark rape case of *DPP v Morgan*.[51]) This right to exclude all others was reluctantly ceded to married women, and then late in the day, with minimal comment and reflection.

When the husband's rape immunity is juxtaposed with another criminal law, the law of abortion, one can see just how powerful state control of women, and their bodies, continued to be. The Offences Against the Person Act 1861 made it a crime punishable by life imprisonment should a woman seek to terminate a pregnancy.[52] Put together, these two criminal laws (an exemption for the man and a proscription for the woman) meant that a man had a lawful right to penetrate and consequently inseminate his wife without her consent and any ensuing pregnancy could lead to life imprisonment for the woman seeking to end it. And as we will see in chapter eight, when I consider the jurisprudence and politics of John Finnis, there has been a tightening of state control of women's reproductive bodies, especially in the United States, undoing the Personhood of American women.

The Second Reform Story of modernisation and reform was told in the early 1990s when the husband's rape immunity was abolished. The immunity was important to male Personhood in law because the right to sex was considered vital to the Legal Person. But it was sex right from the point of view of the man. As it was put bluntly in *Kenny's Outlines of Criminal Law* by JW Cecil Turner in 1962:

> It has been stated that as a general rule of law a husband cannot be guilty of rape on his wife because, upon marriage, the wife gives a consent (which she cannot retract) to the husband's exercising a right of intercourse with her. On this principle there is a general matrimonial obligation imposed on the wife by reason of marriage … The court may, however, intervene to terminate those relations, by an order that the wife be no longer

[50] Ngaire Naffine, *Criminal Law and the Man Problem* (Oxford, Hart Publishing, 2019).

[51] *DPP v Morgan* [1976] AC 182.

[52] The case of *R v Bourne* [1939] 1 KB 687, 694 decided that an abortion was legal if the doctor was 'of opinion, on reasonable grounds and with adequate knowledge, that the probable consequences of the continuance of the pregnancy will make the woman a physical or mental wreck'. In 1967 the Abortion Act made abortion legal in specified circumstances. See HLA Hart, 'Abortion Law Reform: The English Experience' (1972) 8 *Melbourne University Law Review* 388. The Abortion Act has since been amended by the Human Fertilisation and Embryology Act, 1990: see s 37 of that Act.

> bound to cohabit with the husband, and if it does so then the husband is not entitled to have intercourse with her without her consent, and thus could be guilty of rape on her.[53]

As we saw in chapter three, Mill made it clear that self-governance was the most basic human right. In legal terms, this translated into the right to keep others from one's person, from one's body, which is why the crimes of assault and murder were considered basic criminal law, and still are. This right to control the physical self and exclude others from it was considered critical to men. But because of the husband's rape immunity, it was unavailable to women, as soon as they were legally joined with a man. Though bodily integrity was defined as the most important physical characteristic of a Person, women were said not to possess it, legally or naturally. Once she was joined to a man, a woman lost the right to bodily integrity, perhaps the most important, indeed defining, right of a Person. This understanding of women was made law by the removal of the crime of rape from the province of marriage. It entailed the denial to women of what was considered essential to be a respected whole human being. It concomitantly conferred on men what could be called the right to rape because it immunised them from prosecution. Indeed they would be doing no wrong, because they would be asserting a basic male right.

In the 1990s the husband's rape immunity was removed. Within the span of a few years, the courts of Scotland, England and Australia abolished the immunity at common law. The Courts declared that husbands were now Persons chargeable under the Offences Against the Person Act with the offence of rape. And wives became Persons who could complain of rape by their husbands. Hence two correlative populations of Persons were greatly adjusted. This was, in theory, a monumental change to two populations of Persons. All husbands and all wives were brought into the law of Persons for the purposes of the law of rape.

As I observed in *Criminal Law and the Man Problem*, these Reform cases, which abolished the immunity, nevertheless gave slight treatment to what was in theory a major change in law, one that had a direct bearing on central criminal law and its serious Offences against the Person. (After all it greatly expanded the scope of the crime of rape.) The husband's rape of his wife had probably been lawful up to then, and at the insistence of many of the men of law. And yet judges seemed bent on diminishing the scale of the change, distancing themselves from the sentiments of earlier judges.

VI. The Long Arm of Lord Hailsham

Lord Hailsham's determination in *DPP v Morgan*[54] in 1975 (that an unreasonable mistaken belief in consent to intercourse excused an accused) was a catalyst for

[53] JW Cecil Turner, *Kenny's Outlines of Criminal Law*, 18th edn (Cambridge, Cambridge University Press, 1962) 192.

[54] *Morgan* (n 51).

rape law reform, but not in England. The following year, an inquiry into the law of rape, triggered by public concerns about Hailsham's decision, led to an affirmation of Hailsham's definition of the mental element of rape, but failed to consider his quiet affirmation of the husband's rape immunity, which was let stand.[55] An inquiry into rape law in 1984 then explicitly affirmed the husband's immunity.[56] It was not until 1990 that the English Law Commission recommended its abolition.[57]

By contrast, on the other side of the world, at the farthest reach of Empire, the state of South Australia actively responded to public disquiet about *Morgan*.[58] In 1976, the South Australian Parliament criminalised (aggravated) wife rape, making it the first jurisdiction to do so in the common law world.[59] (South Australia had fully decriminalised homosexuality, the previous year.) The other Australian state parliaments followed suit, throughout the 1980s, fully criminalising rape by a husband. Other jurisdictions around the world were also proceeding against the immunity: for example Canada abolished it in 1982. Meanwhile, in the UK, the husband's sex right remained lawful.

Then the courts of the UK finally began to act. In 1989, the Scottish High Court of Judiciary drew on the idea of 'female modernisation' in *S v HM Advocate*[60] to recognise the married woman's right to complain of rape by a husband. In their view the law was bound to change because married women had emerged out of their limiting legal status. The immunity was 'to be understood against the background of the status of women and the position of a married woman'.[61] In the past 'no doubt, a married woman could be said to have subjected herself to her husband's dominion in all things'.[62] But she no longer chose to do this, it seemed (but had she ever? No evidence was adduced about what women actually thought). 'By the second half of the 20th century … the status of women, and the status of a married woman, in our law have changed quite dramatically'.[63] Little was said about the past uses of male power.

In 1991 in *R v R* the English Court of Appeal[64] and then the House of Lords[65] decided to recognise wife rape as the crime of rape. (The Court was necessarily

[55] Great Britain Home Office, *Report of the Advisory Group on the Law of Rape* (London, CMND No 6352, 1976).

[56] Criminal Law Revision Committee, *Sexual Offences* (HMSO No 15, 1984).

[57] See Law Commission, 'Rape within Marriage' (1990) Law Commission Working Paper No 116; Law Commission, *Criminal Law: Rape within Marriage* (HMSO No 205, 1992).

[58] See discussion in PA Sallmann and Duncan Chappell, *Rape Law Reform: A Study of the South Australian Experience* (Adelaide Law Review Research Paper No 3, 1982).

[59] Section 73 of the Criminal Law Consolidation Act Amendment Act 1976 (SA) stated that: 'No person shall, by reason only of the fact that he is married to some other person, be presumed to have consented to sexual intercourse with that other person'. A critical account of the qualified nature of the abolition of the husband's rape immunity is to be found in Naffine (n 50) at 112.

[60] *S v HM Advocate* [1989] SLT 469.

[61] ibid 473.

[62] ibid.

[63] ibid 473.

[64] *R v R* [1991] 2 WLR 1065 ('*R v R*, Court of Appeal').

[65] *R v R* [1991] 3 WLR 767 ('*R v R*, House of Lords').

aware that legislative change had just been endorsed.) As Joanne Conaghan has observed, '[t]he arguments in *R v R* are marked by a surprising degree of doctrinal sparseness'.[66] Again, as the courts effected this major change to the criminal law directed explicitly at men, attention was directed towards the changing status of women and away from the past exercise of male legal power to secure the interests of men. According to the Court of Appeal:

> It seems to us that where the common law rule no longer even remotely represents what is the true position of a wife in present day society, the duty of the court is to take steps to alter the rule if it can legitimately do so in the light of any relevant Parliamentary enactment.[67]

The House of Lords employed similar reasoning, when it spoke of the modernisation of the status of the wife. It approved the statement of Lord Lane that it was time for 'the removal of a common law fiction which has become anachronistic and offensive and we consider that it is our duty having reached that conclusion to act upon it'.[68] Lord Keith of Kinkel, speaking for the rest of the Law Lords, observed:

> It may be taken that [Hale's dictum] was generally regarded as an accurate statement of the common law of England. The common law is, however, capable of evolving in the light of changing social, economic and cultural developments. Hale's proposition reflected the state of affairs in these respects at the time it was enunciated. Since then the status of women, and particularly of married women, has changed out of all recognition in various ways which are very familiar and upon which it is unnecessary to go into detail.[69]

Again the talk was mainly of social and legal reform rather than fundamental legal change. Little was made of the contraction of men's lawful power to use sexual force against women. And so the House of Lords concluded that 'in modern times the supposed marital exemption in rape forms no part of the law of England'.[70]

In 1991, the Australian High Court in *R v L*[71] also declared that by that year, and perhaps even before that, the husband had lost his common law immunity. Chief Justice Mason, and Justices Deane and Toohey described the change in the briefest of terms:

> Without endeavouring to resolve the development of the common law in this regard, it is appropriate for this Court to reject the existence of such a rule as now part of the common law of Australia … The notion is out of keeping also with recent changes in the criminal law of this country made by statute, which draw no distinction between a wife and other women in defining the offence of rape. It is unnecessary for the Court to do more than to say that, if it was ever the common law that by marriage a wife gave

[66] Joanne Connaghan, *Law and Gender* (Oxford, Oxford University Press, 2013) 51.
[67] *R v R*, Court of Appeal (n 64) 1073.
[68] ibid.
[69] *R v R*, House of Lords (n 65) 770.
[70] ibid 776.
[71] *R v L* (1991) 174 CLR 379.

> irrevocable consent to sexual intercourse by her husband, it is no longer the common law.[72]

In 2012 the Australian High Court went further still, and declared that wife rape *was* an offence known to South Australian law in 1963 (the year of the alleged rape by a husband), and probably before that, because Australia was more enlightened than Britain, with respect to the rights of women, notably the franchise.[73] (The Court invoked the fact that in 1895 South Australia became the first jurisdiction in the world to enfranchise women and permit them to stand for Parliament.[74]) Thus the legal past was reassessed and reinterpreted and made to appear better than it was.[75]

VII. Moving on: The Return to Legal Business as Usual

The Reform Stories relied on the power to explain law and legal change: by which I mean the power of the still powerful group, men of legal authority, to control the account of what had happened, the prevailing story. The Reform Stories remained patriarchal. For history was told with men still controlling its telling and, perhaps unsurprisingly, previous judges were excused and the new law was cast as good and principled. The violent engagements between women seeking rights and the men who denied them came to be seen as a gentle road to reform and a wise, even generous, acknowledgement of women's political maturing.

There was little desire for self-reflection about the nature of institutions which had so vigorously supported a one-sex system. The fact that the 'last Persons Case' must, logically, have acknowledged the maleness of law's Persons up to that point in time was left unconsidered in its implications. So they were all men before? Yes. Therefore what? Almost nothing was made of it. And with the Second Reform Story, the fact that husbands could lawfully rape their wives before the abolition cases and then couldn't afterwards was not made the subject of reflective inquiry into the nature of law: before and after.

Having subjugated women, through a denial of their Personhood, a new generation of male legal officials suppressed the fact of that subjugation, and instead told a tale of social and legal maturation and reform. This permitted the doublethink of law. Because male legal authorities, who were still connected with their legal forbears, controlled the explanation of law, they could control the story. They could say that we are nevertheless principled and perhaps always were or at least that in earlier times things needed to be done differently.

[72] ibid 389–90.

[73] *PGA v The Queen* (2012) 245 CLR 355.

[74] Constitution (Female Suffrage) Act 1895 (SA).

[75] See Wendy Larcombe and Mary Heath, 'Developing the Common Law and Rewriting the History of Rape in Marriage in Australia: PGA v The Queen' (2012) 34 *Sydney Law Review* 785. See also my analysis of *PGA v The Queen* in Naffine (n 50).

As Erika Rackley and Rosemary Auchmuty observe, in their sustained case for feminist legal history, there is a need 'to resist and debunk the idea that legal history – and women's legal history in particular – is inherently and inexorably progressive. This myth is a feature of most institutional histories and accounts of the development of legal doctrine'.[76] As Sachs and Hoff-Wilson said, in *Sexism and the Law*, the decision to recognise the Personhood of women seeking admission to the Upper House of the Canadian Parliament was treated as 'the culmination of the smooth and automatic unfolding of an idea' thus 'hiding the wounds of bitter past battles … by pretending they never existed'.[77]

And so according to Sharpe and McMahon, in their assessment of *Edwards v A-G of Canada* and its aftermath:

> [M]ost people simply forgot about the case once the decision was rendered. Prime Minister King appointed a woman … to the Senate, but the country became preoccupied with other pressing concerns. The Great Depression was paramount in the 1930s, followed by the Second World War and the great boom of the 1950s. In those decades of turmoil, the rights of women somehow managed to get lost. The Persons case … was all but forgotten until the 1970s when it was resurrected by a new wave of feminists.[78]

And something similar happened in the 1990s. With the abolition of the marital rape immunity (of husbands) cases, we have the Second Reform Story. A wholesome explanation was given to the changed definition of rape so that it now inculpated the husband. Once again men relinquished some of their male-defining powers over women. In these Reform Stories about the law of rape, both the problem with the law, and the extent of legal change were minimised, as legal men (the almost exclusive holders of legal power) now permitted women to exclude all others from their persons, the husband included. Much was glossed over. Allowing women to be Persons in this most fundamental manner was portrayed as a sensible modernising move, one that effected no great change to law, as a whole.

Now untethered from its masculinist past, legal theory could proceed with a supposedly neutral Individual as the subject of legal analysis. There was no appetite to consider the effects of this legal history of the Person (with its openly acknowledged great skewing towards one half of the population) on the robustness of theory of the Person, or the impartiality or objectivity of theorists of the Person.

The incorporation of women into the concept of the Person was done with so little fanfare, so little self-scrutiny, that the vicious history was pasted over. Attention was directed elsewhere. So by the time of the Second Reform Story, the legal subjection of women through the Persons Cases was all but forgotten. The First Reform Story had worked its magic. The final Persons Case did not do the job of personifying women, for this would have been a legal exercise on a grand

[76] Erika Rackley and Rosemary Auchmuty, 'The Case for Feminist Legal History' (2020) 40 *OJLS* 878, 900.

[77] Sachs and Hoff-Wilson (n 31) 40.

[78] Sharpe and McMahon (n 6) x.

scale, a shaking up of the whole of law, and the Persons Cases did the very opposite. They blocked women until the last case and then it was simply declared that women were now Persons. (Well done ladies.) This was done in the most cursory fashion. The Persons Case, which finally added women to the concept, according to the orthodox story, and which might have triggered a major re-evaluation of law, did not.

Assimilation of women into the world of law, as full legal actors, which was thought to have happened with the final Persons Case, and then later with the abolition of the husband's rape immunity (my two Reform Stories), is all very well. But this way of thinking about law's reforms says little about what women were being brought into and it tells us little about men, law's main characters, as law once understood them to be. Why were men the right fit for the Legal Person? What did it mean for law? What sort of law did it give us? These are substantial jurisprudential matters.

The Reform cases emit a sense of numbness because they show almost no interest in these basic questions. There is a strange brevity to the decision-making, a sense that all is now sorted, so let's move on quickly, without a fuss. But why don't jurists want to know more about what they are dealing with? With the Persons Cases, women (half the population) were positively excluded from major parts of power-conferring law and then finally they were let in. With the marital immunity cases, men (half the population) lost a right which was extraordinarily antithetical to basic legal principle, the right to enter a woman (the other half of the population) at will, and so at last the law endorsed one of its own fundamental principles: that we all have the right to exclude others from our persons. These movements in law are potentially vast in their significance, especially given the sheer numbers involved. Surely they have a lot to tell us about law, then and now. But where is the interest?

Women were denied public power as well as the basic legal avenues of self-protection and self-government. When judges said that it was inveterate usage that women had not been Persons for the exercise of public power, they were exercising both definitional and explanatory power. Certainly when they said that it was one of women's privileges not to have to exercise public power, that it was in women's interests not to be Persons, they were using both sorts of power.

In this reforming legal time, the men of legal authority again used their explanatory power to make sense of law's modernisation, ensuring that law was seen to adjust to the times, in a seemly manner. The suppression of women, they said, was appropriate for former times (even Sankey hinted at this). Again, the men of legal authority oversaw and permitted fundamental legal change (the ceding of rights to women) without addressing the system itself, which had presupposed male Personhood. Thus, the male monopoly of law was concealed or ignored or watered down and legal reputations of the legal patriarchs were sustained. Patriarchal law remained in place, invisible and untouchable. The continuing systemic maleness of law was implicitly denied.

And when the husband's right to rape his wife was removed, again there was no reckoning with the rejected law and its makers: with those who had instantiated and sustained the right. Instead, the law was explained away, and its makers and supporters were let off the hook.

VIII. Protecting and Preserving Male Power and its Uses

When law's maleness was under threat, and it seemed that professional, political and educational rights were to be given to women, some leading men fought hard and loudly to stop this happening. Those legal men, who supported male right, remain respectable legal authorities in the male legal pantheon. When male legal power was slowly and reluctantly ceded, there was little interest in what this meant for law, before and after the concession. Instead of acknowledging these foundational features of law, instead of finding them interesting and informative and in need of understanding and explanation, they were shelved, and still are. There was almost a positive carving out of them, perhaps as a canker, a setting of them aside, a sign of more 'barbaric times' perhaps, so they didn't taint the main body of legal thought. So there was no need to examine the profound sex inequality built into the system, as infrastructure and superstructure. And as I will explain later in the book, this endemic inequality built into law remains profoundly awkward for the main theories of law, for which legal respect for all Individuals is treated as a basic tenet. It may even be existential, in that it places law as a discipline of principle under threat.

Evidence of a seemingly defensive stance, even fear, is to be found in the setting aside of the misogyny of leading theorists of law, so that the rest of their thought can be analysed without this encumbrance. We saw this with Dicey. We will see it again with Finnis. And it is also to be found in the general treatment of law as a discipline and body of knowledge, in which these disturbing facts do not feature and implicitly are assumed not to feature. The silences of contemporary jurisprudence about these patriarchal practices permit these unpalatable truths about law's Persons and characters to be excised, without further mention. Patriarchy is not seen as part of the fabric of law, as integral to it, and in need of investigation and inquiry.

Techniques of dissimulation and deflection were deployed at critical moments of legal decision-making, to defend and advance the reputations of senior judicial officials who openly favoured men and acted against women. A landmark case or decision, which might have provided an opportunity for deep reflection and evaluation of the moral failings of the law to date, came to stand for something benign and even positive. Violation of the human rights of women was supported by leading legal figures, who then came to stand for something else. Hale and Blackstone had their reputations preserved despite their crushing legal formulations about the status of women. Their disdain for women was not seen as integral to their thinking nor as part of their main record. Sankey's very soft recognition of women as Persons in *Edwards v A-G of Canada* was not seen (except by Sachs and Hoff Wilson and perhaps by Lady Hale) as an apologia for the evils of past practices. Instead, Sankey appeared as a reforming hero.

IX. The Power to Tell the Story of Change

The power to tell the story of change is a considerable one. It entails the power to control what is thought to be the truth of what has been happening and what is happening now, and, in a sense, make it historically true. The sheer strength of male legal power steered the story of law's Person along certain channels. The enormity of the (male) political and legal achievement of dividing up the population into the preferred and the non-preferred, here men, there women, and then reversing it, was minimised. The scale and nature of change were downplayed. The so-called personification of women was done with the least disruption to the rest of law, and it was also done with the least disruption to the scholarly understanding of law and to legal theory.

This was by no means inevitable. The decision to admit women as Legal Persons could have signalled a need for great change in legal thought, as the population of Persons enlarged so dramatically; as it acquired people with perhaps different interests and certainly very different legal histories. But there was to be no Kuhnian paradigm shift in thinking, in which the old order was scrutinised and found wanting, because it was so riven with contradictions.[79] There was to be no new paradigm in law about its very subject.

Remarkably little happened in response to the decisions to change the meaning of critical legal terms, pertaining to Personhood: by shrinking the powers of men, so that women could be Persons too. The courts, and sometimes the parliament, responsible for change ostensibly stayed within the conventions of the common law and the interpretation of statutes, while arriving at very different conclusions from their predecessors. There was a looking away, a distancing from what went before, a quick moving on, as if little had happened, and as if nothing were deeply wrong with the law before, and nothing more needed to change once the subjugating law had been removed. There was little appetite for a postmortem of the law and the legal practices which had been removed, let alone open truth-telling or apology.

[79] See Thomas S Kuhn, *The Structure of Scientific Revolutions* (Chicago, University of Chicago Press, 1962).

7

Case Study 2: HLA Hart and *The Concept of Law* – Proceeding with a Clean Slate

I. Introduction

With the Reform Stories, there was almost no reckoning with what had gone before: with the explicit maleness of the Legal Person, as determined by the legal officials. A veil was drawn over this unseemly past and so legal theory could proceed without this unfortunate history, letting it recede from memory. So when HLA Hart became one of the most influential jurisprudential figures of the twentieth century, with his *The Concept of Law*,[1] he could proceed with his theorising *as if* none of this had happened. There was no pressing political or historical need to reckon with the recent past, with its active exclusion of women from much of the legal world and from its population of Persons. There was no need for truth-telling and reconciliation. Theory of law could be detached from these facts and developed in a highly abstract manner, with its characters conceived as abstractions.

When Hart thought up his concept of law in the early 1950s, for publication in 1961, there were no legal ruptures to note, no deep iniquities to be documented, as women at last ostensibly acquired the status of Persons who could inhabit the public world. The active, sustained and vigorous exclusion of women from such Personhood need not be considered. The country from which Hart wrote (England) was imagined as a healthy legal system *de novo*. The vast powers of the husband, still embedded in the rules of criminal law, were overlooked. That the Upper House of the UK Parliament had yet to admit women on the same terms as men was not of note.[2] That women had been completely excluded from the House of Lords up to a few years earlier was not attended to. Indeed that Hart's Oxford

[1] HLA Hart, *The Concept of Law* (Oxford, Clarendon Press, 1961). The book was based on his undergraduate lectures.

[2] Duncan Sutherland, 'Peeresses, Parliament and Prejudice: The Admission of Women to the House of Lords, 1918–1963' (2010) 20 *Parliaments, Estates and Representation* 215, 2015: 'Only after the creation of life peerages, after 1958, were women admitted to the House, and even then the hereditary peeresses had to wait until 1963 for admission.' See also Duncan Sutherland, 'Ladies in a Lords' House: Women in the House of Lords Since 1958' in Bruce Kinzer, Molly Baer Kramer and Richard Trainor (eds), *Reform and its Complexities in Modern Britain: Essays Inspired by Sir Brian Harrison* (Oxford, Oxford University Press, 2022).

College and Hart's colleagues were all male, that he spoke to audiences of young men, was not a cause for concern and certainly was not taken to have a bearing on theory. Nor was the fact that the women of England had yet to be fully enfranchised when Hart became a student at Oxford, in 1926. The maleness of law and the state institutions was simply normal.

As Nicola Lacey explains, in her fine biography of Hart, *The Concept of Law* was intended to 'illuminate all forms of law, wherever or whenever they arose'.[3] So strictly speaking, Hart did not need to deal with the specific norms and ways of any particular legal system, let alone his own, and its dubious legal practices. His theory was determinedly ahistorical.

This is not to say that Hart remained in his philosophical armchair, only ever imagining law outside of place and time. On the contrary, he engaged actively in contemporary debates about law reform in his own country. He was theorist and activist. The problem, for present purposes, is with how Hart implicitly divided up his work and his thinking.

Yes, Hart was an active law reformer, he was concerned about social policy, and he engaged in applied scholarship. And he was certainly concerned about injustices to women, and he tried to do something about them. He was especially concerned about the criminal laws of abortion and their adverse effects on the lives of women. He spoke openly about what he saw as the benefits of liberal law reform in this area.[4] He did this on homosexuality and prostitution as well.[5] He invoked John Stuart Mill on the need for law to keep out of the private sphere and private morality. My concern is that these parts of Hart's thinking were carved off from his more conceptual and theoretical work on the nature of law and its subjects, which was to form the basis of his great reputation: his theory about who law was speaking to, and who could speak for law and recognise it to be true law.

The legal situation and status of women, especially when seeking termination of a pregnancy, were put by Hart and his interpreters into his applied, policy reforming work, not his general theory of law. Thus both Hart and his followers located reproducing legal subjects within special, even difficult law, rather than general law, so that women became a special category of the Person rather than, perhaps, the foundational Legal Person. The perceived social and moral complexities of abortion law were not viewed as problems for law in general and its characterisations of adult, rational persons and subjects, when pregnant. And this remains the

[3] Nicola Lacey, *A Life of HLA Hart: The Nightmare and the Noble Dream* (Oxford University Press, 2004) 4.

[4] See, eg, HLA Hart, 'Abortion Law Reform: The English Experience' (1972) 8 *Melbourne University Law Review* 388. See also Lacey (n 3) 302 in which she discusses his preparations for his Australian delivery as liberal reformer.

[5] Hart was a high-profile figure in what came to be known as the Hart-Devlin debate on the legality and morality of homosexuality. The debate was in response to the Wolfenden Report, *Report of the Departmental Committee on Homosexual Offences and Prostitution in Great Britain* published in 1957 which recommended that 'homosexual behaviour between consenting adults in private should no longer be a criminal offence'. See Peter Cane, 'Taking Law Seriously: Starting Points of the Hart/Devlin Debate' (2006) 10 *The Journal of Ethics* 21.

case today: in theory of law, there tends to be a generic Legal Person, who is never pregnant (for he is implicitly a man), and then there are specific or special persons (women) who often are pregnant.[6]

Nor did Hart's general theory of law – populated as it was by legal officials, familiar with the rules governing rules, and by law-governed and protected citizens – take any account of the fact that until quite recently women had been considered the wrong types of being to be legal officials, let alone Persons endowed with some of the most basic rights of legal subjects to their property and their bodies (in the case of the married woman). The Reform Stories greatly assisted in putting these facts into the background and keeping them out of general theory of law, Hart's included.

II. Hart's Theory

Turning to Hart's general legal theory, *The Concept of Law*, Nicola Lacey explains its essential elements with elegant simplicity:

> The nub of Hart's theory is the startlingly simple idea that law is a system of rules structurally similar, in both form and function, to the rules of games such as chess or cricket. The rules are of different kinds, with complementary functions. Some – 'primary rules' – directly govern behaviour. … The most obvious example of primary rules would be criminal laws.[7]

But there are also, of necessity, 'secondary rules'. These are rules of 'recognition, adjudication and change'. These secondary rules provide for 'the identification, application and alteration of the primary rules'.[8] Such laws 'range from constitutional laws to laws governing the creation of contracts, marriages or wills'.[9]

As Aziz Huq further clarifies:

> On Hart's view, a modern legal system exists where there is a union of primary and secondary rules, and where one of the secondary rules – the rule of recognition – sets out the criteria of legal validity for all other rules. Further, the rule of recognition 'provid[es] the criteria by which the validity of other rules of the system' can be assessed.[10]

From this it follows that the rule of recognition is 'a matter of official practice, that is, the criteria officials converged upon and accept from an internal point of

[6] On the abstracted person of criminal law, see Alan Norrie, *Crime, Reason and History: A Critical Introduction to Criminal Law*, 3rd edn (Cambridge, Cambridge University Press, 2014) 26. See also Celia Wells and Oliver Quick, *Lacey, Wells and Quick, Reconstructing Criminal Law: Text and Materials*, 4th edn (Cambridge, Cambridge University Press, 2010) 95.

[7] Lacey (n 3) 225.

[8] ibid.

[9] ibid.

[10] Aziz Z Huq, 'What We Ask of Law' (2022) 132 *Yale Law Journal* 487, 539.

view'.[11] And Hart tells us who makes up 'the relevant "official world"'. As Huq spells out, Hart's world of legal officialdom encompasses '"the judiciary," "the legislature," and other tribunals'.[12] And these legal officials, who bring their expertise to bear on the law, making it in the right way, recognising it and employing it, are to be distinguished from 'private citizens' whose task it is to obey the law.

Hart's theory ostensibly described law everywhere and anywhere. This is what he had in mind. But particular law and particular legal systems and particular legal subjects were not far from view. For 'legal rules have an internal and external aspect'.[13] As Lacey explains, 'we know that a rule is in existence not only because it is regularly observed, but because those subject to it use it for a standard of behaviour, criticising themselves or others for breaches of the rules'.[14] The internal point of view of 'the citizen' takes the form of this imagined person saying or thinking 'it is the law that …' and so 'I obey the law, or choose not to'. It is more than a habit of obedience, but something absorbed, becoming internal to the person. This means that there are people observing and experiencing the law, using it as their standard for themselves and for others.

So Hart's theory is soon populated. There is the citizenry observing the law and there are expert legal people, the officials telling us what that law is. Thus we come quickly to real people who are hard to imagine outside of times and places, governed by real, specific laws.[15] In fact, Hart gives us a lead on this, ushering us into the real world, as he tells us that 'in a healthy society they [private citizens] will in fact often accept these rules as common standards of behaviour and acknowledge an obligation to obey them'.[16] Hart seems to be thinking of his own society in which general obedience to the law ideally comes with an internal sense of obligation. This is to be distinguished from an outsider view of law, in which the person might think: 'I see that people are generally doing this' and therefore I will. So all these imagined characters within Hart's concept of law soon come to be embodied in real people.

III. Leaving Legal Patriarchy in Place

In his general theory, Hart's laws and legal ways, which are meant to be universal and enduring, begin to look much like the laws and ways of English experts of English law. Hart seems to read off law from English law and necessarily from

[11] ibid 540.
[12] ibid.
[13] Lacey (n 3) 5.
[14] ibid.
[15] On the gravitational force of the real person, when a theorist is trying to deal only in human abstractions, see Kathleen Wilkes, *Real People: Personal Identity without Thought Experiments* (Oxford, Oxford University Press, 1988).
[16] Hart (n 1) 113.

his place within it, for he speaks about, and from within, civilised or mature law and its organising systems. He takes the legal system within which he writes to be healthy.[17] And because he implicitly takes a stand on English law, taking it to be a mature and developed law, from which one can confidently write theory, it could be said that Hart fails to deal with and so perpetuates patriarchy, and the male concept of the Person. It seems very unlikely that this was Hart's intention, but this is how it pans out. That women were actively excluded from the concept of the Legal Person (especially when there was a law that conferred public power),[18] does not enter his analysis. It is neither questioned nor noted. Patriarchy is therefore left in place. Indeed it is presupposed – because Hart necessarily gets his understanding of law from the male-controlled and occupied system of law he inhabits – but not discussed as a patriarchal system. Its male-governed nature is implicitly irrelevant.

In other words, by putting the English legal system (his implicit template for legal systems) in a positive light, Hart necessarily accepts that a legal system that has actively excluded half of society (women) from its political and legal and educational institutions – from parliament, the judiciary and academia – can be treated as a healthy one. An entirely male set of institutions, where only men could be legal officials, where only men could man the legal pumps, is treated as a properly-formed legal system. Women life peers (but not female hereditary peers) acquired the right to sit in the House of Lords the same year that Hart published his famous essay, 'Positivism and the Separation of Law and Morals',[19] that is 1958. In other words when Hart was preparing this paper, women were not permitted to sit in the Upper House of the UK Parliament. The complete maleness of the institution was either invisible or untroubling.

Of course, Hart was not alone in this, in writing from within a legal system he took to be generally fair and civilised, when in truth it was profoundly patriarchal.[20] In some ways it seems harsh to single him out, because Hart was also an important liberal reformer. But as I noted at the beginning of this chapter, his specific reform work was separated from his general theory, which went on to be extremely important to legal theorists who, in turn, have continued to theorise law as if it did not have this deeply divided patriarchal-law-forming history.[21]

Hart's *The Concept of Law* also gives us cause for concern when we start looking into the basic ingredients of its theory of law. For here we find legal officials who recognise and apply the law, making it valid by their actions. These legal officials

[17] I discussed this in Ngaire Naffine, 'The Common Discourse of Hart and Fuller' in Peter Cane (ed), *The Hart-Fuller Debate in the Twenty-First Century* (Oxford, Hart Publishing, 2010) 217.

[18] By this I mean a rule positively endowing the holder, called a Person, to exercise public power.

[19] HLA Hart, 'Positivism and the Separation of Law and Morals' (1958) 71 *Harvard Law Review* 593.

[20] For example Lon Fuller did it too as I also point out in Naffine (n 17).

[21] On the removal or sidelining of female and feminist critiques from legal theory, see Kristen Rundle's lively analysis of Allan Hutchisons's *Hart, Fuller and Everything After*: Kristen Rundle, 'On Politics, Polemics and Performance' (2024) *Jurisprudence*, available at www.tandfonline.com/doi/full/10.1080/20403313.2024.2404356. Rundle points out that Hutchison does this himself.

are not said to be men, though they have nearly all been men, but they also must be men for Hart's theory to make sense. Here are my reasons for saying this.

IV. Women Cannot Supply the Internal Point of View of Hart's Legal Official

Firstly, Hart's internal point of view of legal officialdom, built into his rule of recognition, necessarily presupposes the viewpoint of male officials because, for most of English legal history, women were positively precluded from such positions because they were considered, by legal officials, to be the wrong kinds of beings to exercise such power. Simply put, women in England were not permitted to have the education, the training and the formal access to the role of law-recognised law-recognising officials. True, by the time that Hart was writing there were women practising law and acting as judges.[22] In the latter case, there were very few. It was not until 1956 that Rose Heilbron 'became the first ever woman judge in England when she became Recorder of Burnley'.[23] Moreover, according to her daughter, Hilary Heilbron, KC, '[f]or most of the 1950s and for part of the 1960s she was the only female practising Silk in England and Wales'.[24] Some reality should come into Hart's theory, I suggest. It should have some empirical basis as well as conceptual logic. As we have seen, in the very recent history within which Hart was writing, and at the time of his writing, women were largely excluded from such public offices, by all male legal officials, *and* there was no legal outcry about it, mainly endorsement.

To drive the point home. Legal theory, especially that of Hart, places emphasis on the legal official whose task it is to work with law, to recognise it as legitimate, in effect to give it legitimacy by acting with it and on it. But this legal official would cease to be one, he would cease to be empowered as an official, were there a whiff that he might have had a female legal history, a female legal life. The blocking of women as a class from higher education, from legal practice, from professional and political life, by men of legal authority – by the very legal officials Hart invokes – rendered women incapable of performing the role of the authoritative legal insider, the one who could recognise real law. The legal official needed a male legal life, actually and symbolically. Hart's legal officials could not have women's legal and political character or experience. Legal officials come from a very different place in the system: they come from above, not from below.

[22] The first woman to sit on the English High Court was Dame Elizabeth Kathleen Lane in 1965. See 'Dame Elizabeth Kathleen Lane' (*Britannica*), available at www.britannica.com/biography/Elizabeth-Lane.

[23] Hilary Heilbron, 'Women at the Bar: An Historical Perspective' (*Counsel*, online, 31 May 2013), available at www.counselmagazine.co.uk/articles/women-the-bar-historical-perspective.

[24] ibid.

For Hart's theory of law to stand, men must be his imagined legal officials because he is building on the English legal system for his modern legal system and, for most of its history, only men could occupy these expert positions. Hart looked to legal officials for the authoritative internal point of view and this could only be supplied by men as, for most of its history, only men were on the inside of law: law's expert interpreters and agents.

V. Why Women are not Really Imagined as Hart's Citizen Subjects

But there is more to this. Nor could women be imagined as Hart's ideal type of general rights holders, his 'citizens' positively empowered to act by law, law's central addressees. The reason is that so much of rights-conferring law was not addressed to women, or law actively denied women fundamental rights. Even in the role of citizen, women were often cast as legal outsiders. As Kathleen Hennessy reminds us: 'As late as the 1970s, working women were routinely refused mortgages in their own right, or were granted them only if they could secure the signature of a male guarantor'.[25] Women were generally neither officials nor were they the broadly-empowered subjects of rights-conferring law. This was especially true of married women and women were expected to marry.

So if we were to generate Hart's law and legal system from women's outsider experiences and point of view, it would be grim. It would be a very different, even dystopian, law in which the defining experience was to be muzzled and excluded from positions of authority, from 'public functions', with much of one's private and public life mediated by a man. The legal and political system would be repressive and disabling.

Just a quick thought experiment: if women were the implicit point of view from which law was understood and recognised, then a very different story of law would have to be told. Given that women were actively excluded from Legal Personhood, in so many ways, including from legal officialdom, a law generated from women's experiences of law would be incoherent or perhaps a legal system built upon exclusions. For the experience of women has been that of a legal outsider. Women have had a lowly status created by male legal officials invested in the continuation of that female status and who have brought it into being.

Were women to supply the implicit point of view of Hart's law, everything would alter. In fact the legal officials who represented the internal point of view for the purposes of Hart's rule of recognition would cease to exist, for women were, for so long, actively debarred from this role. This role was seen, by legal officials, to be indelibly male.

[25] Kathleen Hennessy, 'You've Come a Long Way, Jenny' *The Guardian* (Online, 18 April 2004), available at www.theguardian.com/money/2004/apr/18/womenandmoney.observercashsection.

VI. The Heurist Device Brought in Aid

In the final chapter, I will discuss the operation of a silent (that is undeclared) heuristic device which has had some very odd, unacknowledged and no doubt unintended epistemological effects on law and legal theory. It applies to Hart's work, so I will mention it now. The heuristic device entails the theorising of law *as if* women had always been equivalent to men, interchangeable legal units, notionally participating in all areas of law, equally authoritative. When Hart's work is read as an analysis of legal systems in general, especially when they are functioning effectively, this is what is happening. He is using a heuristic device that makes men and women interchangeable.

Rather than write about law as fundamentally divided along sex lines, or writing his theory acknowledging the legal dystopia which in many ways has been the female experience, Hart implicitly treats the entire population as having been brought into law in the same way *ab initio*. His legal world comprises properly and fairly-appointed legal officials and citizen choice-makers and addressees, as if the sex of any of them were quite irrelevant. But it never has been. Instead the legal world has been divided in two, half on the inside and half (in many ways) on the outside.

Hart's theory must stay at a sufficiently high level of abstraction, divorced from real political and legal life, to work. True, he is endeavouring to offer a general theory of law. But nevertheless, he presupposes that any rational adult in his legal world could be an official if qualified; that any rational adult could be an addressee of power-conferring law, as if their sex did not matter. Hart's English legal system has never been as he imagined it – an equitable system with all rational adults, men and women included, treated as equal legal addressees. Hart's legal officials have to be thought of as (unspecified) men for it to work in the way that he describes. Women cannot be read into this role because they were explicitly and vigorously excluded from the positions of rule-recognising officials by the law-recognising officials, as we saw in chapters two and three. But for the theory to work, as general theory, it must be supposed that none of this was true.

VII. Hart's Creatures

There is another way in which Hart imagines a man into his theoretical law and legal system, without realising that he is doing so. Hart recognises 'certain fundamental notions which are "necessary" and "bottomed in the common nature of man"', quoting the nineteenth-century English legal theorist John Austin here.[26] Thus, Hart concedes a minimal content of natural law which requires the criminalisation

[26] Hart (n 19) 621.

of killing and causing harm, in any developed system, because we are soft-skinned vulnerable creatures, not 'giant land crabs'.[27] Hart gives just enough physicality to his Persons, his legal subjects, to acknowledge that they can be injured and injure. In his highly influential lecture delivered at Harvard and published by that law school's review in 1958, Hart explained that as human beings do not have hard carapaces, laws prohibiting violence are always necessary, everywhere and at any time.

> [W]hy we think certain things necessary in a legal system and what we mean by this: suppose that men were to become invulnerable to attack by each other, were clad perhaps like giant land crabs with an impenetrable carapace, and could extract the food they needed from the air by some internal chemical process. In such circumstances (the details of which can be left to science fiction) rules forbidding the free use of violence and rules constituting the minimum form of property – with its rights and duties sufficient to enable food to grow and be retained until eaten – would not have the necessary nonarbitrary status which they have for us, constituted as we are in a world like ours. At present, and until such radical changes supervene, such rules are so fundamental that if a legal system did not have them there would be no point in having any other rules at all. Such rules overlap with basic moral principles vetoing murder, violence, and theft; and so we can add to the factual statement that all legal systems in fact coincide with morality at such vital points, the statement that this is, in this sense, necessarily so. And why not call it a 'natural' necessity?[28]

So Hart has an idea of real embodied men threatening real men, and this potential for violence must be dealt with in any legal system, which must always seek to restrain the threatening man. But Hart has nothing to say here about women. He is unlikely to be thinking of women threatening men. Hart's men are autonomous, potentially dangerous individuals, who need law to keep other threatening men at arm's length (as true Persons do). These men are separate, distinct, sharply delineated and indivisible: they have bodily integrity, but soft skins, which law must protect.

VIII. Ignoring Wife Rape

In fact, women go missing from Hart's story of law in another way. Those predatory beings who we are told must be restrained by law are nevertheless permitted, by law, to do violence in certain circumstances. Despite his insistence on the prohibition of violence, Hart pays no heed to the lawfulness of forced sex within every marriage. Hart insists that rules forbidding violence are so fundamental that they are required by all systems of law, as minimal natural law. But the use of force to achieve sex within a marriage was not a crime in his system of law, which he cast

[27] ibid 623.
[28] ibid.

as advanced and effective. And such force remained lawful for decades after *The Concept of Law* was published. The lawfulness of wife rape was general and legal knowledge, but it was knowledge of which little was made.[29] (Hart was not a lone offender but part of the zeitgeist.)

So again, if law were told from the standpoint of the woman, especially the wife, the law would be seen as incapacitating, even evil. Certainly it would fail Hart's own minimal requirements of law. The governing law was openly against the woman's own interests and its very purpose was to deny her bodily integrity, not to protect it. The married woman of the 1950s, given a legal voice, might say that, on a daily basis, the law failed to protect both her person (in light of her husband's immunity from rape prosecution which persisted until the 1990s) and, going back not too long before, say to the life of her grandmother, law did not protect her property of which she was essentially divested upon marriage. She could say that she had not been afforded the legal carapace needed by all soft-shelled human beings unable to draw sustenance from thin air.

If protection of bodily integrity and confidence about ownership go to the heart of any civilised legal system, forming its minimal content of good law, even to a positivist such as Hart who did not otherwise believe in the necessary overlap between law and morality, then it can be said that the justice concerns of English married women reveal a different face of law. Given a voice, they would have presented him with a genuinely different way of thinking about law, as rights removing, rather than rights conferring.

IX. The Pregnant Legal Subject

There is another, related, reason for saying that Hart was necessarily imagining men into his concept of law. As noted already, Hart's Persons, his general subjects of law, were never imagined pregnant, even though someone had to have been pregnant for these men to come into existence. Hart did not consider how his Persons reproduced, though it was surely a vital feature of their minimal physicality. After all, their perpetuation was essential to their survival as a species.

An account of the way in which these soft-skinned creatures reproduced themselves would have brought into the discussion the physicality of women and how their capacity for child-creation and child-bearing played out in theories of the free Legal Person, Hart's choosing subject. But Hart's Persons are always whole and complete. They stay themselves as they ward others off; they never divide; they never reproduce as humans do, though it is a given that someone is doing this, off stage, outside the purview of general legal theory. With their natural and

[29] This is my precise point in Ngaire Naffine, *Criminal Law and the Man Problem* (Oxford, Hart Publishing, 2019).

legally-protected bodily integrity, Hart's Persons are never imagined bringing another into being, with their own body. Women (the missing characters) do this.

The continuing failure of legal theory to consider pregnant women as full and typical Legal Persons is a persistent problem for theory. Theories of the Person involving pregnant women still tend to move swiftly to a discussion of the Personhood of the foetus, as we will see in chapter eight, when I consider the theory of John Finnis. Yes, there may be discussion of the rights of the pregnant woman but not explicitly her Personhood, though Personhood is very much at the centre of discussion, just not hers. Theorists of general jurisprudence continue to assume that they do not need a theory of the reproducing subject because their implicit Legal Person and Individual and Human does not personally reproduce. Their subject, and Hart's subject, is a free chooser, a legal agent, as well as a physical being who can hurt and be hurt; but he is never pregnant.

X. Needing Persons to be Men (For the Sake of Theory)

Hart's theory proceeded as if his Person could be any human being and his legal theory, in the way that it was manifested, needed this to be true. Hart relied on a generic anyone Person who was imagined at a sufficiently high level of abstraction that it did not settle on any one type of human being. It depended on an assumption that it was meaningful and productive to theorise as if there were only one form of human life and one sex.

But Hart invested this being with certain minimal characteristics, and perhaps the primary one was the ability to engage with law, to be addressed by law,[30] to act in law, and to act in relation to Persons in a lawful manner. Hart then added another characteristic. Because we are not giant land crabs with impenetrable carapaces, law and legal systems had to protect us from one another: from physical invasion and harm. This idea of physical vulnerability seemed to permit one to imagine a generic fleshy soft human being. The problem is that Hart did not factor in human reproduction, which would seem to precede vulnerability, as without reproduction there would be no vulnerable human. But an acknowledgement of human reproduction would split his population in two: biological men who cannot reproduce[31] and women who generally can. Implicitly, Hart treated his human unit as an indivisible, choosing, autonomous individual. Men were indivisible. But women could divide biologically. The divisible human had no place in his general theory. In general, theory of law and theory of the Person, Hart's

[30] Hart famously referred to adult humans, confronted with the law, as choosing subjects, as people with the capacity for choice. On capacity versus character theory in criminal law, see Nicola Lacey, *In Search of Criminal Responsibility: Ideas, Interests and Institutions* (Oxford, Oxford University Press, 2016).

[31] A qualification may be needed here. A woman who has transitioned to become a trans man may still have a functional uterus, in which case a pregnancy may still be possible.

approach is still adopted. It is still taken to be meaningful to talk about Individuals or subjects or Persons as if there were a generic person and as if there had always been one. Hart was a prominent figure who engaged in this practice.

We are not giant land crabs and nor are we cassowary birds, or emus, whose females lay the eggs and then leave them to the male birds to incubate (which might have produced a very different set of incubation laws had humans been of this ilk). We are human beings whose female population is especially vulnerable to violence from the male population, especially in the domestic context,[32] and who are also vulnerable to unwanted pregnancy. According to the UK National Police Chiefs Council:

> The harm caused to victims and society by violence against women and girls (VAWG) in all its forms – including but not limited to harassment, stalking, rape, sexual assault, murder, honour-based abuse, coercive control – is immeasurable. While men and boys also suffer from many of these forms of abuse, they disproportionately affect women. A woman is killed by a man every three days in the UK. Domestic abuse makes up 18 per cent of all recorded crime in England and Wales. In the year ending March 2022, there were 194,683 sexual offences, of which 70,330 were rape.[33]

Violence by men directed at women has been an enduring social and legal problem which tends not to find its way into theory of law, even though theory of law is about human regulation. Harmful conduct is highly sexed. John Stuart Mill spelled this out clearly in *The Subjection of Women*,[34] as we saw in chapter three. And the rape of wives by husbands has been a known evil and positively accepted and excused by law.[35] Again Mill wrote of this and expressed his outrage with this social and legal state of affairs.

These harsh facts were not factored into Hart's law and legal system which was implicitly a civilised system in a relatively civilised society. This is not how law's people were cast by Hart, and of course he was not alone in this. As we will see, Ronald Dworkin did it too. And so did many theorists of criminal law, to the present day.[36] Hart spoke for jurisprudence at large. And this jurisprudence was cast with biological men in mind, but not openly recognised as such. The subject of general jurisprudence, its actor, its agent, its Person, its Individual, indeed its human being, was implicitly a forceful man (rather than a forceful woman) who might threaten other men (and women) and their property, and so law needed to constrain him. And he was biologically a man in another sense, in that he did not reproduce but had another being do it for him. So Hart's minimal natural law,

[32] See World Health Organization, 'Violence Against Women' (25 March 2024), available at www.who.int/news-room/fact-sheets/detail/violence-against-women, which states that: 'Violence against women – particularly intimate partner violence and sexual violence – is a major public health problem and a violation of women's human rights.'

[33] National Police Chiefs Council, 'Violence Against Women and Girls' (March 2024), available at www.npcc.police.uk/our-work/violence-against-women-and-girls/.

[34] John Stuart Mill, *The Subjection of Women* (London, Longmans, Green, Reader and Dyer, 1869).

[35] As I said at length in Naffine (n 29).

[36] See my analysis in ibid.

which he said was about human beings who were physically vulnerable and could harm others, rather than giant land crabs, in truth presupposed the physiology and reproductive life of the male for whom reproduction occurred off site, in a woman.

In the twentieth century, Hart became a giant of theory,[37] and Anglo-American jurisprudence did not consider what was going on. It was not seen that at Hart's time of writing there were powerful and effective measures to control and limit the legal viewpoint, making sure that it was almost exclusively male. It was not seen that the legal officials and thinkers who provided the internal official viewpoint, who were part of the very pedigree of law, were protecting their patch. That they were nearly all men and had to be men for the theory to work.

Hart's theory developed in an intellectual space in which the maleness of legal life had no bearing. But of course he was far from alone in this. Though he famously said that his was a sociological jurisprudence, the most basic facts about law and society were shelved. So too were the most basic biological facts about the perpetuation of the species and the manner in which law regulated it. Hart set his theory above, or in isolation from, these constituting facts about the male monopoly of law[38] and the polity and the internal legal forces used to sustain it. His biographer Nicola Lacey agrees:

> [T]hat philosophical analysis of key legal and political concepts needs to be understood both historically and institutionally and that Hart's relative lack of interest in this sort of contextualization marks a certain limit to the insights provided by his legal and political philosophy.[39]

And though Hart's theory acknowledged what he considered to be the minimal facts about human physiology, these minimal facts did not include sex difference, and reproduction. For all we know, the beings at the heart of his theory might reproduce by parthenogenesis. Though that can't be right because then his central characters would be divisible. They were not giant land crabs but nor were they men and women.

The Concept of Law did not consider the way law was used by one half of the population to suppress and control the lives of the other. Nor did it consider the preservation of positions of legal authority for men, the positions which would supply the point of view, from which law would be recognised and given validity. And since Hart published *The Concept of Law*, which is now about 65 years ago, at the time of writing, very little has been said about his implicit acceptance of almost total male control and occupation of the legal system and his selective inclusion of basic facts of human physiology which do not cater for species reproduction.

[37] Hart's legacy was marked by a book which grew out of a British Academy Symposium commemorating Hart's contribution to legal theory, on the centenary of his birth: Matthew Kramer et al (eds), *The Legacy of HLA Hart: Legal, Political, and Moral Philosophy* (Oxford, Oxford University Press, 2008).

[38] This is the term used in Albie Sachs and Joan Hoff-Wilson, *Sexism and the Law: A Study of Male Beliefs and Legal Bias in Britain and the United States* (Oxford, Martin Robertson, 1978).

[39] Nicola Lacey, 'Philosophy, Political Morality, and History: Explaining the Enduring Resonance of the Hart-Fuller Debate' (2008) 83 *New York University Law Review* 1059, 1062.

There has been almost no testing of *The Concept of Law* in the light of it, probably because his presuppositions persist in modern theory.

That said, by separating the conditions of valid law from the morality of law, Hart created an important intellectual space for the critical evaluation of actual law. Hart was aware that law could be immoral, that it could be made with bad intentions by those with the power to implement those intentions, and still be law. It could still have the right pedigree. His separation of law from morals was therefore a considerable achievement.[40] It enabled immoral law to be acknowledged as actual law, law with a recognised pedigree, but still subjected to moral and political critique, and Hart did this himself in his policy work. This is an important liberal legacy of Hart.

XI. Legacy and Aftermath: Ronald Dworkin and Hercules

The immediate successor to Hart's Chair at Oxford, Ronald Dworkin (who was also Hart's student), would seek to close this intellectual space for critical legal evaluation of law and the uses of power. As Dworkin's obituary observed, in 1969 'Hart, who had been one of Dworkin's examiners at Oxford, [and] was by then approaching retirement, … was able to persuade the Oxford law faculty to appoint Dworkin as his successor as professor of jurisprudence.'[41] There was a close connection between Hart and Dworkin, though their thinking was to diverge on what made law law.

For the purposes of his general theory of law, Dworkin created an imaginary judge 'Hercules', whom he placed at the heart of his theory. Hercules was the wisest of legal men and the bearer and diviner of legal values.[42] As Dworkin explained his creation: 'I have invented … a lawyer of superhuman skill, learning, patience and acumen, whom I shall call Hercules.'[43] This wisest of judges could find the principles underpinning law, and so integrate law, and find its internal moral meaning and integrity, even in hard cases. As Lacey explains, Dworkin's legal principles (as opposed to legal rules) could be determined 'by their degree of "fit" with institutional history, and their support within institutional, background (social), or even the judge's view of critical morality'.[44] The task of the Herculean judge, especially in a hard, that is complex, case, one with no straightforward legal answer, 'was to draw on the available principles to come up with the solution which fitted in the

[40] And he was insisting on this before the appearance of *The Concept of Law*. See Hart (n 19).

[41] Godfrey Hodgson, 'Ronald Dworkin Obituary' *The Guardian* (Online, 15 Feb 2013), available at www.theguardian.com/law/2013/feb/14/ronald-dworkin.

[42] Hercules is an important figure in the immensely influential Ronald Dworkin, *Law's Empire* (London, Fontana Press, 1986).

[43] Ronald Dworkin, *Taking Rights Seriously* (London, Duckworth, 1977) 105.

[44] Lacey (n 3) 331.

overall account or "theory" which best justified the content of the legal system to date'.[45] And thus the wise judge could find the apposite existing law.[46] And he could get to the heart of 'law as integrity'. As Dworkin spelled out:

> Law as integrity asks judges to assume, so far as this is possible, that the law is structured by a coherent set of principles about justice and fairness and procedural due process … That style of adjudication respects the ambition integrity assumes, the ambition to be a community of principle.[47]

To Dworkin, law was 'a seamless web of principles which … dictate "one right answer" waiting to be found by judges in virtually every case in a reasonably sophisticated legal order'.[48] As Sandra Berns further illuminates Dworkin's central character:

> The judge assumes the role of deus ex machina, superimposes a rational and coherent structure upon the accidents and struggles of social life … The ideal offered us, that of the judge as hero, emphasizes disengagement, detachment, distance … The judge attains pure and undiluted rationality through his devotion to the ideal of law, an ideal in whose creation he is engaged. To realize his task, he must, in Dworkin's vision, transform the messily haphazard and historically determined materials with which he works into a unified and coherent fabric, a seamless web.[49]

This prompts one to contemplate how those highest of judicial officials in England, the Lord Chancellors, who included Loreburn and Birkenhead, measured up against Dworkin's Hercules? They were certainly represented as sage judges.[50] Were they getting the deep principles of law right, recognising law's integrity? Were they finding the one right answer? Or was Sankey closer to the mark? Were the Persons Cases hard cases? Were the anti-woman principles espoused by the judges themselves woven into the law and part of law's identity and integrity, or perhaps part of its institutional background?

But Dworkin's wise judge was not imagined in this less ideal but more realistic manner, as a wielder of power, and certainly he was not a man advancing the interests of men. Rather he was the sage or even ideal judge, ascertaining the best version of the existing law.[51] And so the uses of power, and the advance of vested (male) interests, by the highest legal officials were unconsidered by Dworkin, Hart's successor, who was also to become an immensely influential theorist. These were matters not attended to by Dworkin, though Loreburn, Birkenhead and Sankey were all judicial officials in England, operating at the highest level, and deciding

[45] ibid.

[46] ibid 332.

[47] Dworkin (n 42) 243.

[48] Lacey (n 3) 333.

[49] Sandra S Berns, 'Hercules, Hermes and Senator Smith: The Symbolic Structure of Law's Empire' (1988) 44 *Bulletin of the Australian Society of Legal Philosophy* 35, 42–43.

[50] See RFV Heuston, *Lives of the Lord Chancellors 1940–1970* (Oxford, Claredon Press, 1987).

[51] See the concise analysis of Dworkin's theory of law and his central character Hercules in Lacey (n 3).

on the very Personhood of men and women: the two deciding one way (men were Persons, not women), one the other (women were Persons too).

And would Dworkin's ideal judge, his Hercules, be able to do the theoretical work which Dworkin gave him to do if he had called him Helena? Would Dworkin's theory look the same with an ideal female judge? Would she be permitted to perform the role of an ideal gender-neutral judge, which I imagine Dworkin was setting out to bring into being, but with a male name? As Erika Rackley reflects:

> [H]owever hard she tries, the woman judge cannot easily wear Hercules's bespoke suit; she simply does not look like a superhero. Her unavoidable deviance from the aesthetic norm disrupts the homogeneity of the judiciary and troubles traditional understandings of legal authority. As a result, she is unable to speak as a judge unbracketed; distance and authority collapse, and the legitimacy of her judgment … is always open to question.[52]

Were Hercules to become Helena, she would look like a woman, and might draw in women's unfortunate legal history, while Hercules is probably not meant to be sex specific, though he has the implicit benefit of a man's legal history. Again, we have the problem of a sex-divided legal system not recognised as such and the means of avoiding that recognition is, interestingly, to put a male judge (who has the sex of legal power) at the heart of theory.

While Hart evaluated his legal system as advanced, and implicitly did so on liberal principles, he also acknowledged that law could be made by powermongers and still be law. Law and morality were different things.[53] Contra Dworkin, valid law was not necessarily understood as law of integrity. By contrast, in the jurisprudence of Ronald Dworkin, 'questions of membership and power are quite simply not on the theoretical agenda',[54] as Lacey observed, for the very reason that they might undermine the idea of the integrity of legal principle, upon which his theory of law relied, with its wise judge Hercules. As Lacey further teases out his thinking, Dworkin imagined a shared community of interpreters who formed a 'community of principle', one 'characterised by its commitment to a cluster of values which ensure and facilitate its pursuit of "integrity"'.[55] However, Dworkin's interpretive community was not in reality an open community.

> The interpretive community whose voice can be heard is, after all, a professional community, access to membership of which is carefully policed in terms of an historically embedded set of norms, rites of passage, social and technical qualifications. Like all communities, its identity is marked by exclusionary criteria.[56]

[52] Erika Rackley, 'When Hercules Met the Happy Prince: Re-Imagining the Judge' (2005) 12 *Texas Wesleyan Law Review* 213, 221–22.

[53] This comes out strongly in the Hart-Fuller debate. See Cane (n 17) 217.

[54] Nicola Lacey, *Unspeakable Subjects: Feminist Essays in Legal and Social Theory* (Oxford, Hart Publishing, 1998) 147.

[55] ibid 140.

[56] ibid 142.

Indeed, these were the very things shared by Hart's legal officials. And of course it was men who historically had exclusive membership rights to this community.

Like Hart, Dworkin entered the public policy arena and debated the rights and wrongs of particular laws, considered controversial. He dedicated an entire book to an analysis of the laws of abortion and euthanasia[57] and also spoke up in general public fora.[58] Also like Hart, his writing on abortion entailed a defence of a woman's right to terminate a pregnancy. Also like Hart, this more policy-related work did not feed into his general theory of law; nor did it openly address the character and sex of law's Persons, which the Persons Cases had so closely entwined. Nevertheless (like Hart), he characterised his legal system as reasonably sophisticated. Hercules might have his work cut out for him, but he could find the integrity within existing law.

XII. Drawing Up to the Present

Another major figure in the legal canon, with a direct line to Hart is John Finnis, the subject of the next chapter. (Hart was not only the doctoral supervisor of Finnis but Hart also commissioned *Natural Law and Natural Rights* in which Finnis advanced his general theory of law.) Contra Hart, Finnis sought to bring together law and his own understanding of morality, but this time in a manner which did a positive ill service to women, especially in the sphere of reproduction. As we will see, for Finnis, his general goods of life, what made life worthwhile, and so should therefore be protected by law, were generally to be denied to women as soon as they were pregnant because then the foetus became the Person of priority.

As I explain in the next chapter, in the 1960s Finnis started writing about the law of abortion and what he saw as the rights of the foetus, but in a very different manner from Hart and from Dworkin.[59] Unlike Hart and Dworkin, Finnis saw abortion as a fundamental wrong which must be criminalised and, as we will see, he proved to be highly political and influential in his views. Not surprisingly, the uses of law to advance male power did not feature explicitly in Finnis's analysis, even though Finnis himself was recommending and advancing legal power over women.

Although the sex-divided nature of law was far from done with, Hart proceeded in his general theory without reference to it. And so, too, did his successors, as they formulated their competing theories of law. The legal Individual who remained at the centre of legal analysis was endowed with none of this history. And, of course, the idea of the liberal legal Individual itself misrepresented the bloated

[57] Ronald Dworkin, *Life's Dominion: An Argument about Abortion, Euthanasia, and Individual Freedom* (New York, Alfred A Knope, 1993).

[58] See Ronald Dworkin, 'The Great Abortion Case' (1989) 36 *The New York Review of Books* 49.

[59] JM Finnis, 'Abortion and Legal Rationality' (1970) 3 *Adelaide Law Review* 431.

legal personality of men (especially as husbands), as they extended outwards, into the bodies and property of women and gave themselves exclusive access to public positions of authority. It was as if this control and subjection of women by leading men of law never happened. Now attention was generally directed away from this history of the makings of English law.[60]

The silences in mainstream legal philosophy about the maleness of law's institutions and people, and the explicit exclusion of women from property, from higher education, from public life, from legal life, from the very possibility of becoming legal authorities, from Personhood, are revealing. It is not as if these things are not known. But orthodox philosophy and history of law do not make these raw facts part of their theories. Nor do they affect mainstream legal philosophers' thinking about the morality of law and about the principles which are said to guide law.

A common legal life and common legal concerns of men and women are historical fictions, for men and women have not been permitted, by law, to be the same kinds of legal being, living the same kinds of legal lives. Or rather, implicitly, the community that comes to mind for mainstream legal scholars, as they work on their theories of law, is a community of men who may all look pretty similar. The major male figures of the legal canon are themselves celebrated as fair minded. And jurisprudence proceeds, paradoxically, without acknowledging its history, but with confidence in its leading men as we will see in the next chapter, when I consider the theory of John Finnis.

[60] The Feminist Judgments Projects have sought to reverse this trend and thinking. See the discussion of the Projects and the sidelining of feminism in the final chapter.

8

Case Study 3: Women as Intermittent Persons (and Men as Continuous Persons) in the Work of John Finnis

I. Introduction

My third case study is John Finnis. He was born in 1940. He won a Rhodes Scholarship while at Adelaide Law School where he was awarded his first degree. His name is displayed in the law school foyer. Finnis went on to study for his doctorate at Oxford. He was supervised by HLA Hart who was to commission his book *Natural Law and Natural Rights*[1] ('*NLNR*') published in 1980, in the esteemed Clarendon Series.[2] *NLNR* established Finnis's reputation as a legal theorist. The book has been described as 'a major restatement of classical natural law theory'.[3] Finnis has remained a prominent interpreter and advocate of the natural law position (as he understands it) over many years and in many places. At the time of writing, he is Professor of Law and Legal Philosophy Emeritus at Oxford having been Professor of Law and Legal Philosophy from 1989 to 2010. He became a prominent theorist of law and continues to be one. Not incidentally, since the early 1960s, John Finnis has been an avowed Catholic and at times an advisor to the Vatican. His commitment to Catholic theology has strongly influenced his theory, especially through its deferral to, and promotion of, the religious thinking of Thomas Aquinas.[4]

In 2017 Queen Elizabeth II appointed Finnis honorary Queen's Counsel for his 'prolific and peerless contribution to legal scholarship'.[5] In 2019, he was appointed

[1] John Finnis, *Natural Law and Natural Rights*, 1st edn (Oxford, Clarendon Press, 1980) ('*NLNR* 1st edn'). This text was republished in 2011 with the author's further thoughts: John Finnis, *Natural Law and Natural Rights*, 2nd edn (Oxford University Press, 2011) ('*NLNR* 2nd edn').

[2] Many years on, Finnis was chosen as lead author in a book to commemorate Hart's work, 100 years after his birth: Matthew Kramer et al (eds), *The Legacy of HLA Hart: Legal, Political, and Moral Philosophy* (Oxford, Oxford University Press, 2008).

[3] Raymond Wacks, *Understanding Jurisprudence*, 4th edn (Oxford, Oxford University Press, 2015) 30.

[4] Finnis is something of an Aquinas expert and devotee. See John Finnis, *Aquinas: Moral, Political, and Legal Theory* (Oxford, Oxford University Press, 1998).

[5] Kevin Allen, 'Professor Emeritus John Finnis Made a Commander of the Order of the British Empire' (*University of Notre Dame*, 6 January 2023), available at law.nd.edu/news-events/news/professor-john-finnis-2023-commander-order-british-empire/.

a Companion in the General Division of the Order of Australia, Australia's highest civilian honour, for his eminent service as a jurist and legal scholar. In 2023 King Charles made Finnis a CBE 'for services to legal scholarship'.[6] Finnis is squarely within the pantheon of legal theorists,[7] both publicly and within the academy, where his theory of law continues to be acknowledged and examined.[8]

II. Finnis as a Theorist of Male Persons and their Basic Goods

Finnis is explicitly a theorist of Persons. He has stated that 'persons are the most important part of law's concerns and law's nature'.[9] Thus he places the concept of the Person at the heart of legal theory and its explication of the nature of law. As a legal scholar and theorist, Finnis has sustained an interest in Legal Personhood and presents himself as a Personhood expert;[10] he insists also that the concept of the Person is central to jurisprudence, because law is for Persons. He explains that

> prior to all legislation and prior even to constitutional text, we and our courts ought to have a realistic and just account of what persons are and who are persons, and ought then to interpret legal and constitutional provisions so as to align them as far as possible with that just and realistic juridical, juristic, legal account and principle.[11]

And yet the Legal Personhood of women (but not of men) is highly problematic in Finnis's writings, as I will make clear in this chapter. Finnis does not supply 'a realistic and just account of what persons are', when Persons appear in his work *as* women. Women are not cast as self-constituting and self-directed Individuals possessed of practical and free reason, the sort of Persons that he says

[6] ibid.

[7] On the idea of a legal pantheon, this time among the judiciary, see Charles Alan Wright, 'A Modern Hamlet in the Judicial Pantheon' (1995) 93 *Charles Michigan Law Review* 1841.

[8] See, eg, the festschrift for Finnis to which some of the most distinguished legal theorists contributed: John Keown and Robert P George (eds), *Reason, Morality, and Law: The Philosophy of John Finnis* (Oxford, Oxford University Press, 2013); 'The Legacy of John Finnis: Contemporary Engagements and Developments' (2022) 67 *American Journal of Jurisprudence* 141. The introduction to this special issue of the journal explains that 'the papers … advance contemporary inquiry by drawing on, or responding to, Professor Finnis's scholarship, thereby demonstrating his enduring contributions to jurisprudence and philosophy'. The two universities to which Finnis is attached, Oxford University and the University of Notre Dame, both describe his contributions to jurisprudence.

[9] John Finnis, 'The Priority of Persons Revisited' (2013) 58 *The American Journal of Jurisprudence* 45, 45. This text is a sequel to John Finnis, 'The Priority of Persons' in Jeremy Horder (ed), *Oxford Essays on Jurisprudence* (Oxford, Oxford University Press, 2000).

[10] In 2022 in his amicus brief to the US Supreme Court in *Dobbs v Jackson Women's Health Organization, Dobbs v Jackson Women's Health Organisation* 597 US 215 (2022), Finnis again declared his expertise as a scholar of legal personality. I will return to this case later in the chapter.

[11] Finnis, 'The Priority of Persons Revisited' (n 9) 46.

his theory is for.[12] Indeed, as he portrays them, women are more appropriately characterised as Intermittent Persons, an idea I will shortly explain.

In his theory of law, Finnis declares that all 'human persons' are 'ends in themselves'[13] who require a set of basic goods. Human beings both deserve and require these goods to live and to be properly respected as Persons. And, in fact, there is a divine ordinance behind this personification of the human, a 'divine causing, shaping and sustaining of the universe'.[14] A detailed account of the basic goods that law naturally (and perhaps supernaturally) should respect and protect, according to Finnis, if it is to respect us as Persons, is set out in *NLNR*. No evidence is supplied in support of his selection of goods, nor the order of their listing. But then Finnis says that he does not and indeed cannot provide such supporting evidence because, as he asserts, they are 'indemonstrable' and 'self-evident'.[15] So we must take them on trust, or perhaps on faith.

Finnis's goods are life, knowledge, play, aesthetic experience, practical reasonableness, friendship and religion and he tells us that law should be put in service to these values.[16] We are all, he says, entitled to these fundamental goods of life, including life itself and also the ability to make decisions about how our life should be lived (practical reasonableness). To Finnis, '[a] first basic value … is the value of life'.[17] So life is his first good. And then he tells us that this includes our will to live and to save the lives of others through medical schools and 'the resuscitation of suicides', as well as 'the transmission of life through the procreation of children' as well as 'keeping the child alive and well until it can fend for itself'.[18] So far this looks quite benign, potentially compatible with a secular orientation, and indeed perhaps self-evident, in its apparently liberal claims. Finnis seems to be espousing the essential and equal value of every human Individual and their right to live a life of their choosing. And he goes on to tell us how the human Individual should live, with 'practical reasonableness', so as to realise their own 'freely ordered evaluations, preferences, hopes and self-determination … involving freedom and reason'.[19]

So the freedom of the Individual, to set their life course, is vital according to Finnis. However, 'Religion' is also listed as a good and by this he means 'the establishment and maintenance of proper relationships between oneself …. and the divine'.[20] The religion from which Finnis draws his idea of the divine is Catholicism, made explicit in the final chapter of his book. And though Finnis says that his goods are not listed in any particular order, that all are 'equally fundamental',[21] he

[12] See Finnis, *NLNR* 2nd edn (n 1) 168.
[13] ibid 425.
[14] ibid 425.
[15] Finnis, *NLNR* 1st edn (n 1) 85.
[16] ibid 88.
[17] ibid 86.
[18] ibid 87.
[19] ibid 88.
[20] ibid 89.
[21] ibid 92.

proceeds to give 'life' a preeminent role and also to give it a strongly theological dimension. He has done this throughout his career, to the present day. This starts to introduce a fundamental contradiction in his work, and women bear the ill-effects of this contradiction.

III. The Problem of Women as Individuals

The catch comes for women, understood as liberal Individuals, possessed of practical reasonableness, with Finnis's declaration that the Person does not start at birth, as law generally times the beginning of a Legal Person (mindful of the location of the foetus). Throughout his career, Finnis has maintained the position that 'people begin at their conception – neither earlier nor later';[22] that is, conception is when a person becomes an ensouled being, who must be protected at almost all costs. This is, to Finnis, one of 'the realities of personal existence'.[23] Finnis offers an essentially theological, rather than a scientific, account of the development of human life.[24] This account does not square with modern biological science. (Indeed the term 'conception' and also 'conceptus', another term Finnis uses, is more religious, than scientific in nature.[25]) Because the Person begins at conception, in Finnis's theory, when a woman becomes pregnant, she immediately 'houses' another human Individual, another Person, who has the rights of any other Individual. It follows that the woman herself can no longer be regarded as a liberal Individual, as Finnis imagines the Individual.

Finnis's understanding of the beginnings of human life, and the human Person, does not accord with modern embryology. According to leading embryologist, Scott F Gilbert, '[t]here is no consensus among biologists as to what embryonic stage represents the time when independent human life begins. Different biologists have proposed that personhood begins at such events as fertilization, gastrulation, the acquisition of an EEG pattern, and birth'.[26]

[22] See the abstract to John Finnis, *Intention and Identity: Collected Essays*, vol 2 (Oxford, Oxford University Press, 2011) ch 16.

[23] Finnis, 'The Priority of Persons' (n 9) 9.

[24] On the scientific view, see Richard J Paulson, 'The Unscientific Nature of the Concept that "Human Life Begins at Fertilization," and Why it Matters' (2017) 107 *Fertility and Sterility* 566; Scott F Gilbert, '"When Does Human Life Begin?" Teaching Human Embryology in the Context of the American Abortion Debate' (2024) 515 *Developmental Biology* 102.

[25] As biologist and embryologist Scott Gilbert explains, 'conception is a religious notion that was coined more than a millennium before scientists discovered fertilization (in the mid-1800s), and it need not have anything to do with the union of sperm and egg. Rather, "conception" is a statement that Divine permission or soul is needed for embryos to form in the womb. Whereas fertilization concerns the union of egg and sperm, conception involves three parents – female material, male material, and divine soul.': Gilbert, ibid 104.

[26] Scott F Gilbert, 'Pseudo-embryology and Personhood: How Embryological Pseudoscience Helps Structure the American Abortion Debate' (2022) 3 *Natural Sciences*, available at onlinelibrary.wiley.com/doi/full/10.1002/ntls.20220041.

Finnis made his position clear, that women when pregnant could not be regarded as Individuals or as discrete Persons, well before the publication of *NLNR*. In 1973 he declared that

> if we are going to use the wretched analogy of owning houses, I fail to see why the unborn child should not with justice say of the body around it: 'That is my house. No one granted me property rights in it, but equally no one granted my mother any property rights in it.' The fact is that both persons share in the use of this body, both by the same sort of title, viz., that this is the way they happened to come into being.[27]

Finnis has never departed from this view, though in his subsequent writing he has used more temperate language. In essence, the woman is the 'house' or perhaps vessel of the embryo.

The legal nature of a woman, her very Personhood, once pregnant, is thus radically altered, in the eyes of Finnis. It is almost reversed. She is now no longer the rightful and respected recipient of the basic goods of life, and law's fundamental protections, able rightfully to set her own life's course. Now she is a being of a different nature, no longer an Individual. She is someone who potentially poses a dire threat to the basic rights of another (as Finnis sees it) who is within herself. As we will see, Finnis's argument actively villainises women who would seek a termination, calling them 'mothers' who would destroy their '(unborn) children'. Finnis deploys the term 'mother' to indicate the grotesque nature of the woman who would seek a termination. The 'mother', who is conventionally seen as a protective figure, is cast as a potential assailant of her own (unborn) child. She is no longer an Individual but a human being cast in relation to another. The 'father' seems not to feature in these vilification processes. Nor are men defined or delimited by their role in reproduction. After the act of insemination, they can get on with being Individuals and Persons.

To Finnis, women (as women) are divinely destined, and perhaps even designed, for wifehood,[28] and motherhood, and the two defining statuses are inextricably linked. Women as wives are meant to embrace what Finnis calls 'procreation' (they are meant to engage in unprotected sexual intercourse with their husband) and then, once pregnant, they are meant to carry any ensuing embryo to term, at almost any personal cost, for in the view of Finnis (but not of law) the fertilised egg is immediately a Person who should be protected by law. Indeed this embryo is now in need of powerful criminal legal protection (according to Finnis) especially from the woman herself, who (according to Finnis) 'houses' it.[29] Thus the woman, if pregnant (and indeed whether married or single) is cast by Finnis as a potential

[27] John Finnis, 'The Rights and Wrongs of Abortion: A Reply to Judith Thomson' (1973) 2 *Philosophy & Public Affairs* 117, 142.

[28] On the idea of wifehood, see Anna Funder, *Wifedom: Mrs Orwell's Invisible Life* (Penguin, Random House, Australia, 2023).

[29] On the pregnant woman as the house of the embryo, see Finnis (n 27) 142.

threat to life itself, a potential destroyer of her 'unborn child' (which is what Finnis repeatedly calls the fertilised egg or zygote, the embryo and the foetus).[30]

Finnis does not present his work and his thinking in this way, as highly differentiated in its implications, according to whether his subject is a man or a woman. He does not say that he is setting out the basic goods of a male life. Rather he purports to be developing a general theory of law for all human beings, for everyone, not just for men. (We are not meant to think that he is doing men's law or men's theory of law.) Mostly he says that his theory is about humans, individuals or persons, for these are the terms he employs to denote his legal subject. In *NLNR* he declares that '[a]lmost everything in this book is about human rights'.[31] But the only humans who can consistently, over a lifetime, be the bearers of his natural rights, and the goods they are meant to secure, are men.

Finnis derives his understanding of the basic human goods and basic human rights (for men) from theology. In *NLNR* Finnis is, for most of the book, relatively muted about his theology and his consequent belief in the soul as the essence of law's Persons. But then he dedicates his final, and arguably most important, chapter to 'Nature, Reason, God' where he explicitly aligns his theory with Catholic theology. In later publications, Finnis is, if anything, more loquacious about his religion, and his belief in the soul as the essence of the Person. In the lead chapter of a collection of essays entitled *Oxford Essays on Jurisprudence*, in what is described as a 'long-established series [which] brings together some of the leading contributors to Oxford's course on the Philosophical Foundations of Common Law for the Bachelor of Civil Law',[32] Finnis spells out what he considers to be 'the priority of persons' and insists that

> the essence and powers of the soul seem to be given to each individual complete (as wholly undeveloped, radical capacities) at the outset of his or her existence as such. And this is the root of the dignity we all have as human beings.[33]

Here Finnis draws his understanding of what he sees as 'the "natural facts" which should inform juristic thought about the persons whom law exists to serve', that is human biology, or 'bodily makeup' or 'bodiliness',[34] not from modern science, but from Aristotle and Aquinas. There is no editorial concern expressed in this collection of essays about Finnis's use of ancient and medieval sources for the facts of life.

Finnis is consistent on the point that the outset of the soul and of the human being and of the moral and Legal Person[35] is the moment of fertilisation. Thus,

[30] John Finnis refers to women who would 'destroy their unborn children', meaning seek a termination, in John Finnis, 'Public Reason, Abortion, and Cloning' (1998) 32 *Valparaiso University Law Review* 361, 377.

[31] Finnis, *NLNR* 1st edn (n 1) 198.

[32] See the online abstract to Horder (n 9), available at academic.oup.com/book/50633.

[33] Finnis, 'The Priority of Persons' (n 9) 15.

[34] ibid 13–14.

[35] We may see Finnis using the term 'human being' and 'person' as synonyms and interchangeably.

'from the moment of the insemination of the ovum … the specifically human, rational (and sensitive and vegetative) animating form and act (soul) – and therefore personhood … can be and doubtless is present'.[36] Again, Finnis does not justify this claim with any biological science, which has developed apace since the thirteenth century.[37] Moreover, to Finnis, the soul and its powers are 'the root of the dignity we all have as human beings'.[38] This is, to him, an unalterable universal timeless metaphysical truth; it is the natural but underived fact 'which should inform juristic thought about the persons whom law exists to serve'.[39]

Because life, the soul, and the Person, all commence at what Finnis calls 'conception', with 'the conceptus' (again a religious rather than scientific term), Finnis is convinced that any law permitting a woman to terminate a pregnancy sanctions the destruction of innocent 'unborn children'. Finnis has been explicit, even proselytising, from the beginning of his scholarly career, about what he sees as the evils of abortion,[40] especially about the perceived evils of the American Supreme Court decision of *Roe v Wade*[41] which (once) protected a woman's right to abortion in the early stages of pregnancy.[42] Over a lifetime, Finnis has campaigned vigorously against almost any sort of right of a woman to terminate a pregnancy, at any stage. At the same time, he has offered himself up as a legal scholar, expert in the nature and theory of Legal Persons, and their fundamental natural rights. Legal Persons, law's fundamental rights holders, he says, are notionally anyone, any human being. But this cannot be the case because he readily takes women out of the concept. To my mind, this is the fundamental contradiction and flaw in his theory.

IV. Heterosexual Marriage as the Only Moral Form of Marriage (to Finnis)

To the present day, Finnis has also sustained a deep conviction in the essentially and exclusively heterosexual nature of marriage in which sexual intercourse should

[36] John Finnis, '"The Thing I Am": Personal Identity in Aquinas and Shakespeare' in Ellen Frankel Paul, Fred D Miller Jr and Jeffrey Paul (eds), *Personal Identity* (Cambridge, Cambridge University Press, 2005) 253.

[37] Again see the extensive writings on the science of embryology of Scott F Gilbert.

[38] See above n 33 and accompanying text.

[39] Finnis, 'The Priority of Persons' (n 9) 13.

[40] See, eg, Finnis (n 27); John Finnis, 'The Legal Status of the Unborn Baby' (1992) 43 *Catholic Medical Quarterly* 5; John Finnis 'Abortion, Natural Law and Public Reason' in Robert P George and Christopher Wolfe (eds), *Natural Law and Public Reason* (Washington, Georgetown University Press, 2000).

[41] *Roe v Wade* 410 US 113 (1973).

[42] See his discussion of this case in Finnis, 'The Priority of Persons' (n 9) 15.

be 'open to procreation'.[43] Heterosexual marriage, sexual intercourse and procreation are, and should be, necessarily connected, he says, and Finnis has sustained this position. In 2023 Finnis, described as 'professor emeritus of law and legal philosophy at the University of Oxford', and as 'the renowned professor of natural law' attended 'a conference of international Catholic theologians and jurists in Rome' where he explained 'that the Church's doctrine on contraception fulfills the four conditions required for a teaching to be infallible'.[44] Here Finnis affirmed the 'wrongness of contracepting conjugal intercourse'.[45]

Heterosexual marriage is the fundamental form that intimate relations, committed to the production of life (his first good), should take, in Finnis's view. And it places women and men in highly orthodox positions and relations and villainises those who engage in same-sex relations who cannot have 'procreation' as their purpose. He writes of

> The assault on social justice entailed by *the epochal disconnect between sexual intercourse and procreation* which is characteristic of our age ... One of its most important elements obtains wherever same-sex relationships are held out by a society and its laws as marriages, that is, as publicly and privately approvable. For: approval of the pseudo-marital sex acts of same-sex couples, or of any of the many kinds of non-marital sex act, entails a kind of conditional willingness to engage in sexual activity in a way that is in truth non-marital, that is, in a way that does not allow the parties to the act to thereby actualize, express and experience their marriage as a committed, permanent, *exclusive friendship open to procreation*. Such willingness, while it endures, is incompatible with genuinely marital acts, and thus wounds the marriage of those couples one or both of whom has such a willingness, however remote and conditional (emphasis added).[46]

Procreative heterosexuality, within marriage, is the correct and natural form of sex, to Finnis and all this is part of his theology, as he makes clear in the final chapter of his book. His doctoral supervisor HLA Hart, who commissioned *NLNR* and even gave the book its title,[47] advised Finnis to put his theological chapter into an appendix, so as not to 'undermine the book as a work of philosophy'.[48] Finnis did not do this. Instead he made his theology and his commitment to the Catholic Church and its teachings the denouement of his book and still this tome was received as a work of scholarly jurisprudence.

[43] Finnis, 'The Priority of Persons Revisited' (n 9) 56.

[44] Edward Pentin, 'John Finnis to Pontifical Academy for Life: Church's Infallible Teaching Against Contraception Is "Certainly True"' (*National Catholic Register*, Vatican, 26 January 2023), available at www.ncregister.com/news/john-finnis-to-pontifical-academy-for-life-church-s-infallible-teaching-against-contraception-is-certainly-true.

[45] ibid.

[46] Finnis, 'The Priority of Persons Revisited' (n 9) 56.

[47] Finnis, *NLNR* 2nd edn (n 1) 414.

[48] Nicola Lacey, *A Life of HLA Hart: The Nightmare and the Noble Dream* (Oxford, Oxford University Press, 2006) 347.

V. Finnis's Characterisation of Female Life and the Female Legal Subject

In a fairly small compass, Finnis indicates how a woman should live her life. She should be wedded to a man; she should only have sexual intercourse with this man; she should have an eye to procreation which means that she should not employ contraception; and she must not terminate the pregnancy, which is likely to ensue given the absence of contraception. The reason is that from the moment of fertilisation there is 'a conceptus', as Finnis (unscientifically) terms the fertilised egg. There is a Person who must itself be fully respected and protected: which must have the benefit of the goods Finnis has delineated. How women, who have 'the conceptus' within them, are now meant to have the goods themselves, he does not say. The ramifications of this new Person (the conceptus) for women, but not for men, are vast, though they are not considered here. To put it simply, the Personhood of the woman is interrupted, and it cannot resume until birth has been achieved. The woman is put on hold.

Having put life at the start of his seven goods, Finnis then avows that the creation of life should be the goal of sexual intercourse or at least in contemplation. He tells us that abortion is a grave wrong akin to torture. Indeed his first reference to abortion in *NLNR*, which is placed within an argument against utilitarianism and its supposed evils, puts the following horrors in a list with abortion at the end of them, hence placed in clear juxtaposition.

> Thus the calculus is forced through to provide a determinate solution (the quickest, cheapest way of getting what was first focused upon: hence the forced collectivization and liquidation of the farmers, the nuclear or fire-storm bombing of the enemy's hostage civilians, the inquisitorial torture of suspects or informers, the fraudulent cover up and obstruction of legal process, the abortion of unborn and 'exposure' of newly born children …).[49]

It would seem that women who seek to end an unwanted pregnancy are to be viewed in the same light as those who forcefully collectivise and liquidate the farmers, who engage in 'the nuclear or firestorm bombing of the enemies' hostage civilians', who engage in 'the inquisitorial torture of suspects or informers', and, bringing his assessment of women directly into the legal arena, those who abuse legal process by 'fraudulent cover up and obstruction'. Women wanting to end a pregnancy are placed alongside the purveyors of the worst evils.

Finnis' expressions of disgust and horror of women who would seek a termination are not buried in *NLNR*. The first item in the index of the book is 'Abortion' and the first page reference under that heading contains these claims. Moreover, Finnis refers explicitly to the Catholic Church as the expounder and keeper of

[49] Finnis, *NLNR* 1st edn (n 1) 117.

these principles, including the wrongness of 'anti-procreative sexual acts'.[50] This does cause one to reflect on who are Finnis's intended interlocutors. Who is his intended audience? *NLNR* is a work of jurisprudence in the esteemed Clarendon series commissioned by HLA Hart. Is Finnis writing his book for women as well as for men? Is he thinking of the female legal scholar? If so, what is he telling her? Is this really a broad scholarly engagement with both women and men?

What Finnis does not choose to discuss is the dramatically different effects of his characterisation of the good of 'life', and how it comes into being, on the Personhood of women (and their freedoms and right of self-determination, their rights to the good of 'practical reasonableness'), as opposed to the Personhood of men. In fact, women understood as Legal Persons, as separate and discrete Individuals possessed of practical reason, are barely mentioned throughout the entire book. For most of the book, his subject is designated a human or Individual, really fudging the issue. His goods such as freedom and play, and choice are called 'human' values. For he claims that this is a book about natural law and humanity, not a book about the natural rights and goods of men. It is presented as a work of general jurisprudence and it is still presented and analysed as such. Finnis says that 'the basic goods are human goods and can in principle be pursued, realized, and participated in by any human being'.[51]

And yet Finnis leaves us in no doubt about his Catholicism and his consequent views about the reproductive lives of women. And so, to make his theory work, he keeps women as Individuals, and their female-human lives and female-human freedoms, out of his analysis. For women are not seen to be freely choosing Individuals, though all humans are said to be. Thus there is no open explicit tension between the lives he prescribes for women and the lives he prescribes for his Individual Persons, who are meant to be everyone and anyone. Again this is a basic contradiction in his theory.

Finnis's jurisprudential successors also accept that his subject is the human as Person.[52] *NLNR* is regarded as a book about the fundamental human goods. And in fact Finnis declares this to be so. He refers to the human being's right to 'survival, his [sic] coming to know, his creativity, his all-round flourishing'.[53] He also insists on 'fundamental impartiality among the human subjects who are or may be partakers of those goods'.[54] But Finnis does not in fact display a 'fundamental impartiality among [his] human subjects'.[55] His goods play out very differently for men and women. Life for a woman if pregnant, especially if it is an unwanted pregnancy, is hardly compatible with her pursuit of the other values and goods. This he does not discuss.

[50] ibid 124.
[51] ibid 106.
[52] See, eg, the treatment of Finnis in Gerald J Postema, *Legal Philosophy in the Twentieth Century: The Common Law World* (Dordrecht, Springer, 2011).
[53] Finnis, *NLNR* 1st edn (n 1) 106.
[54] ibid 107.
[55] ibid.

In the postscript to the second edition of *NLNR*, Finnis is explicit that:

> Marriage is a distinct fundamental human good because it enables the parties to it, the wife and husband, to flourish as individuals and as a couple, both by … the most radical and creative enabling of another to flourish, namely, the bringing of that person into existence as conceptus, embryo, child and eventually adult fully able to participate in human flourishing on his or her own responsibility.[56]

So (again) the Person begins and exists as 'conceptus' and as 'embryo', necessarily located within the woman, not the man, though he does not spell this out. The woman is supposedly a human Individual, with the right to flourish, as is the man. But she, not the man, in Finnis's thinking, is potentially also the location for another Person who it seems also has the rights of a flourishing Individual. From the moment of fertilisation, there is another Person of consideration and that Person is found in the woman, not the man. The woman's Personhood is therefore interrupted and suspended. What is to be made of this sex difference and how does it play out in his theory? In fact how can the theory hold? We are not told.

Finnis does not refer to these fundamentally different experiences and roles of men and women and what they mean for their respective Personhood. In his way of thinking, men and women are Individuals and then they are a couple and then they procreate. The woman then seems to transform into a Person-bearing human who ceases to be a Person herself. These implications of his analysis are stepped over. But Finnis makes clear that his imagined woman should have almost no say over whether or not her pregnancy is to continue. For she is no longer a self-governing sovereign Person.

VI. Same Sex Relations

In his postscript to the second edition of *NLNR*, Finnis also speaks powerfully of what he regards as the evils of homosexuality. He spells out what he thinks of Persons who wish to 'copulate' with Persons of the same sex, rather than the other sex, within a heterosexual marriage. As he did with 'abortion', he expresses his views, this time of homosexual people, by placing the objects of his opprobrium in a list of profoundly unacceptable human beings and actions. So, condemnation is achieved by placing homosexual people among those with horrific inhuman desires, a list of desires apparently dreamed up by Aristotle, thus giving this taxonomy an esteemed and ancient pedigree. Homosexual people are listed with those who would 'copulate with beasts' or eat coal or other human beings. Here are Finnis's exact words:

> The fact that I find in my make-up a regular and strong inclination to [Aristotle's four stock examples] eat coal or other people or copulate with beasts or people of the same

[56] Finnis, *NLNR* 2nd edn (n 1) 447. Here Finnis is quoting and endorsing himself from John Finnis, 'Marriage: A Basic and Exigent Good' (2008) 91 *The Monist* 388, 396.

> sex as myself, does not provide a reasonable or even an intelligent basis for thinking that the satisfying of those inclinations is a good either as end or means.[57]

So the Person who would prefer intimacy with someone of their own sex is condemned by the power of association. Such men and women are likened to those who would eat coal or eat other people or copulate with beasts.

Elsewhere, in a sustained argument on what he takes to be the evils of homosexuality, Finnis has said that:

> Those who propound 'gay' ideology or theories of same-sex marriage or 'sexual activity' have no principled moral case to offer against (prudent and moderate) promiscuity, indeed the getting of orgasmic sexual pleasure in whatever friendly touch or welcoming orifice (human or otherwise) one may opportunely find it.[58]

This is offensive language, designed to denigrate and dismiss its subjects. It is not a language of legal principle and nor is it scholarly.

For nearly all of *NLNR* Finnis is largely silent about his conviction that the basic goods (and evils), as he interprets them, are prescribed by God and that pursuit of the goods aid our relationship with God. But he does put his theology at the end. Thus 'the human person's way of realizing the proposed friendship with God builds on all the requirements of practical reasonableness in the pursuit of, and respect for, all the basic forms of human good'.[59]

VII. Aquinas and Aristotle and the Primacy of Men

John Finnis generates a strange and dark world. It is populated by ancient and medieval authorities, who calmly and wisely but verbosely roam his pages. Finnis looks to Aquinas and Aristotle,[60] over and again, for their enduring wisdom on the goods (and evils) of life, to tell us how men and women in the twentieth and twenty-first century should conduct themselves according to his natural law. 'Between antiquity and modernity stands Thomas Aquinas (ca. 1225–74).'[61] Aquinas himself looks back to antiquity for much of his thinking, especially to Aristotle (384–322 BCE). Both men are invoked throughout *NLNR* as men of indisputable reputation and knowledge. They are Finnis's guides to the eternal meaning of life. As Valerie Kerruish observed, in a contemporaneous review essay of *NLNR*: 'Finnis' classical

[57] Finnis, *NLNR* 2nd edn (n 1) 449.

[58] John Finnis, 'The Good of Marriage and the Morality of Sexual Relations: Some Philosophical and Historical Observations' (1997) 42 *American Journal of Jurisprudence* 97, 133. See also John Finnis, 'Law, Morality, and "Sexual Orientation"' (1994) 69 *Notre Dame Law Review* 1049.

[59] Finnis, *NLNR* 2nd edn (n 1) 410.

[60] So famous that they need only one name.

[61] 'Thomas Aquinas' (*Stanford Encyclopedia of Philosophy*, 7 December 2022), available at plato.stanford.edu/entries/aquinas/#:~:text=Between%20antiquity%20and%20modernity%20stands,of%20the%20newly%20founded%20universities.

scholarship is put to the service of updating Aquinas and the timeless, placeless truths of natural law theory.'[62]

Though Finnis purports to be writing about men and women, especially as understood by his distant predecessors, for much of *NLNR* he seems to have men in mind as his main subjects. Men, guided by natural law, can pursue his basic goods of a freely-lived life, governed by practical reason, freedom, play, aesthetics and religion. The lives of women seem to be of a different order: they are to have a more cramped and limited existence, especially because of their assigned role in reproduction.

Both Aristotle and Aquinas made it clear that women were inferior beings. On one translation, to Aristotle 'the female is … a deformed male';[63] on another, she is 'a mutilated male'.[64] Aquinas, following Aristotle, had this to say about women:

> [W]oman is defective and misbegotten, for the active force in the male seed tends to the production of a perfect likeness in the masculine sex; while the production of woman comes from defect in the active force or from some material indisposition, or even from some external influence; such as that of a south wind, which is moist, as the Philosopher [Aristotle] observes.[65]

Aquinas was also of the view that women's primary (perhaps only) purpose was to procreate. To wit:

> On the other hand, as regards human nature in general, woman is not misbegotten, but is included in nature's intention as directed to the work of generation. Now the general intention of nature depends on God, Who is the universal Author of nature. Therefore, in producing nature, God formed not only the male but also the female.[66]

Finnis does not say that women are defective and misbegotten, but he does seem to share the Thomistic view that species regeneration is perhaps the most important female function. For it is in this sphere – the sphere of reproduction – that he openly discusses the lives of women, as women. And in this role of reproduction, women lose a fundamental personifying good of life: the right to decide and set its course (practical reason).

Finnis takes his cues on sex, contraception, reproduction and the natures of women and men from a Dominican friar of the thirteenth century who rose to a Chair in Theology (Aquinas) and an ancient philosopher (Aristotle). As Valerie Kerruish observed:

> [W]hereas a student of natural science will not be called on to take serious note of Creationist theory, the publication of John Finnis' *Natural Law and Natural Rights*

[62] Valerie Kerruish, 'Philosophical Retreat: A Criticism of John Finnis' Theory of Natural Law' (1983) 15 *University of Western Australia Law Review* 224, 225.

[63] Aristotle, *Generation of Animals* (translated by AL Peck) (London, William Heinemann Ltd, 1943) 175.

[64] Aristotle, *De Generatione Animalium* (translated by JA Smith and WD Ross) (Oxford, Clarendon Press, 1912) 737.

[65] Thomas Aquinas, *Summa Theologica*, vol IV (translated by the Fathers of the English Dominican Province) (London, Burns Oates & Washbourne Ltd, 1922) 275–76.

[66] ibid 276.

in the prestigious Clarendon Law Series indicates that for ethics and jurisprudence, Francis Bacon lived in vain.[67]

Regarding biology, Aquinas had yet to acquire the benefits of modern scientific knowledge, though this is not a deterrent to Finnis. Aquinas had an ill-formed understanding of embryology (which had yet to be developed) from which he drew his understanding of the nature and purposes and respective value of men and women. Women came off badly.

To Aquinas, men and women had a natural hierarchy, one which was to be found in the Bible: 'Woman is naturally subject to man [within the household] … because by nature man possesses more discernment of the reason.'[68] He adds that 'in all things in which there is a difference between the sexes, the active principle is in the male and the passive in the female.'[69]

Aquinas's understanding of human reproduction was drawn from Aristotle. As John Wijngaards explains, Aquinas

> considered the semen to be the active principle in conception. Only men produced seed and therefore only men were responsible for procreation. They taught that semen was cast into the womb as seed into the soil. The process of embryonic development was activated by the semen and nourished by the blood of the mother.[70]

None of this is discussed, but nor is it disputed, by Finnis, or regarded as a concerning feature of the thinking of his inspirational figure. Finnis says remarkably little about biological sex difference and the respective roles of men and women in human reproduction, as it is now understood and known. He says nothing about pregnancy and the modern science of embryology, how cells differentiate, and the scientific indeterminacy about when a human life comes into being,[71] though he does talk of 'procreation' and the Person it produces, at the moment of fertilisation (which is scientifically quite hard to know and identify).

Like Dicey, but for different reasons, John Finnis is vehemently opposed to the liberal rights of women, understood as Individuals, and in a manner which represents a great contradiction within his main ideas on natural law. His advocacy of the self-determining rights of the Person and his opposition to female reproductive autonomy is clear from the 1960s to the present. He does not call it opposition to female rights, but this is what it is. And like Dicey, his work is sustained, by himself and by others. He is of, and stays in, the pantheon of legal theorists and is rewarded with the glittering prizes.

[67] Kerruish (n 62) 225.

[68] Thomas Aquinas, *The Summa Against the Gentiles* (translated by Paul Sigmund) (New York, WW Norton & Company, 1988) 38.

[69] ibid 40.

[70] John Wijngaards, *The Ordination of Women in the Catholic Church: Unmasking a Cuckoo's Egg Tradition* (London, Darton, Longman & Todd, 2001).

[71] See earlier references to the works of embryologist Scott F Gilbert and especially Gilbert (n 26).

VIII. Gerald Postema Endorsing Finnis and Aquinas

Finnis's enduring canonical status is evident from Gerald Postema's history of 'legal philosophy in the twentieth century', with its strong endorsement of Finnis and his contribution to legal thought.[72] Postema, himself, is a major jurisprudential figure, widely published and influential in the world of legal theory.[73] We are told, by Postema, that: 'More than any other theorist of his generation, [Finnis] gave new life to classical natural-law jurisprudence, systematically developing insights and arguments from the rich Thomistic tradition.'[74] Postema tells us approvingly that 'Finnis ... gave contemporary expression to Thomist legal theory.'[75] He accepts that Finnis's principles 'are rooted in basic human goods'[76] and that these goods instantiate 'the flourishing, of individual human persons',[77] that their ideal 'is the fulfillment of each human being'[78] and that the choice of these goods is 'self-evident'.[79]

Postema himself endorses what he calls a true legal philosophy, '*vera philosophia*', which transcends time and place, and is populated by humans and their generic lives, which somehow transcend the local. He refers approvingly (but not with the greatest clarity) to 'the synechist inclination toward integrating phenomena, practices, and concepts used to manage them into a systematic framework of comprehensive explanation'.[80] And then he tells us where to find the right guide to this wise approach and we are returned to Aquinas who is described as one of the philosophers 'setting their accounts of the nature of law in a broad, systematic, and *rigorously developed philosophical (and theological)* context' (emphasis added).[81]

> To get a sense of this, one must read Aquinas's theory of positive law, the so-called 'Treatise on Law' (Summa Theologiae IaIIae Qq 90–97), in its context – alongside the vast philosophical-theological Summa and, in particular, his discussion of lex, we should also read his illuminating discussion of ius ('right' or 'right order,' especially, Summa Theologiae IIaIIae Qq 57–58), government, and cognate discussions, and later elaborations of it in the scholastic tradition (for example, those of Suarez). See Thomas Aquinas, Political Writings 76–192 (RW Dyson ed & trans, 2002).[82]

[72] Postema (n 52). This work is also notable for its construction of a male genealogy of legal theorists: see Ngaire Naffine, 'Postema's Persons' (2017) 8 *Jurisprudence* 588.
[73] See, eg, the tribute to Postema offered by Thomas Bustamante and Thiago Lopes Decat (eds), *Philosophy of Law as an Integral Part of Philosophy: Essays on the Jurisprudence of Gerald J Postema* (Oxford, Hart Publishing, 2020).
[74] Postema (n 52) 548.
[75] ibid 550.
[76] ibid.
[77] ibid 551.
[78] ibid 552.
[79] ibid 551.
[80] Gerald J Postema, 'Jurisprudence, the Sociable Science' (2015) 101 *Virginia Law Review* 869, 895.
[81] ibid 882, fn 53.
[82] ibid 895, fn 82.

This is quite a reading list, all theological in nature. Postema advocates a philosophical jurisprudence which is purportedly located in time and place, but its population of Persons are remarkably vague. They supposedly all share a general human experience, but they are not sex differentiated.

Postema's '*vera philosophia*' is said to be a universal true philosophy of law and a 'sociable science', because it has room for philosophy and theology.[83] But Postema is not talking about the actual modern lives of women and men under law. Instead Postema looks into the far past and different cultures for his indicators of the one true law. He is a time traveller, uninterested in the men and women near him, in place and time. Postema advocates

> sympathetic reading of systematic philosophers like Aquinas [which] should proceed on the Silliness Reflection Principle: If a proposition attributed to an author looks silly on its face, it is likely that the silliness lies not in the author or the text but in the attribution.[84]

And yet here is Aquinas on the nature of human reproduction (which needs to be checked against the silliness principle):

> This active force which is in the semen, and which is derived from the soul of the generator, is, as it were, a certain movement of this soul itself: nor is it the soul or a part of the soul, save virtually; thus the form of a bed is not in the saw or the axe, but a certain movement towards that form. Consequently there is no need for this active force to have an actual organ; but it is based on the (vital) spirit in the semen which is frothy, as is attested by its whiteness. In which spirit, moreover, there is a certain heat derived from the power of the heavenly bodies, by virtue of which the inferior bodies also act towards the production of the species as stated above. And since in this (vital) spirit the power of the soul is concurrent with the power of a heavenly body, it has been said that *man and the sun generate man*.[85]

According to Postema, the legal past of legal thinkers retains its 'moral presence' and he supports 'the idea of keeping faith with our past and with each other'.[86] In 2021, Postema offered a vision for a philosophical jurisprudence, one that would draw on the leading characters of philosophy, theology and law, of the past and long past, as he saw them. He listed them off:

> It will include exploration of the attempts by theoretically-inclined observers of the various 'forms of law' to give articulate expression to the inherited and practiced understandings implicit in them. Such theorists might include card-carrying philosophers like Aristotle, Kant, and Bentham, philosopher theologians like Al Farabi, Aquinas, Ockham, and Hooker, and theoretically inclined practitioners and jurists like Marsilius

[83] See ibid 871.
[84] ibid 892 n 79.
[85] Thomas Aquinas, *Summa Theologica* vol V (translated by the Fathers of the English Dominican Province) (London, Burns Oates & Washbourne Ltd, 1922) 189 (citations omitted).
[86] Gerald J Postema, 'On the Moral Presence of the Past' (1991) 36 *McGill Law Journal* 1153, 1153.

> of Padua and Matthew Hale. Reflecting on their work can bring into focus dimensions or aspects of law.[87]

In this vision for law, Postema sees the wisdom of bringing together theology and law. He defers, respectfully, to Aquinas as a 'philosopher theologian'.[88] Aquinas is described as one of the 'card-carrying' religious thinkers, whose work 'can bring into focus dimensions or aspects of law'.[89] Postema suggests that law and its understanding can be enriched by this theologian who has been so important to the thinking of Finnis and to the Catholic Church. This is worrying. Aquinas was not a believer in the human rights of women, and nor did he believe that women had the same value as men. Nor did Aristotle and Hale, who also feature on Postema's list of esteemed thinkers of the past (all men), who could enrich jurisprudence. In view of their advocacy of men, and men's interests, and their poor treatment of women, these supposed greats of the past need to be treated with particular scepticism, not openly endorsed.

As Blair Williams has observed in the context of political history writing, 'the Great Man narrative is an enduring problem. It leads to an overemphasis on so-called "foundational patriarchs" and overlooks the impact of political players who don't conform to this stereotype'. She continues:

> This inevitably calls to mind the enduring myth of the 'Great Man' as the architect of historical change. This is best described by 19th century historian Thomas Carlyle, who believed 'the history of the world is but the biography of great men'.[90]

IX. Respecting Theology

Religious understandings of the supposedly complementary and hierarchical nature of men and women have fed the legal view. And legal deference to religious views has helped to preserve the male legal and social order.[91] Such deference has given Finnis a good deal of licence. In *NLNR*, Finnis's supporting theology is evident in the body of his text (and it is confirmed in the final chapter):

> The principal bearer of an explicit theory about natural law happens, in our civilization, to have been the Roman Catholic Church. … that Church has stringently elaborated the

[87] Gerald J Postema, 'Philosophical Jurisprudence: A Vision' (2021) UNC Legal Studies Research Paper, 8.

[88] ibid.

[89] ibid.

[90] Blair Williams, 'I Studied 31 Australian Political Biographies Published in the Past Decade – Only 4 were About Women' (*The Conversation*, online, 14 September 2021), available at theconversation.com/i-studied-31-australian-political-biographies-published-in-the-past-decade-only-4-were-about-women-167448.

[91] See Ngaire Naffine, 'How Religion Constrains Law and the Idea of Choice' (2009) 30 *Adelaide Law Review* 15, reprinted in Paul Babie and Neville Rochow (eds), *Freedom of Religion under Bills of Rights* (Adelaide, University of Adelaide Press, 2011).

> implications of the seventh requirement, as those implications concern *the basic values of life (including the procreative transmission of life)*, truth (including truth in communication), and religion. And it has formulated those implications in strict negative principles such as those declaring wrongful *any killing of the innocent, any antiprocreative sexual acts*, and lying and blasphemy. (The ecclesiastical formulations are more complex; but that is their gist.) Those strict negative principles have thus become popularly regarded as the distinctive content of natural law doctrine. But in fact, as the term 'natural law' is used both in this book and, it seems to me, in the pronouncements of the Roman Catholic Church, everything required by virtue of any of the requirements discussed in this chapter is required by natural law (emphasis added).[92]

Finnis has sustained the one Catholic view of women if pregnant (that the foetus is the main Person of concern, not the woman) for nearly 60 years. There has been no scholarly openness or revision. If anything, he has dug deeper into the past for his understandings of biology, human development, morality and law. The improvements in women's legal lives as Persons are depicted as a terrible threat to true and absolute values. To Finnis, the zygote (or in his language 'the conceptus') is a Person and a human being who therefore attracts the right to life and life is Finnis's first basic good.[93]

Finnis, as legal scholar, has advocated vigorously all his academic life for a legal endorsement of the idea of human sanctity of the 'conceptus'.[94] He has proselytised what is essentially a conservative Catholic religious paradigm: and more importantly, he believes that the idea of the uniqueness and sanctity of a human being demands that law directly reflect this human sacred nature. Absent from his writing is frank and open consideration of the direct impact on the Personhood of women when pregnant, as a direct consequence of the supposed Personhood of the embryo, which is imagined as a free-standing sacred or biological being – in the spirit of liberal Individualism. To state what should be obvious but is often overlooked: for every embryo or foetus that is regarded as a sacred Person there is a woman whose status as an autonomous self-governing Person is in jeopardy, as a direct consequence. Finnis writes about pregnancy or rather the Personhood of the embryo, treated as an individual Person, but not about women as Individuals and their Personhood.

With no jurisprudential explanatory system which makes sense of pregnancy, of the woman if pregnant, the most powerful human archetype remains that of the (male) non-reproducing Individual and this idea of an Individual is applied by Finnis to the embryo, but not to the woman. Finnis never deals with the pregnant woman as Individual. Finnis believes that pregnant women's decisions about their own bodies always involve another Person and so women are not sovereign subjects. Hence his natural law theory of the basic goods is designed for men, but not for women.

[92] Finnis, *NLNR* 1st edn (n 1) 124.

[93] Finnis (n 22) 287.

[94] For Finnis, these are the metaphysical truths and 'the "natural facts" which should inform juristic thought about the persons whom law exists to serve.': Finnis, 'The Priority of Persons' (n 9) 13.

Finnis takes us back to ancient ways of thinking about the legal subject, invoking Aristotle, Aquinas and the Catholic God. He resists positive consideration of women and their Legal Personhood, steering analysis away from women as legal actors and Persons, and the necessary conditions for their lives as Individuals, while professing to be an expert on Personality and within his natural law theory, to have identified the basic goods of life which it seems that the pregnant woman is not to have. Finnis does not openly consider women as Individuals in law. His sustained concern for orthodox marriage and its retention, as an exclusively heterosexual institution; his demand that intercourse between a husband and wife should always be open to reproduction; his insistence that at conception there is a new Person; his preoccupation with the status of this 'unborn child'; and then the setting aside of the consequential effects on the Personhood of women, but not of men, of this understanding of the embryo, are all designed to return us to earlier legal ways of thinking about women, before they came out of coverture. And Finnis has been remarkably successful at steering the debate.

X. State Restraint and Respect for the Religious

Finnis has moral absolutes which he says are simply in the world and divined by reason but they also rely heavily on Catholic theology, which he also makes plain.[95] Women bear the brunt of his moral absolutes as they must be willing, almost unconditionally, to create and bear life. The dramatically different effects of his theory on women and men are ignored. Women are not allowed their own lives, their pursuit of the basic goods. And yet a life of uncontrolled reproduction does not square with those basic goods. This contradiction is built into his theory but generally not challenged by mainstream theorists.[96]

The theorists of law who invoke Finnis, as an important theorist of the legal canon, do not consider how he renders problematic the very Personhood of women. There is a forbearance, possibly out of respect for his religion.[97] HLA Hart himself was careful not to cause religious offence to Finnis. As Nicola Lacey remarks, 'his avoidance of the topic of religion in encounters with Finnis, was typical of both his liberalism and his concern not to cause offence'.[98] And as Tamas Pataki has

[95] Finnis has published in Catholic fora for many years and makes no secret of his allegiance to this Church and its influence on his thinking. See, for eg, Finnis, 'The Legal Status of the Unborn Baby' (n 40).

[96] Although mainstream analytical jurisprudence has not seen the problem, feminist writers have noted the patriarchal and other ideological assumptions of Finnis within his theory of law. See especially Lynne Henderson, 'Whose Nature? Practical Reason and Patriarchy' (1990) 38 *Cleveland State Law Review* 169; Kerruish (n 62); Valerie Kerruish, *Jurisprudence as Ideology* (London, Routledge, 1991).

[97] On restraint based on respect for religious faith, see Naffine (n 91).

[98] Lacey (n 48) 347.

observed, 'religious tolerance is largely a creature of secular humanism, and in its spirit the majority of critics manqué have simply declined to fire'.[99] Nicolas Bamforth and David Richards have made this very point in their sustained critique of the religious underpinnings of natural law theory.[100] They note the tendency among legal theorists to take the claims of Finnis at face value, accepting that his natural law theory can be understood without the aid of theology, and so they set aside the theology. Most legal theorists, they maintain, seem 'to accept without question the notion that Finnis's account of law is of a secular character'.[101] And so Finnis's religious claims are on the whole left unexamined.

Theorists of law, in liberal spirit and perhaps out of respect for the religious, have typically declined to criticise the contents of religious belief and have even treated such belief as intellectually respectable, including when it is discriminatory and damaging to certain sectors of the population, especially to women. There is a great legal reluctance to challenge directly what are taken by religious believers, such as Finnis, to be foundational (but unevidenced) truths. Legal scholars seem unwilling to say, in true humanistic spirit, that religious tenets can be positively harmful, especially to women, and that theology does not belong in jurisprudence.[102]

By contrast, the Catholic Church offers a strong defined dogmatic metaphysics, especially in relation to the intimate sphere of life and at the edges of life. Moreover, it does not hesitate in coming forward, because it is a proselytising faith trying to impose a universal conception of the good. Liberal legal restraint and respect for religious belief countenances a respectful, even forbearant attitude, to such interventions. This has not been good for women. As Bamforth and Richards observe,

> many of Finnis's arguments ... presuppose a commitment to religious belief and might, more specifically, be seen as constituting a reflection and a defense of the authoritarian and patriarchal views propounded by the Roman Catholic Church hierarchy, most notably under the doctrinally conservative Papacies of John Paul II and Benedict XVI.[103]

Finnis's goods are male goods, which only the male Individual can and should sustain (and to Finnis he should sustain them as a heterosexual man). But this has generally not registered in jurisprudence. Thus in his major survey of twentieth century jurisprudence, Postema treats Finnis with great respect as a theorist and applauds him for enriching jurisprudence with 'the Thomistic tradition', that is with the theology of Thomas Aquinas.[104]

[99] Tamas Pataki, *Against Religion* (Melbourne, Scribe Short Books, 2007) 11.
[100] See Nicholas Bamforth and David AJ Richards, *Patriarchal Religion, Sexuality, and Gender: A Critique of New Natural Law* (Cambridge, Cambridge University Press, 2008).
[101] ibid 3.
[102] Bamforth and Richards are honourable exceptions.
[103] Bamforth and Richards (n 100) 5.
[104] See Postema (n 52).

XI. Why does Finnis Matter Now? Women as Intermittent Persons

To Finnis, women are Intermittent Persons.[105] Despite Finnis's insistence that we should all be able to engage in practical reasoning about the conduct of our lives, as Persons, he necessarily denies this to women, because of the conditions he imposes on their lives. For the woman married to a man, which to Finnis is the only moral form of marriage, there is an expectation of sex without contraception (because marital sex should always be 'open to procreation' as he calls it) and then almost no possibility of termination of any resulting pregnancy (for abortion, he insists, entails the destruction[106] of what he terms a '*prenatal human individual*'[107]). Then there should be birth and child care; and then this process all over again, and again. It follows that women cannot be guaranteed the essential basic goods of Persons, but men can be.

To Finnis, 'the essence and powers of the soul seem to be given to each individual complete … at the outset of his or her existence as such'.[108] And for Finnis this is the moment of conception when, for the purposes of his analysis, the woman with the fertilised egg ceases to be a self-governing Individual. Finnis's sustained vocation has been to assert the Personhood of the embryo and to bring that Personhood into law.[109] In his way of thinking, a woman is necessarily suspended as an Individual Person the moment one of her eggs is fertilised, and this is what she should be striving to achieve. This means that the very Personhood of women cannot and should not be sustained and continuous. Any and every pregnancy should interrupt a woman's Personhood. The moment of insemination has none of these implications for men. This remains unsaid.

Finnis insists on the universality of the basic goods for all human beings, understood as moral and legal Persons. But then he also insists on the exclusion of women from that universality of Personhood any time they are pregnant. Finnis leaves unstated the suspension of the Personhood of women if pregnant, though his analysis means that pregnancy has this effect (of suspending Personhood).

Finnis has been commended for his work on natural law, at the highest levels, and very recently, despite its cruel consequences for women. And his reputation as a leading scholar, especially of Legal Personality, has been sustained. There has been no scholarly doubt or revision by Finnis himself on these basic points.

[105] I advanced this argument in Ngaire Naffine, 'Policing the Legal Person: How John Finnis and Other Jurisprudential Figures Continue to Unperson Women' (2024) 45 *Adelaide Law Review* 21.

[106] John Finnis, 'Abortion is Unconstitutional' (*First Things*, online, April 2021), available at www.firstthings.com/article/2021/04/abortion-is-unconstitutional.

[107] Thus are the embryo and foetus referred to in his amicus brief to the US Supreme Court. See John Finnis and Robert P George, 'Equal Protection and The Unborn Child: A Dobbs Brief' (2022) 45 *Harvard Journal of Law & Public Policy* 927.

[108] Finnis, 'The Priority of Persons' (n 9) 15.

[109] See, eg, Finnis (n 27); Finnis 'Abortion, Natural Law and Public Reason' (n 40).

This matters for women, for law, and for jurisprudence. Finnis has pressed his legal-religious views in amici brief and as an expert witness in court.[110] He has associated with and helped to shape the thinking of some of the most influential judges. United States (US) President Trump, in his first term (and 38 days before the Presidential election) nominated Amy Coney Barrett for a position on the US Supreme Court.[111] Barrett was a colleague of Finnis at Notre Dame University (a place 'where the Church does its thinking').[112] Finnis was the doctoral supervisor of Neil Gorsuch[113] who was also successfully nominated for a place on the US Supreme Court by President Trump. Gorsuch was questioned at his confirmation hearing about his relationship with Finnis and his views on abortion but assured the Committee of his independence from his former supervisor and also from the President.[114]

XII. The *Dobbs* Brief

In 2021 Finnis, with former student, Robert George, submitted an amicus brief to the US Supreme Court in the case of *Dobbs v Jackson*,[115] in which they stated that abortion should be considered a serious crime, a variety of homicide, because life 'begins in contemplation of law' at conception, at which point there is a child and a Person. According to the amicus brief, once there is 'a prenatal human individual',[116] or a 'child in utero',[117] there is 'unborn personhood',[118] and the woman immediately becomes 'a mother' of 'an unborn child'. So the woman's

[110] See Randall Baldwin Clark, 'Platonic Love in a Colorado Courtroom: Martha Nussbaum, John Finnis, and Plato's Laws in Evans v Romer' (2000) 21 *Yale Journal of Law & the Humanities* 1.

[111] Her nomination was confirmed two days before the election.

[112] According to the website of Notre Dame University, it 'is a place born of vision and defined by its Catholic character'. The site continues: 'Notre Dame continues to be a place where the Church does its thinking.'

[113] Gorsuch's thesis maintained the wrongness of the intentional taking of human life in the context of voluntary assisted suicide. He went on to consolidate his thoughts in Neil Gorsuch, *The Future of Assisted Suicide and Euthanasia* (Princeton, Princeton University Press, 2006). On the concerning implications of Gorsuch's thesis for his probable thinking on abortion (which proved correct), see Dena Davis, 'Neil Gorsuch, Aid in Dying, and Roe v Wade' (*The Hastings Center*, 24 March 2017), available at www.thehastingscenter.org/neil-gorsuch-aid-dying-roe-v-wade/.

[114] Committee on the Judiciary United States Senate, *Confirmation Hearing on the Nomination of Hon Neil M Gorsuch to be an Associate Justice of the Supreme Court of the United States* (No J-115-6, March 2017). See also Oliver Laughland and Molly Redden, 'Neil Gorsuch Distances Himself from Mentor who Compared Gay Sex to Bestiality' *The Guardian* (Online, 22 March 2017), available at www.theguardian.com/law/2017/mar/21/neil-gorsuch-hearing-legal-mentor-gay-sex-bestiality.

[115] *Dobbs v Jackson* (n 10).

[116] John Finnis and Robert George, 'Brief of Amici Curiae Scholars of Jurisprudence John M Finnis and Robert P George in Support Of Petitioners Amicus Brief', Submission in *Dobbs v Jackson Women's Health* Organization 597 US 215 (2022), 29 July 2021, 16.

[117] ibid 28.

[118] ibid 31.

identity is now defined by a relation, with her so-called 'child in utero',[119] now considered a 'prenatal person'. She is no longer a self-governing Individual, with practical reason, deciding her life's course; rather she seems to be cast as the uterus containing a child, for that child is now 'in utero', now in her or of her.

Finnis is fully consistent with himself. In his thinking, the woman's welfare and choices are subordinate to the wellbeing of the foetus, unless she is in mortal danger.[120] He declares that 'fairly balancing the child's humanity', here referring to the foetus, and its 'unique physical dependence and impact on her mother' would be satisfied by requiring 'States to allow urgent or life-saving medical interventions even when these would unavoidably result in fetal death.'[121] This is the full extent of his recognition of the rights and Personhood of the woman who is pregnant.

In this brief, Finnis, with George, takes us back to old, ancient and scientifically discredited ways of thinking about the nature of human reproduction, invoking Blackstone and Aquinas. While professing to be an expert on Legal Personality, again he resists positive consideration of women and their Legal Personality, steering analysis away from any talk of women as legal actors and individual Persons. Women with their intermittent status as Persons are not fully Individuals, in his understanding of natural law. According to Mary Ziegler:

> By far the most influential personhood Supreme Court brief in *Dobbs v. Jackson Women's Health Organization* came from the conservative scholars Robert George and John Finnis. George is a professor at Princeton, the former chairman of the National Organization for Marriage, a group opposed to same-sex marriage, and one of the drafters of the 2009 *Manhattan Declaration*, a document in which conservative Christians promised to resist efforts to involve them, their churches or charities, in abortion, stem cell research or same-sex marriage. George had trained under Finnis, a prominent Australian scholar of law and legal philosophy who had taught at both Oxford and Notre Dame, and who had written previously that same-sex intimacy was never 'a valid, humanly acceptable choice and form of life.' In 2021, Finnis had made a widely publicized argument in the conservative journal *First Things* making an originalist case that liberal abortion laws were unconstitutional.[122]

As we know, the US Supreme Court (with Associate Justice Gorsuch and Associate Justice Coney Barrett in the majority) reversed *Roe v Wade*.[123] The Court held 'that the Constitution does not confer a right to abortion. *Roe* and *Casey* must be overruled, and the authority to regulate abortion must be returned to the people and

[119] ibid 28.
[120] ibid 33.
[121] ibid.
[122] Mary Ziegler, 'The Endgame in the Battle Over Abortion: The Arc of the Fetal Personhood Movement Signals where Republicans may be Headed' (*Politico Magazine*, online, 24 March 2024), available at www.politico.com/news/magazine/2024/03/24/personhood-abortion-legal-fight-00147138. Mary Ziegler is Martin Luther King Professor of Law at UC Davis.
[123] *Roe v Wade* (n 41).

their elected representatives'.[124] This meant that the American states could remove the right to abortion as many were waiting to do, in anticipation of the judgment. In essence, the Court found in a manner which was consistent with the intentions of Finnis's and George's amicus brief. The consequences for women have been dire. According to Human Rights Watch:

> The consequences of the *Dobbs* decision are wide ranging. Restrictions on access to healthcare places women's lives and health at risk, leading to increased maternal mortality and morbidity, a climate of fear among healthcare providers, and reduced access to all forms of care. *Dobbs* also enables penalization and criminalization of healthcare, with providers, patients, and third parties at risk of prosecution or civil suit for their involvement in private healthcare decisions.[125]

Legal theorists have tended not to challenge the religiously-inflected and highly differentiated 'facts of life' of women and men, as espoused by Finnis. And there has also been a reluctance to comment on the patriarchal nature of the religious institutions to which he subscribes, which treat men and women as very different kinds of being. And it would seem that men are more holy than women, at least in an authoritative way. The Catholic Church, extolled by Finnis, has an all-male hierarchy. The Pope has very recently endorsed this policy of excluding women from the ranks of religious officials. Finnis himself does not speak of this in a clear and comprehensible way. Finnis does not discuss this policy; but he has nevertheless endorsed the Catholic Church and regards it as consonant with his theory of natural rights. And so he manages to be a respected theorist of law and an advisor to the Vatican. He can promulgate his Catholic views, which do great damage to the Personhood of women, while putting himself forward as an expert on Legal Personality and as Emeritus Professor of Law from Oxford. In the next chapter I will consider where such thinking, and support for it, leaves us, in law and legal theory.

[124] As per the headnote to *Dobbs v Jackson* (n 10). The majority judges were Justice Alito, joined by Justices Thomas, Gorsuch, Kavanaugh, and Barrett.

[125] 'Human Rights Crisis: Abortion in the United States After Dobbs' (*Human Rights Watch*, 18 April 2023), available at www.hrw.org/news/2023/04/18/human-rights-crisis-abortion-united-states-after-dobbs. See also Emily Badger, Margot Sanger-Katz and Clarie Cain Miller, 'States with Abortion Bans are Among Least Supportive for Mothers and Children' *New York Times* (Online, 28 July 2022), available at www.nytimes.com/2022/07/28/upshot/abortion-bans-states-social-services.html.

9

Where We are Now and What's Still Wrong

I. Introduction

According to the Oxford legal philosopher Leslie Green, gender has nothing to do with general theory of law. To wit:

> gender is of no relevance to general jurisprudence for, as far as anyone has shown, there is nothing about 'the very forms of law' that warrants calling them 'gendered', and no answer to leading problems in general jurisprudence depends on any thesis about gender.[1]

It would seem that jurisprudence only concerns the conditions by which human beings are regulated, without a gender, without a sex. I have found the opposite to be true. Law has been an institution controlled by men, and with them in mind, with their very Personhood placed at the centre of it. This has been explicitly the case well into the twentieth century, all done with a straight face and apparently good intentions. As Joanne Conaghan has observed:

> Close scrutiny suggests that the extent of gender's involvement in legal terrain goes well beyond the bricks and mortar to encompass significant aspects of legal architectural design. In particular, many of the conceptual and categorical structures of law have been revealed to have gender dimensions or implications: the distinction between public and private, the paradigmatic model of the legal subject, and tortious conceptualizations of harm, to name but a few.[2]

This book has focused on what Conaghan calls 'the paradigmatic model of the legal subject'. It has closely scrutinised his making and his nurturing, and found him to be consistently male.

My inquiry arose from a concern about the quality of legal scholarship and the quality of law. Legal scholarship (like other scholarship) is meant to be independent, based on a steady and fearless inquiry into the actual nature of its subject

[1] Leslie Green, 'Gender and the Analytical Jurisprudential Mind' 83 (2020) *MLR* 893, 911. See also Joanne Conaghan's powerful reply to Green in Joanne Conaghan, 'Gender and the Analytical Jurisprudential Mind: A Response to Leslie Green' (*The Modern Law Review Forum*, 20 August 2020), available at www.modernlawreview.co.uk/conaghan-green.

[2] Joanne Conaghan, *Law and Gender* (Oxford, Oxford University Press, 2013) 245–46.

(law), based on robust evidence about law and alert to its biases and how they might interfere with these requirements of good scholarship. Law itself is meant to be principled, fair, neutral, rational, committed to the equality of all and in service to society: in it, not above it; for it, not against it. What I found in writing this book is judicial and parliamentary reasoning and prominent legal scholarship about the nature of law which is still not of this kind. It is not robust, because it is not attentive to its orientation and its biases. And I have found law which is still not neutral and principled because it is not scrutinised for its fairness and neutrality, but is instead taken to be fair.

II. Controlling the Point of View and so Controlling the Story

Law's Persons, law's rights-bearing subjects, those with the best set of rights, have been made by powerful men who have been powerful because of the law that they have made. They have made the Legal Person in their own image, as they understood themselves to be. There is ample evidence that men of legal authority believed themselves powerful because of their innate superiority, not because of laws which worked in their interests, laws which they themselves forged. This circular and flawed reasoning calls for inspection.

Much of the male legal thinking I have considered leans on the idea that there is a prelegal being suitable for Personhood, and that being is a man, who is thought of as naturally and already superior (to women) before he enters the realm of law. The orthodox view is that these legal men first stood outside law, with all their superior qualities already formed, and then law was matched to these superior abilities. Mill was alert to the deficiencies of this thinking when he said that we do not know what women would be like in a world without patriarchy. Similarly with men. We do not know what men would be like in a world without patriarchy, a world in which they did not have built-in advantages, including the power to define and explain these basic existential matters of law.

Some of the most recognised jurists, right up to the twentieth century, actively opposed the personifying rights of women and promoted those of their own sex, which makes us doubt their objectivity and commitment to fundamental legal principles. This powerful bias calls into question the quality of all their scholarship, especially if we are to continue to turn to them for the exposition of general legal principle. However, the problem of legal patriarchy and its implications for law *in toto* is greater than this. It is bigger than the problem of individual jurists who maintained their reputation despite their active legal stance against women. It goes to law itself and to the way it has been populated, examined and understood, conceptualised and explained.

Much of the male control of women, and the promotion of men, through law, has been achieved by legal definition: by what goes inside and outside of basic legal concepts such as the Legal Person and the explanation and justification of these concepts. It has been achieved by the official interpretation of legal terms. Men of legal authority have controlled the definition and explanation, the very story or narrative, of the Legal Person, in a manner that has hugely strengthened male interests, while often saying that they were doing the very opposite: that rights-stripping was in the interests of women.[3]

This inquiry has found that leading men of law controlled the stories of law, the definitions and the explanations, and deployed them to advance male interests and suppress those of women. Men of legal authority, at the highest levels, did this over centuries. They selected the boldest means possible to advance male interests and to erase or suppress the interests of women: they said who was and was not a Person and enforced it through law. Simply put, they employed their powers of control of legal definition and explanation of the concept of the Legal Person to erase women from important parts of law, especially those parts which entailed the exercise of public power, and so they preserved their own power and interests. They also tightly controlled the sex and reproductive lives of women, but not of men. And then they made very little of these unpleasant facts.

What I have discovered in the writing of this book is almost a female dystopia. As I pursued my inquiries, things just kept looking worse and worse for women and better and better for men, because of male legal decision-making and power, right up to the present day. Each time I pursued an avenue of investigation, I found that what leading legal men were doing to women, as opposed to what they said they were doing to women, was offensive and full of cant. I kept uncovering the highly deliberate actions of men of legal authority to block women from the polity and from the economy, from education and from law, and to curtail and control their sexual and reproductive freedom, using basic legal concepts.

This strenuous legal subjugation of women has inevitably shaped law: its orientation, its focus, its priorities, its very sense of a Person. I have not tried to solve or settle these matters of skewed and faulty reasoning because, simply put, this hard problem of law, its man problem, needs a good deal of thought and attention. We don't have the answers yet because the problem rarely features on the agenda of contemporary analytical jurisprudence. In the next chapter, however, I will suggest some lines of inquiry.

III. Wilful Blindness and the Cognitive (Limiting) Effects of Being with Like Minded and Like People (All Men)

As the philosopher-psychiatrist Iain McGilchrist observed, 'we see, at least consciously, only what we are attending to in a focussed way', such that our

[3] William Blackstone did this; so did James Fitzjames Stephen; and so did the judges in nearly all of the Persons Cases.

attention 'is guided by our expectations of what it is we are going to see'.[4] In other words, we experience what we know already and we do not experience what we do not expect to experience, so that changing how and what we see is difficult.

> Our incapacity to see the most apparently obvious features of the world around us, if they do not fit the template we are already working with … is so entrenched that it is hard to know how we can ever come to experience anything truly new.[5]

Or as the psychologist-philosopher William James similarly observed some time before, any change in thinking only ever represents a tiny graft on one's existing body of thought and knowledge.[6] The impression gained that there is broad (and rational) agreement between users of legal language has been the result of the suppression of different and less powerful points of view, especially those of women. It has been a function of patrilineal obligation to male predecessors and an unwillingness of the more powerful members of the dominant legal community to step outside of their own narrow, but influential, community of meaning, and to question their own way of seeing the world.

At the heart of law and its analysis has been a sustained neglect of its anti-woman history, a wilful blindness, an acting as if this were not true. Women have been, in many ways, shut down by law and by its leading representatives and expounders and explainers. And then the fact of women's active exclusion from the legal power institutions has also been shut down, and then law has been declared to be a fully fleshed out and fair system, with fully-informed and wise authorities. When adjudicating on the membership of the population of Legal Persons, there has been little to no reflection on the fact that men have consistently been the preferred Persons and that men of legal authority have justified the sustained legal subjugation of women, from a position of self-interest, advantage and immense power. This is a compromised speaking position.

It is highly likely that the men of law saw and found what they wanted and expected to find, which was the superiority of their own sex and the inferiority of the other. After all male legal authorities were exclusively in charge of legal definition and explanation and what they were defining and explaining was their own powers and Personhood, to which they were completely accustomed and in which they had powerful vested interests. These are fertile conditions for confirmation bias.[7] As Raymond Nickerson explained: 'Confirmation bias, as the term is

[4] Ian McGilchrist, *The Master and his Emissary: The Divided Brain and the Making of the Western World* (New Haven, Yale University Press, 2009) 163.

[5] ibid.

[6] See William James, *The Principles of Psychology* (New York, Henry Holt and Company, 1890), ch 11 of which is on the nature of attention.

[7] For an account of Peter Wason's development of the idea of what has come to be known as confirmation bias, see Jonathan Evans and Philip Johnson-Laird, 'Editorial Obituary: Peter Wason (1924–2003)' (2003) 9 *Thinking and Reasoning* 177. Here Wason is described as 'one of the founders of the modern study of thinking and reasoning': at 178. See also PC Wason, 'On the Failure to Eliminate Hypotheses in a Conceptual Task' (1960) 12 *Quarterly Journal of Experimental Psychology* 129. Wason published pathbreaking work on this topic.

typically used in the psychological literature, connotes the seeking or interpreting of evidence in ways that are partial to existing beliefs, expectations, or a hypothesis in hand.'[8] This is what I have found consistently in law and its analysis.

Confirmation bias, group thinking and socially-patterned, rather than scientifically-derived, understandings are now well known impediments to good thinking.[9] As Dan Kahan and associates have established, in their psychological investigations into what they term 'cultural cognition', there is a powerful 'disposition to form perceptions of fact congenial to one's values'.[10] There is an 'unconscious influence of individuals' group commitments' on perception.[11] People tend to perceive in the same way that others in their social cohort tend to perceive. Kahan's experiments have shown that cultural values and interests affect perception and reasoning, though the perceiver may remain ignorant of this fact and convinced of their utter neutrality and perceptual accuracy. Kahan has called this 'cognitive illiberalism'.[12] Despite a genuine sense of their impartially, and despite even a genuine endeavour to be impartial, tested observers have been shown to make their assessment of what they are seeing 'along cultural lines'.[13] This is what I have found to be so in law.

There is a considerable body of evidence on how social affiliations and sympathies affect thought and the capacity to reason impartially. What may appear to the thinker, the reasoner, as objective, independent and rational decision-making turns out to be influenced by the thoughts of others one likes, trusts and associates with. In other words, reasoning is not independent and individual but social, so what one's friends and associates take to be true, and I would also say acceptable, one also takes to be true, and acceptable.[14] Reasoning and fact finding therefore take a short cut, drawing on the thinking of trusted others. Men of legal power have operated in an 'echo chamber', with other men of their ilk, causing what is now labelled 'group think', to use the modern vernacular. They have been talking to themselves about themselves, without seeing themselves because they have been the only sex with power, to address and consider and answer to. There has been no comparator with sufficient power to subject them to official critical analysis.

[8] Raymond Nickerson, 'Confirmation Bias: A Ubiquitous Phenomenon in Many Guises' (1998) 2 *Review of General Psychology* 175, 175.

[9] There is a considerable literature on this phenomenon. As the Britannica entry on 'confirmation bias' states, '[r]esearch has shown that confirmation bias is strong and widespread and that it occurs in several contexts': Bettina J Casad and JE Luebering, 'Confirmation Bias' (*Britannica Encyclopedia*, 17 December 2024), available at www.britannica.com/science/confirmation-bias.

[10] Dan M Kahan et al, '"They Saw a Protest": Cognitive Illiberalism and the Speech-Conduct Distinction' (2012) 64 *Stanford Law Review* 851, 901.

[11] ibid 851.

[12] ibid 854.

[13] ibid 860. This point is developed in Dan Kahn and Donald Braman, 'The Self-Defence Cognition of Self Defence' (2008) 45 *American Criminal Law Review* 1.

[14] See Steven Sloman and Philip Fernbach, *The Knowledge Illusion: Why we Never Think Alone* (New York, Riverhead Books, 2017), cited in Elizabeth Kolbert, 'Why Facts Don't Change our Minds' (*The New Yorker*, online, 19 February 2017), available at www.newyorker.com/magazine/2017/02/27/why-facts-dont-change-our-minds.

Therefore, there is ever more reason for legal scholars to contemplate and to raise concerns about the intellectual implications of the all-male and socially-homogeneous constitution of their discipline for their understandings of law. We must examine law's 'implicit ways'.[15] As Susanne Langer put it, such ways

> are not avowed … but simply followed … They are what a German would call his 'Weltanschauung', his attitude of mind, rather than specific articles of faith. They constitute his outlook; they are deeper than facts he may note or propositions he may moot.[16]

As Thomas Kuhn observed about the development of knowledge in science: 'When the individual scientist can take a paradigm for granted, he need no longer, in his major works, attempt to build his field anew, starting from first principles and justifying the use of each concept introduced.'[17] One could say this has happened in law, especially with its concept of the Legal Person.

There are few signs that the men of law imagined women as interlocutors or addressees: as those who needed to be engaged with and persuaded; as those whose interests needed to be also represented and satisfied; whose feelings needed to be considered. There are fewer signs that the incumbents of power reflected on the moral implications and effects of their incumbency. Could the men of law imagine women as the powerful ones, the status quo reversed? Actually, Dicey did, and when he did the numbers, he recoiled in horror. Or rather, he issued strong warnings about the threat that women posed to the well-running of the state. And so he opposed the legal empowerment of women.

If we pay attention to attention, how much attention is given to something, how much it is thought something needs to be attended to, and what is not attended to, then we can learn much. The male control of law and the effects of that control have been poorly attended to. This book has considered speaker and audience, that is, who has been imaginatively in the room of listeners and interlocutors and how this has affected both what is said and the nature of attention. It has considered how legal techniques and terms have been deployed and manipulated. It has considered the style and brevity of judgments and the tone adopted. It has considered the uses of time, with judgments whipping back centuries and then back to the present. And also the suspension of time, with principles floating outside of time and place.[18]

Having expected a rupture, a discontinuity, in the history of the common law, as women were Personified; having anticipated reflection on fundamental legal change, as the legal population effectively doubled; and having anticipated curiosity about the significance of this doubling of the population by the inclusion of

[15] Susanne K Langer, *Philosophy in a New Key: A Study in the Symbolism of Reason, Rite, and Art*, 3rd edn (Cambridge, Harvard University Press, 1971) 4.

[16] ibid.

[17] Thomas S Kuhn, *The Structure of Scientific Revolutions*, 1st edn (Chicago, University of Chicago Press, 1962) 19–20.

[18] For some intriguing work on the relationship between law and time, see Emily Grabham, *Brewing Legal Times: Things, Form and the Enactment of Law* (Toronto, University of Toronto Press, 2016).

women, for law generally, what I have found instead are continuities. As Sachs and Hoff Wilson once said: 'The judgment of Lord Mansfield's court outlawing the holding of slaves on English soil is famous; the many judgments rejecting women's claims to equality of treatment are not even known. Posterity too has its biases.'[19]

Lines of male legal authority have remained intact, reaching into the deep past and those ancient authorities can be called up at any time. They are rarely questioned. The reputations of legal and also religious men long past, if anything, have strengthened over time, even though their understandings of law and of human nature were derived not only from different times and places and peoples, but from different cosmologies, and even though each one of them avowed the natural superiority of the male and the natural inferiority of the female. Women have no legal lines of authority to draw upon, no authoritative forbears speaking for them to whom they can turn, because women were precluded from such authoritative roles, until recently. This author enjoys the new benefits.

Male partisanship in law, through the deployment of its basic concepts, described thus far, has been clear, pronounced, unprincipled and actively sustained, over centuries. It raises fundamental questions about the impartiality and the integrity of law and legal theory and especially about the formulation and the application of the principles of equality, legality and even the rule of law. These are all matters which should concern theorists of law. And yet the uses of law to secure male interests and to suppress those of women, all well documented (for the relevant cases, treatises and legislation are all on the record), are still treated as mundane and of little intellectual interest to those who theorise law and its conditions. They are set outside the order of business of mainstream legal theory.

The Persons Cases, which actively empowered men as Legal Persons and disempowered women (saying they were non-Persons), are of remarkably little jurisprudential concern, even though legal theorists are keenly interested in the nature of their legal subject: the legal actor, the bearer of rights and duties. Why didn't the so-called final Persons Case lead to a re-evaluation of law? Why hasn't the anti-woman thinking of some of law's most senior officials and theorists raised serious concerns about what has been going on in law's heartland and at the highest levels? Is it a matter of not seeing or not wanting to see or choosing not to deal with it? That is, not wanting to face the facts?

As Alfred North Whitehead once said, it is the claims and convictions and judgements which don't even come to mind as in need of defending which are often the most in need of inspection and most intractable to assessment.[20] It is vital to consider what is put into the realm of judgement, reasons, challenge and argument and what is the unconsidered setting of that judgement. In a monocultural world of male legal officials and legal thinkers, much has been placed outside the

[19] Albie Sachs and Joan Hoff Wilson, *Sexism and the Law: A Study of Male Beliefs and Legal Bias in Britain and the United States* (Oxford, Martin Robertson, 1978) 50.

[20] See Alfred North Whitehead, *Science and the Modern World* (Cambridge, Cambridge University Press, 1925) ch 3.

realm of open inspection, reason, assessment and challenge, because what was said by legal men about themselves and about women was thought to be incontrovertibly so. Male dominance and control have been just the normal state of law and its order; they have appeared right and natural and given sense to judgement; as Wittgenstein might call it 'a seeing as' or as 'seeing an aspect'.[21] And this limited seeing remains a problem and impairs legal thinking.

IV. Male Legal Power as Banal

Male power and its uses in law are still treated as normal, just part of the warp and woof of legal life. Men populating virtually all the positions of power in law, positions made exclusive to men by law and also the very active efforts of legal men to keep it that way, has hardly turned a hair. Albert Venn Dicey brought law's maleness to the fore. But his positive endorsement of that male domination was too much for his later analysts to cope with. And so they largely ignored Dicey's accurate observation that law was dominated and controlled by men. The maleness of law is perhaps its most defining feature, but it is not considered an interesting jurisprudential topic, in its own right, though it should be.

Male legal power has been so endemic, so implicitly accepted, that when there has actually been active plotting against women, by men of legal authority, the plotters have been treated not as male supremacists but as undiplomatic men who can be a little trying. That is doing patriarchy, but in ways that are too obvious. And the neglect of this male monopoly, the failures to object to the efforts of prominent men to sustain specific laws which controlled, excluded and demeaned women, means that the messages are still there, not in all their detail, but in the inheritance and atmosphere of law.

The fact that men of legal power have always addressed a male audience (other men of legal power) about the exercise of their own power, as Legal Persons, helps to explain an insensitivity to the effects of the perquisites of power on the quality of judgement. The Legal Person has been theorised and understood from an entirely male point of view, that of elite men of law. When point of view is tightly controlled by an elite, as it has been in law, much is not put into the zone of inspection and challenge. Incompatible ideas can be suppressed: ideas that would challenge the dominant view can be silenced or rendered unreliable, because they have no official vehicle for expression. The dominant or even exclusive cast of an argument or claim, the framing of a problem in a certain manner, becomes simply how things are. It becomes the natural reality, taking much as given, instead of a particular way of seeing, which is that of the powerful.

[21] See Ludwig Wittgenstein, *Philosophical Investigations*, 3rd edn (translated by GEM Anscombe) (New York, MacMillan Publishing, 1958) 205, 213. See also David B Seligman, 'Wittgenstein on Seeing Aspects and Experiencing Meanings' (1976) 37 *Philosophy and Phenomenological Research* 205.

And so there has been a tendency to naturalise the background patriarchal assumptions, the great sea of meaning in which the jurist swims, with his tribe or shoal of fellow believers. It is perhaps experienced as objective truth (the best, most reasoned and supportable understanding), because there have been so few effective voices of dissent, which have been allowed to count. Miranda Fricker has called this 'epistemic injustice': the silencing of the dissenting views of the less powerful group, by rendering them incredible and unreliable.[22] Even though women vigorously protested their reduced legal state,[23] and even though the stripping of female rights was brutal and thorough,[24] women's views and interests have, perversely, been treated as naturally congruent with the lives of men.

There has been a silent understanding that the personification of men and the unpersoning of women do not need dealing with as real legal historical facts, and of some recency in their operation. It is taken as given that law can be theorised and understood as if these brutal facts are irrelevant: as if everyone had always come into the world in the same manner and was sent down the one law-enabling channel. This assumption is implicit every time a work of legal theory invokes a Legal Person without reference to their sex, or possible sex. The idea of an Individual as basic legal unit casts out of discussion the sustained maleness of law's subjects.

V. Male Power and Faulty Historical Reasoning

As a consequence, some very odd reasoning has been permitted, even endorsed and repeated. There has been a reliance on almost magical thinking, which is still not questioned seriously, as a package of ideas, in contemporary jurisprudence. These male-affirming stories of law have been sketchy, stretching over unreal time. Especially in the case law on the Legal Person, they have drawn on Roman, medieval, and ancient common law. They have taken place in vague places, lacking a sense or air of reality. They have not been tied to particular times or places, to specific jurisdictions and specific (real) laws and people.[25]

There has been unconventional periodisation, as an historian might think of it. In the contemporary search for legal wisdom, for the deep principles of law,

[22] See Miranda Fricker, *Epistemic Injustice: Power and the Ethics of Knowing* (Oxford, Oxford University Press, 2007).

[23] See, eg, Erika Rackley and Rosemary Auchmuty (eds), *Women's Legal Landmarks: Celebrating the History of Women and Law in the UK and Ireland* (Oxford, Hart Publishing, 2018).

[24] See Jane Purvis, 'What was the Cat and Mouse Act? The Reason why Suffragettes were Force-Fed' (*History Extra*, online, 10 July 2024), available at www.historyextra.com/period/edwardian/cat-mouse-force-feeding-suffragettes-hunger-strike/; Ian Miller, *A History of Force Feeding: Hunger Strikes, Prisons and Medical Ethics, 1909–1974* (Basingstoke, Palgrave Macmillan, 2016).

[25] This point has been well made by Lindsay Farmer and Nicola Lacey. See Lindsay Farmer, *Making the Modern Criminal Law: Criminalization and Civil Order* (Oxford, Oxford University Press, 2016); Nicola Lacey, *In Search of Criminal Responsibility: Ideas. Interests, and Institutions* (Oxford, Oxford University Press, 2016).

lines are still cast freely into the past, to millennia ago, to foreign lands and vastly different societies. (This is especially true of the writing of John Finnis, whose work I considered in the previous chapter.) The times and places of the production of legal knowledge seem irrelevant. The lines of legal learning might go back to three centuries before the common era, or to medieval times, to the early modern period or to the late Victorian. The deep or middle past and the present have been treated in essentially the same manner, especially in their understandings of the natures of men and women. Men have been thought of as innately, and hence timelessly, superior; women, in equal measure, have been thought inferior, and so ill-suited to the exercise of public authority. From Aristotle, to Aquinas, from Hale to Blackstone and to the twentieth century theorists, it has been treated as perfectly natural that men should govern and control women (including their sexuality) and that men should occupy exclusively all positions of influence. Equally, it has been unthinkable that women should govern men (and their sexuality) or exercise control over the explanatory systems of public and legal power.

The sustained and vigorous drive to keep women out of legal and political life, while retaining a sense of law as a fair and open, just and principled, institution has produced some startling history, odd periodisation, and curious reasoning. It has helped to preserve the reputations of ancient legal historical figures whose prejudiced and superstitious thinking have carried over from the pre-modern to the modern and even to the present day. This is not the official story of law, which tends not to see patriarchy as a defining characteristic of the legal world. But this unsaid account of law is fully supported by the evidence. Vested interests have led to fundamental flaws in legal perception and legal thought, in the deep past and up to the present.

The history of law and its Person has been a history by and for men and it is also a history of men: of half the population. However it has not been presented as such. According to prevailing explanations of law, it is a whole history even though implicitly half the population has been deemed irrelevant. As Gerda Lerner once observed:

> By making the term 'man' subsume 'woman' and arrogate to itself the representation of all humanity, men have built a conceptual error of vast proportion into all of their thought. By taking the half for the whole, they have not only missed the essence of whatever they are describing, but they have distorted it in such a way that they cannot see it correctly. … The androcentric fallacy … cannot be rectified by simply 'adding women'. What it demands for rectification is a radical restructuring of thought and analysis which once and for all accepts that humanity consists in equal parts of men and women and that the experiences, thoughts, and insights of both sexes must be represented in every generalization that is made about human beings.[26]

This point is fundamental. The history of women's legal lives has been removed *ab initio*, as barely counting, because women were deemed not to be Persons, for so

[26] Gerda Lerner, *The Creation of Patriarchy* (New York, Oxford University Press, 1986) 220.

many legal purposes, and the subjects of law were Persons, for to be a legal subject was to be a Person. So the story of law has been a half story. It has therefore been defined by its limitations, its exclusions, what it has taken out from the start. The concept of the Person has done a good deal of this work of instating men as The Story and ejecting women. But all the way along, there have been women living lives. As unpersons or quasi-persons, women have been living lives shaped and defined by law, though lives often damaged by law. So the deleted story is not so savoury. But logically women's legal lives are equally the story – and, based on the numbers, at least half the story – but still this is not how it has been seen. There remains a remarkable inattention to the historical facts of both women's and men's legal lives. Or we could say that the facts themselves have simply not changed legal minds.[27]

If one considers the first few decades of the twentieth century, when women were trying to get the franchise, and so participate in political power, and were still being firmly pushed back, a little may be said of these political struggles over the retention of male power, and then much will be said about other political struggles, such as those of the Irish to achieve home rule. Numerically the man versus woman problem is vastly greater. It is not seen in this way. The political and legal lives of women, which were frankly a train wreck, are not discussed, merely accepted.

The successful efforts of the most senior legal official, the Lord Chancellor, to keep women out of the Upper House of Parliament in 1922 (whose effects endured for 40 years) does not rate a mention. The efforts to keep Ireland within the United Kingdom, which were occurring at the same time, are of great interest. The fact that the same person was embroiled in both matters (that is helping to secure independence for the Irish while securing the continued exclusion of women from the Parliament), is not noticed. As Bruce Lincoln has remarked, 'the frequent repetition of the same authoritative story can help to maintain society in its regular and accustomed forms'.[28]

VI. Lessons from Other Disciplines

Law is not alone in its patriarchalism. In fact an alarming want of objectivity about men and women has been detected across disciplines.[29] An illustration of embedded patriarchal thinking in the discipline of history is to be found in EP Thompson's *The Making of the English Working Class* whose very purpose was to show the agency of the English Working Class, who were said to be 'present' at their own making. That is, they were active thoughtful parties to it. Thompson's aim was

[27] And on why facts do not necessarily change minds, see Kolbert (n 14).

[28] Bruce Lincoln, *Discourse and the Construction of Society: Comparative Studies of Myth, Ritual, and Classification* (Oxford, Oxford University Press, 1989) 25.

[29] See, eg, Caroline Criado-Perez, *Invisible Women: Exposing Data Bias in a World Designed for Men* (London, Chatto & Windus, 2019).

to demonstrate their active history, to bring them in. This is a dignifying book about a group of people ill served by historians, intended to elevate an ignored or denigrated group and demonstrate their active involvement in the 'making' of their 'class'.

As historian Sandra Stanley Holton explains: 'EP Thompson remains a powerful influence in British social history, with his *The Making of the English Working Class* long ago achieving canonical standing among radical historians.'[30] And yet Thompson's classic book has 'absences and silences'[31] when it comes to women. Simply stated, 'EP Thompson entirely leaves out of his account women domestic servants, despite their ubiquity in the period under consideration.'[32]

According to Thompson, '[n]ext to the agricultural workers the largest single group of working people during the whole period of the Industrial Revolution were the domestic servants'.[33] And these workers were mainly women. However, this large population of female workers is noted but not discussed; they are not part of the story of the making of the working class. Thompson by necessary implication removes female domestic servants from the working class, from his class of workers (because he does not see them as workers). Holton regards this as 'an example of gender blindness that may include women within a historical account without interrogating the meaning of their presence'.[34] Women are both present and absent.

VII. Women as Anomalies in New Theories of the Person

If the position, the location, the context, the human coordinates have consistently and stably been from the point of view of men, if the point of view of law has always been not only from the male point of view but also relative to men, in community with other men, then law takes the male sex as its reference point. Men's position, their place in the world, their composition, their coordinates, their very biology, will appear the logical and necessary points of reference. In theory of the Person, this has happened and it is still happening. Men are treated as the standard Individuals, the reliable and physically stable beings in space (who have stayed the same) and the continuous beings over time (who have stayed the same). Women by contrast are problematic Persons, who are thought to form poor subjects for orthodox legal analysis.

This way of thinking – this exceptionalising of women – is apparent in two books on Legal Personhood by Visa Kurki which seek to offer a new definitive

[30] Sandra Stanley Holton, 'Challenging Masculinism: Personal History and Microhistory in Feminist Studies of the Women's Suffrage Movement' (2011) 20 *Women's History Review* 829, 831.

[31] ibid.

[32] ibid.

[33] EP Thompson, *The Making of the English Working Class* (London, Victor Gollancz, 1963) 211.

[34] Holton (n 30) 831.

account of the concept.[35] Though striving to be comprehensive in his coverage, Kurki excises women from his account of orthodox thinking about the Legal Person. The non-paradigmatic nature of women as Persons is the very reason he finds for setting women aside, from the outset, rather than investigating the treatment of this half of the population as apparently anomalous and therefore interesting beings. Implicitly the more paradigmatic man is instated as the subject. I am highlighting the work of Kurki because it illustrates the continuing problem in legal theory of excising women from the general analysis of the Legal Person, logically leaving us with the analysis based on men, as the archetypal Persons. Conceptual analysis is therefore skewed.

Another concerning effect of this skewed analysis is the failure to consider the use of male legal power to define and constitute law's subject, law's Person, thereby strengthening the rights of men and weakening the rights of women. These basic historical facts are commonplace legal knowledge and yet mainly neglected. With the Persons Cases, women were declared inferior beings in law, consistently ousted from positions of public power and legal authority in favour of men. In Kurki's first book, *A Theory of Legal Personhood*, this disabling of women as Persons is mentioned, euphemistically. We are told: 'The legal status of women has historically varied quite a bit from jurisdiction to jurisdiction, which is why it will not be a focal case when I assess the problems of the Orthodox View.'[36] However foetuses are to feature in this book, along with rivers, artificial intelligence and animals and whether they do, and should, qualify as Persons. As I said elsewhere, in a commentary on this book:

> Though women are … cast out of the analysis, curiously, foetuses are allowed in as awkward legal entities to be sure, but nevertheless considered informative. Their location in the world (inside, or as part of, a woman), and the nature of their dependence for life (on a woman), is not mentioned. To spell out the problem … once you start talking about foetuses, you are talking about women, whether you refer to them or not. And so, women come right back into the analysis, but without acknowledgement of their reincorporation. Logically they become the invisible housing of the foetus. Foetuses are then implicitly treated as free-standing entities, as if you might perhaps encounter one when walking down the street. This individualisation of the foetus happens throughout the book.[37]

This reluctance to consider women's Personhood is evident again in Kurki's follow up Cambridge Elements book, *Legal Personhood*,[38] which is largely silent about the relative legal statuses of women and men. We are told, in the Introduction,

[35] Visa AJ Kurki, *A Theory of Legal Personhood* (Oxford, Oxford University Press, 2019); Visa AJ Kurki, *Legal Personhood* (Cambridge, Cambridge University Press, 2023).

[36] Kurki, *A Theory of Legal Personhood* (n 35) 15. And see my discussion of this problem in Kurki's theory of the Person in Ngaire Naffine, 'Hidden Presuppositions and the Problem of Paradigm Persons: Visa AJ Kurki's "A Theory of Legal Personhood"' (2021) 44 *Revus* 127.

[37] Naffine (n 36) 131.

[38] Kurki, *Legal Personhood* (n 35).

after a brief reference to slaves, that '[w]omen have also historically been denied some aspects of legal personhood in many Western jurisdictions, even though the status of women has varied from jurisdiction to jurisdiction.'[39] This instability and inferiority of female Legal Personhood, vis a vis men (who are the necessary and implicit comparator), is no longer given as a reason to set aside women, as Kurki did in his previous book. There he indicated that women were too atypical in their Personhood to deal with. In fact, the mention of women's unstable and variable legal status on the first page of the later book could lead one to anticipate that the problematic Personhood of women would now call for active consideration in a work of this nature and that it would be given due attention. Kurki even refers briefly to the doctrine of coverture, acknowledging its contraction of the Personhood of women. But he does not refer to the equal and opposite effect: the profound enlargement of men's Legal Personality, given that it was into the Personhood of men that women were absorbed.

Women and their non-paradigmatic Personhood then quietly drop from view (as does the paradigmatic Personhood of men), but not so the possible 'personhood' of the foetus, which is called a 'classical' subject in the Law of Persons. We are told that 'the legal status of foetuses remains highly controversial, primarily because of its connection to the question of abortion rights'.[40] Having said this, the foetus is then treated as an analytically distinct and discrete legal entity, absent the woman whose foetus it is. The foetus is conceptually detached and separated from the woman; it is implicitly treated as a free-standing conceptual and physical entity, despite its necessary location within a woman, who is bringing it into being. The implications of the Personhood of the foetus for the Personhood of the woman are not examined, despite their intimate connection.

Later in this book, John Finnis is cited as a natural law thinker, expert in the law of Persons. Finnis is quoted, at length, expressing his objections to *Roe v Wade* for its denial of Personhood to foetuses, which Finnis calls 'unborn children'.[41] Kurki does not align himself with this position, but equally he raises no objection to Finnis's consistent, long-term, and religiously-oriented personification of the foetus and his efforts to make his view of the foetus law.[42] Kurki starts to employ the term 'unborn children' himself, when referring to foetuses,[43] which seems to import some of Finnis's way of thinking into Kurki's own work.

The overturning of *Roe v Wade*[44] is mentioned by Kurki, and so too is its stated effect: that is the removal of women's constitutional right to abortion, so that 'states now enjoy significantly more freedom in determining the legal status of foetuses

[39] ibid 1.

[40] ibid.

[41] See, eg, John Finnis, 'The Rights and Wrongs of Abortion: A Reply to Judith Thomson' (1973) 2 *Philosophy & Public Affairs* 117, 142; John Finnis, 'Public Reason, Abortion, and Cloning' (1998) 32 *Valparaiso University Law Review* 361, 377.

[42] Kurki, *Legal Personhood* (n 35) 29.

[43] ibid 34.

[44] *Roe v Wade*, 410 US 113 (1973).

and embryos'.[45] Again, from this, it might seem that women's non-paradigmatic, unstable and diminished Personhood, especially when pregnant, is ripe for discussion. Some analysis of the legal status of women would surely throw light on the concept of the Person, which forms the subject of this book. But nothing more is said about the effects of these new American laws on the Personhood of women, if pregnant, as these laws reconfigure the legal status of the foetus.[46] The necessary effect on female Personhood is never teased out, even though it cries out for analysis by a Personhood scholar who wishes to provide an authoritative account of the concept of the Legal Person and especially of its most troubling parts.

The legal personification of the foetus is actually occurring in the United States and it is criminalising the lives of women if pregnant. As a writer for *The Guardian*, Carter Sherman observes: 'In 2018, Alabama became the first state in the country to enshrine a fetal personhood clause into its state constitution, after voters backed a measure to recognize "the rights of the unborn child", including the right to life.'[47] More recently, the Alabama Supreme Court decided that Alabama's Wrongful Death of a Minor Act applied to frozen embryos.[48] According to the Alabama Chief Justice:

> In summary, the theologically based view of the sanctity of life adopted by the People of Alabama encompasses the following: (1) God made every person in His image; (2) each person therefore has a value that far exceeds the ability of human beings to calculate; and (3) human life cannot be wrongfully destroyed without incurring the wrath of a holy God, who views the destruction of His image as an affront to Himself.[49]

To Mary Zeigler, an American expert on the law of Persons and reproduction:

> [T]he Alabama ruling provides a roadmap for where the anti-abortion movement is now headed. That destination is enshrining 'fetal personhood' as the law of the land, giving fetuses the same rights as all other persons under the 14th Amendment – an outcome that would have extraordinary consequences.[50]

These consequences, which will especially be felt by women, are not explored by Kurki. Having referred to the conceptual possibilities of 'foetal personhood', but not to the potential and actual implications of such Personhood for the Legal Personhood of women, Kurki moves on to consider the legal status of children

[45] Kurki, *Legal Personhood* (n 35) 1–2.
[46] ibid 30.
[47] Carter Sherman, 'States Push "Fetal Personhood" Bills Despite Outrage at Alabama IVF Ruling' *The Guardian* (online, 20 March 2024), available at www.theguardian.com/society/2024/mar/20/states-fetal-personhood-bill. See also Mary Ziegler, 'The Endgame in the Battle Over Abortion: The Arc of the Fetal Personhood Movement Signals where Republicans may be Headed' (*Politico*, online, 24 March 2024), available at www.politico.com/news/magazine/2024/03/24/personhood-abortion-legal-fight-00147138; Mary Ziegler, 'Personhood: The New War over Reproduction' (Yale University Press, April 2025).
[48] The case is *LePage v Center for Reproductive Medicine*, So 3d, WL 656591 (16 February 2024) involving the death of frozen embryos.
[49] ibid 37–38.
[50] Ziegler, 'The Endgame in the Battle Over Abortion' (n 47).

and people with cognitive disabilities (a longstanding juxtaposition in the law of Persons, when dealing with those of reduced legal status). Then a good deal is said about the 'emerging categories of legal personhood [which] have upset traditional boundaries of legal personhood'.[51]

Kurki considers the potential and actual Legal Personhood of animals, nature and artificial intelligence which he sees as the interesting development in the Law of Persons, perhaps the cutting edge of theory. He refers to 'the traditional boundaries of personhood' and how, in the context of these new candidates for Personhood, these boundaries are shifting, but he leaves unconsidered the shifting Personhood boundaries of women (and correlatively the boundaries of men), first mentioned, and only mentioned, on the first page. While foetuses and their Personhood receive some attention, remarkably perhaps, the Legal Personhood of women, as women, and especially when pregnant, is missing from the analysis.

This writing and theorising removes from basic and applied theory of the Person a good deal of women's lives, while leaving in the lives of men, the unstated default subjects. This is not only a conceptual and analytical problem, but it also has a direct bearing on the fundamental human rights of women. Legal theory is not separate from legal life. Conceptual analysis matters. Definition and theory matter. Accounts of the post *Dobbs* experiences of American women seeking life-saving health care when pregnant, and relief from the courts, make for gruelling and frightening reading.[52] The decision is having broad deleterious effects on the health care of American women. As Claire Brindis et al report in *The Lancet*:

> The *Dobbs* decision has ushered in a new era of uncertainty for reproductive rights and health-care access in the USA. The consequences extend far beyond the ability to choose abortion and impact diverse aspects of women's lives, health, and wellbeing. Indeed, access to contraception and in-vitro fertilisation is already under threat.[53]

And as the dissenting judges asked in *Dobbs*:

> Must a state law allow abortions when necessary to protect a woman's life and health? And if so, exactly when? How much risk to a woman's life can a State force her to incur … short of death, how much illness or injury can the State require her to accept consistent with the [Fourteenth] Amendment's protection of liberty and equality?[54]

[51] Kurki, *Legal Personhood* (n 35) 2.

[52] See Diana Kasdan, 'Two Years After Dobbs: Pregnant Peoples' Lives are Still on the Line and the Texas Supreme Court Looks Away' (*American Bar Association*, 23 June 2024), available at www.americanbar.org/groups/crsj/publications/crsj-featured-articles/two-years-after-dobbs/.

[53] Claire D Brindis et al, 'Societal Implications of the Dobbs v Jackson Women's Health Organization Decision' (2024) 403 *The Lancet* 2751, 2753. See also Claire D Brindis et al, 'Health-Care Workforce Implications of the Dobbs v Jackson Women's Health Organization Decision' (2024) 403 *The Lancet* 2747. These authors report that '[h]ealthcare providers are increasingly constrained from delivering timely and effective care to pregnant individuals who need abortions, even when those procedures are medically necessary to safeguard their life or health.': at 2747.

[54] *Dobbs v Jackson Women's Health Organization* 597 US 215 (2022) 35–36 (Breyer, Sotomayor, and Kagan JJ).

The evidence emerging is disturbing. According to the US Secretary of Health:

> In the two years since *Dobbs*, we have witnessed the devastating impacts. Many women, especially those in states with stringent abortion restrictions, have found themselves navigating care deserts, forced to travel great distances to receive essential services. These barriers disproportionately affect marginalized communities, exacerbating existing health disparities.[55]

So legal theory of the Person, translated into law, shapes and limits and controls lives. And it is important for the legal theorist to acknowledge and to reflect on this. Holding truth to power is a vital part of the scholar's remit.

Another reason for taking up these two books by Kurki and inspecting their theories of the Person is that they illustrate the method by which the sex-divided nature of law, and the uses of legal power to advance male interests, are kept out of analysis. In the next and final chapter I will say more about this method, which I term a heuristic device, for it is a continuing analytical technique in legal theory. Put very simply, the method is to say almost nothing about the active uses of law to suppress the interests of women, through the deployment of its basic concepts. And then to proceed as if these legal deployments of power had never happened, by declaring that both women and men are now Persons; all has been dealt with. We are all Persons now, and for the purposes of analysis, we always were.

We see this in Kurki's short book-length analysis of Legal Personhood. Women do appear, quite frequently, as characters, and we know that they are women because they are given female names. We have women as Legal Persons entering contracts, looking over fences, owing money, being legal guardians and so on. Indeed, these invented Persons, created for the purposes of analysis, are implicitly treated as interchangeable with men. They could be women; they could be men. This implicit interchangeability of male and female characters is an heuristic device which enables theory to proceed unencumbered by the profoundly sex-divided history of the law of Persons and its continuing sex divisions. It looks like women have entered the story, fully, but this illusion is created by placing women only in particular settings where their sex, and their historically reduced status in law, does not seem to matter. I will explain this heuristic device more fully in the next chapter.

In 2020, Joanne Connaghan issued 'an invitation to the analytical jurisprudential community to engage more visibly and vigorously with questions of power, domination and inequality and to take more seriously the social and historical contexts within which jurisprudential questions take form, meaning, and

[55] 'Statement by the Secretary of Health and Human Services on the Second Anniversary of Dobbs v Jackson Women's Health Organization' (US Department of Health and Human Services, 24 June 2024), available at www.hhs.gov/about/news/2024/06/24/statement-secretary-health-and-human-services-second-anniversary-dobbs-v-jackson-womens-health-organization.html.

significance'.[56] This is a generous and important offer. She added: 'Students today quite properly have an appetite for knowledge which speaks directly and explicitly to pressing issues of concern in a deeply troubled, patently unjust, and dangerously unstable politico-legal environment.'[57]

Conaghan's invitation has yet to be taken up. There is continuing complacency about the fact that male legal power has been almost total and a tacit understanding that legal analysis need not take this into account, though it has been the fundamental precondition. It is just what is. This habit of thought is not confined to law. It is to be found across the disciplines, if looked for. But this intellectual habit matters especially in law because of law's almost ontological commitment to equality, fairness, and principled justice.

Without this attention to both halves of the population, and their very different legal roles and lives, the suppression of one half by law, and the advancement of the other by law, there is a serious risk of legal intellectuals repeating another variety of coverture. Without a positive effort to make women genuine subjects of concern, within the understanding of law, there is an intellectual extinguishment of women. Similarly, without proper recognition of men as men within law, men too are not seen and understood for their place in law and how they have made themselves through it.

[56] Conaghan (n 1).
[57] ibid.

10

Populating Law Fairly and Accurately

I. Introduction

Modern orthodox jurisprudence proceeds on a model of society and of law which takes out of consideration the two-sex system of law documented in this book. This is one of the concerning effects of the Persons Cases, the Reform Stories, and the legal reasoning of some of the most influential legal thinkers, as we saw in the case studies. The prevailing jurisprudential story is not a neutral account or explanation of law and its Persons, though it purports to be. Rather, the dominant story of law still fails to consider the historical maleness of its Legal Person and the vigorous efforts to sustain his male character and to keep women in their place. It is therefore flawed.

Theory of law must have a theory of the Person, and in fact it does have a theory of the Person, because the Person is who law is for. And yet in the orthodox jurisprudential story, the profound maleness of this Person, and the maleness of law's institutions and its officials are not the stuff of basic analysis. These defining facts about law are stepped over and men and women are treated *as if* they had always been Individuals, each Person a basic and equivalent unit of analysis. But this is not historically true.

II. The Heuristic Device: The Interchangeability of Men, Women, the Individual and the Person in Legal Theory

The legal technique, the heuristic device, the mode of legal analysis, which enables legal theory to be done, still, without reference to the maleness of the past and present Legal Person and to the maleness of his makers, is the treatment of law's Individual as an 'anyone', with the embedded assumption that he has always been anyone. This enables legal theorists to bypass law's almost ontological commitment to the maleness of its Person and so avow their own neutrality, which may well be their more noble aim. It also enables the male to be instated at any time, because the Legal Individual has not been described and explained accurately: that is, as a man with a male pedigree.

Within this mode of legal analysis, men, women, Individuals, and Persons are ostensibly interchangeable beings, but this requires some careful foot work. A veil is drawn over the past in which this interchangeability was not within contemplation, indeed was openly and vigorously rejected because women were, openly, treated as, and made into, lesser Legal Persons. Law is typically theorised without this history. It is theorised without a time and a place, a past or a present.[1] This ahistorical legal theory achieves a great deal. It silently deems the actual past to be irrelevant for the purposes of theory.

Abstract individualism is what we have now, in place of the differential Personhood of men and women, and the open treatment of women as lesser legal beings, which I have documented throughout this book. And this has its own falsehoods, including suspension of place and time.[2] By abstract individualism I mean that law and its dominant theorists formally treat us all as equal interchangeable, sexless Individuals. In my main legal subdiscipline, criminal law, this is often done. As I noted in *Criminal Law and the Man Problem* about criminal law theory, and its model of its subjects: 'The language of the individual, of persons, now prevails, the language which invokes anyone.'[3] Theories of criminal responsibility talk of 'harm by and to "persons", wrongs by and to "individuals" or "citizens", and there is hardly a man or woman in sight. The two sexes are generally dispensed with in these understandings and portrayals of the subjects of criminal law.'[4] For example, in his theorising about criminal law and its persons, the distinguished legal philosopher Anthony Duff has referred variously to 'members' of a polity, 'citizens' and 'individuals'.[5] Despite the highly sexed nature of crime, men and women are not referred to, on the whole, as the subjects of analysis. And Duff is far from alone in this practice.[6]

Women are now characterised as Individuals and, by silent implication, by a silent deeming, they have always been Individuals. Abstract individualism contains this idea that we are all equivalent and equal legal units.[7] As I also observed in *Criminal Law and the Man Problem*, this brings with it incongruities, as well as denials of what should be central matters of concern.

> The paradoxical idea of the individual as a non-sex-specific type of human is a critical and continuing problem for criminal law because men's specific propensity to offend, to

[1] See Leslie Green, 'Gender and the Analytical Jurisprudential Mind' (2020) 83 *MLR* 893.

[2] See my analysis of the abstract individual in Ngaire Naffine, *Criminal Law and the Man Problem* (Oxford, Hart Publishing, 2019) 148.

[3] ibid 149.

[4] ibid.

[5] See RA Duff, *Answering for Crime: Responsibility and Liability in the Criminal Law* (Oxford, Hart Publishing, 2007). And for a critical discussion of Duff, see Ian Leader-Elliott, 'A Critical Reading of Duff Answering for Crime' (2010) 31 *Adelaide Law Review* 47.

[6] For a discussion of the operation of abstract individualism in criminal law, see Alan Norrie, *Crime, Reason and History: A Critical Introduction to Criminal Law*, 3rd edn (Cambridge, Cambridge University Press, 2014) 26–29.

[7] For a discussion of this practice in other disciplines, see Steven Lukes, 'Methodological Individualism Reconsidered' (1968) 19 *British Journal of Sociology* 119; Steven Lukes, *Individualism* (Oxford, Basil Blackwell, 1973); Geoffrey M Hodgson, 'Meanings of Methodological Individualism' (2007) 14 *Journal of Economic Methodology* 211.

> behave in anti-social ways, the sort of ways which create a need for a social contract, are not inspected as male behaviour. Therefore the central problem of criminal law, the man problem of criminal law, what makes men more criminal than women, why they (men) may need regulating in certain male-specific ways, is not inspected.[8]

As a consequence, criminal legal theory has often not been based on the real lives of women and men. Nor has it openly addressed the main problem of crime (which I have called 'the man problem'). Criminal law and theory have focused on and presupposed male forms of violence and predation, but without openly acknowledging these preoccupations.[9]

In general legal theory, in general jurisprudence, the Individual or Person or citizen are now also invoked, as the basic units of analysis. There is a suspension of time and place and we lose sight of law's historical sexual divisions, which in some ways persist. In his general legal theory on Persons, Visa Kurki has taken this technique a step further, by typically making his imaginary Persons women, as we saw in the last chapter. The implication is that, for the purposes of peopling his invented legal world of Persons, the female case can now cover the male case,[10] because men and women are interchangeable legal units, and so the sex of the Person is necessarily irrelevant, now.

This human interchangeability move is a conceptual leap. It employs a fiction that men and women were always equivalent Individuals and that they are still. It is a fiction in two senses. It is a legal fiction in that it is deemed into existence by law, with the knowledge that the facts are otherwise, but law will take them to be true. In this manner it is a true legal fiction.[11] But it is also a fiction in an ordinary language sense. It is a falsehood purveyed in law and its analysis to the point that the falsehood ceases to be seen as one. Historical female subjugation by law and by legal officials is glossed over. It is an inconvenient truth which is therefore set aside.

The final Persons Case of *Edwards v A-G of Canada*[12] acknowledged that the Legal Person was till then a man but with the decision became a woman as well. What did not occur, because of the Reform Story, was an open consideration of the implications for law and for men and women and the Legal Person of this change: men before; now men and women. So what now? The Reform Story, with its message of the thoughtful assimilation of women, rather than rupture, enabled jurisprudence to proceed as normal, without analysis of past practices, in particular

[8] Naffine (n 2) 181.

[9] See a discussion of this very problem in Sharron Fitzgerald and Anna Carline, 'Problematising the "Man Problem" in the Domestic Abuse Act: Discursive Co-option and the (In)Visibility of Gender' (2024) *Social and Legal Studies*, available at journals.sagepub.com/doi/epub/10.1177/09646639241288528. Here it is demonstrated (through a close study of the parliamentary Hansard on the Act) that the very problem which the Act was meant to address, so-called domestic violence committed by men against women, has been silenced by the Act itself.

[10] This is an interesting reversal of the Interpretation Act, 1850, also known as Lord Brougham's Act.

[11] See the analysis of legal fictions in Lon L Fuller, *Legal Fictions* (Stanford, Stanford University Press, 1967).

[12] *Edwards v A-G of Canada* [1930] AC 124.

the exclusive exercise of power by men of legal authority to define and explain law's subjects. The idea of the interchangeability of women and men as Individuals was then an analytical move which removed the need to consider the implications for law of the entire sex-divided system. It permitted analysis to proceed without consideration of the active legal moves against women. It meant that theory need not refer to the long-standing control and occupation of the system by one sex, men, and the casting of women as legal inferiors.

Because of the Reform Stories, a Legal Individual has emerged in legal theory who does not have the history to which we have been witness in the previous chapters. It is now essential for the theories that the Individual is anyone, because these are delivered as general theories of law, not theories of men and their laws about themselves. So 'the Individual' is necessarily an anyone. The language assiduously employed seems to keep him an anyone.

Though we are now encouraged to think of law's actor as an unsexed Individual, his history has been indisputably a male one and the hard work yet to be done is to find out what law would look like if both men and women had provided models for its Person. Or if women had supplied the template Person, not men. What would these counterfactuals look like?[13]

III. Questioning the Background

This leaves the legal inherited background of patriarchal thinking about the Legal Person unacknowledged and so uninspected.[14] Persistent background thinking that maleness is either irrelevant or just too ordinary a feature of law and its Persons to be interesting is blunting curiosity. Something so normal and ubiquitous is not striking; it does not call for sustained inquiry. It is the excessively familiar wallpaper of law.

Men's supposed stability and reliability as Legal Persons, the fact that they have consistently been treated as paradigmatic Legal Persons over long historical time, has made men the proper stuff of supposedly neutral legal analysis. Men have provided the legal model of human physicality, with their apparently strong, forceful, clearly-delineated bodies and hence natural boundaries.[15] A primary attribute of law's assumed being is still bodily integrity, thought of as strength, wholeness and completeness, and women have been thought not to qualify here. The right to bodily integrity is taken to be the most fundamental right, sometimes

[13] On the concept of the counterfactual, see Richard J Evans, *Altered Pasts: Counterfactuals in History* (Chicago, Brandeis University Press, 2014).

[14] On the idea of the background of theory, see Susan Heckman, 'Backgrounds and Riverbeds: Feminist Reflections' (1999) 25 *Feminist Studies* 427.

[15] See my analysis in Ngaire Naffine, *Law's Meaning of Life: Philosophy, Religion, Darwin, and the Legal Person* (Oxford, Hart Publishing, 2009). See also Ngaire Naffine, 'The Body Bag' in Ngaire Naffine and Rosemary J Owens (eds), *Sexing the Subject of Law* (London, Sweet & Maxwell, 1997).

called the right to non-interference, to self-government, to non-entry, and this cluster of rights within a right has been built into the sort of creature law is meant to be for.[16] (James Fitzjames Stephen and Albert Venn Dicey were quite explicit about it.)

The Legal Person has been cast as (a male) someone who is self-contained, robust and considered at a distance from others, physically, socially, and even morally. These men stop at their skin, and then the outside world (of other men) starts. This has been the repeated rhetoric in legal theory. Man is a stable unit or being, somehow integrated, who finishes with his skin and who has no right to meddle with others, who also start with their skin.[17] The Individual is his own self, and all self, and no-one else. He thus forms a robust reliable research subject.

A sustained account of this somehow-integrated and bordered Legal Individual has been provided by Jennifer Nedelsky.[18] Working in the fields of law and philosophy, Nedelsky has conducted extended character analyses of the liberal Legal Individual, and his 'self-determining, self-making nature'.[19] She has thrown light on '[t]he prevailing liberal conception of the self' which she has described as 'an autonomous self with rights', with law cast in the role of protecting 'equal, autonomous, rights-bearing selves from harm by each other and by the state'.[20] She has called this the 'bounded self', and found it to be present in different branches of law, especially American constitutional law but also in criminal law and property law. According to Nedelsky, 'the image of protective boundaries as essential to the integrity and autonomy of the self is deep and pervasive in Western culture'.[21] In this way of thinking, the most autonomous Individual is the one with the strongest right and ability to secure separation from others: to exclude others from their person and their property.

Women have been thought to fail these tests of an integrated bounded stable being, what with their permeable borders, with their pregnancies and capacity for cell division in reproduction. Men, by contrast, have been thought to satisfy the basic demands of a biologically stable, autonomous subject. Men have thus supplied the constant point of scholarly reference. But as writers across the disciplines have begun to observe, increasingly, the implicit male point of reference

[16] The idea of bodily integrity and the need to protect it is built into the offences against the person.

[17] On this legal idea of the male body, see Naffine, 'The Body Bag' (n 15); Ngaire Naffine, 'The Legal Structure of Self-Ownership: Or the Self-Possessed Man and the Woman Possessed' (1998) 25 *Journal of Law and Society* 193; Ngaire Naffine, 'Women and the Cast of Legal Persons' in Jackie Jones et al (eds), *Gender, Sexualities and Law* (Routledge, 2011).

[18] See Jennifer Nedelsky, 'Reconceiving Autonomy: Sources, Thoughts and Possibilities' (1989) 1 *Yale Journal of Law & Feminism* 7; Jennifer Nedelsky, 'Law, Boundaries and the Bounded Self' (1990) 30 *Representations* 162; Jennifer Nedelsky, *Private Property and the Limits of American Constitutionalism: The Madisonian Framework and its Legacy* (Chicago, University of Chicago Press, 1990), culminating in Jennifer Nedelsky, *Law's Relations: A Relational Theory of Self, Autonomy, and Law* (Oxford, Oxford University Press, 2011).

[19] Nedelsky, 'Reconceiving Autonomy' (n 18) 8.

[20] Nedelsky, *Law's Relations* (n 18) 5.

[21] ibid 98.

within scholarship skews research, it skews thinking and it skews knowledge formation.[22] As one recent study found: 'Male subjects (cells, animals) still dominate in preclinical research and it has detrimental consequences for women's health and the quality of science.'[23]

Moreover, '[a]ssumptions that females as cohorts are more variable' than males have been 'proven wrong'.[24] This sort of research bias and orientation, with its implicit assumption that women are variable and atypical beings, which makes them unsuitable subjects for general research, is being examined in science. There are serious concerns that this understanding of women is undermining the quality of scientific knowledge and, as a consequence, impairing social policy that is informed by such impaired knowledge.[25]

This same gender bias needs to be openly acknowledged and examined in law and considered for its effects on legal theory and on law. After all, law is an institution that controls and regulates the lives of all, and it is backed by force. Theory of law matters.

Law's overwhelming historical maleness – its dominance by men and its peopling by men – should trigger a number of research questions. For example, what has this basic constituting fact about law done to law and to the understanding of law? How has it shaped law's priorities and the very sense of what law is thought to be and its basic institutions? These are basic questions about the nature of law and, if pursued robustly, with intellectual rigour, they could tell us a great deal about law, and how to change it, so that the full population is incorporated

[22] See Caroline Criado-Perez, *Invisible Women: Exposing Data Bias in a World Designed for Men* (London, Chatto & Windus, 2019); Anita Holdcroft, 'Gender Bias in Research: How Does it Affect Evidence Based Medicine?' (2007) 100 *Journal of the Royal Society of Medicine* 2; Gabrielle Jackson, *Pain and Prejudice: A Call to Arms for Women and their Bodies* (Sydney, Allen & Unwin, 2019).

[23] J Plevkova et al, 'Various Aspects of Sex and Gender Bias in Biomedical Research' (2020) 69 *Psychological Research* 367, 367.

[24] ibid.

[25] See Severine Lamon and Olivia Knowles, 'Why are Males Still the Default Subjects in Medical Research?' (*The Conversation*, online, 4 October 2021), available at theconversation.com/why-are-males-still-the-default-subjects-in-medical-research-167545; Lea Merone et al, 'Sex Inequalities in Medical Research: A Systematic Scoping Review of the Literature' (2022) 3 *Women's Health Reports* 49; Gabrielle Jackson, 'The Female Problem: How Male Bias in Medical Trials Ruined Women's Health' *The Guardian* (Online, 14 November 2019), available at www.theguardian.com/lifeandstyle/2019/nov/13/the-female-problem-male-bias-in-medical-trials. And the list goes on and on. See further Natasha May, 'Learning CPR on Manikins Without Breasts Puts Women's Lives at Risk, Study Finds' *The Guardian* (Online, 22 November 2024), available at www.theguardian.com/australia-news/2024/nov/21/learning-cpr-on-manikins-without-breasts-puts-womens-lives-at-risk-study-finds. So why does the lack of manikin breasts matter? 'Most CPR manikins don't have breasts, which contributes towards women being less likely to receive life-saving first aid from bystanders.' And then there is the finding that personal protective equipment (or 'PPE') for health workers during COVID-19 was designed for men, even though women were the majority of front line health workers and the poorly-designed clothing compromised the protection of female workers: Katy Hessel, '"What if Women Ruled the World?" Judy Chicago's Latest Show Feels Very Timely' *The Guardian* (Online, 6 November 2023), available at www.theguardian.com/artanddesign/2023/nov/06/women-ruled-world-judy-chicago-herstory-covid. See also Matthew Weaver, '"Absence of Humanity": Helen MacNamara's Evidence to Covid Inquiry' *The Guardian* (Online, 2 November 2023), available at www.theguardian.com/uk-news/2023/nov/01/absence-of-humanity-helen-macnamara-evidence-to-covid-inquiry.

into legal thought. Such inquiries would of course turn up a far less positive view of the law than jurists are perhaps accustomed to. It would not look like Dworkin's law of integrity.

The consistency with which legal scholars and jurists have turned away from these questions about law's maleness is not only anti-intellectual but baffling; perhaps it even speaks of fear. Open curiosity lies at the heart of good scholarship. We are not seeing this here. As Gerda Lerner made clear,

> [a]s long as men believe their experiences, their viewpoint, and their ideas represent all of human experience and all of human thought, they are not only unable to define correctly in the abstract, but they are unable to describe reality accurately.[26]

IV. Questioning the Greats of the Canon

I am not suggesting that the work of major theorists of law be set aside as inherently flawed, and so unusable, because of their negative and unevidenced characterisations of women. On the contrary, I am suggesting that their work be looked at in their totality, so that it is possible to identify and assess contradictions in their thinking. Then one can make an informed assessment of their work. I have tried to conduct some of this analysis in this book. According to Robert Bernasconi, writing about racism rather than sexism, but the point is transferable:

> My question is whether there is not an institutional racism within contemporary philosophy that emerges in our tendency to ignore or otherwise play down their racism [of Locke and Kant] while we celebrate their principles. It is to my mind shocking to see how little thought contemporary philosophers give to this issue, although there are definite signs that there is now at least a recognition of the problem, just as the sexism of so much philosophy is also now being more carefully scrutinized.[27]

And then Bernasconi suggests what might be done about it.

> My point is not that we should now bypass these thinkers, but that, given their unquestioned importance, such that we cannot afford not to read them, we should make their racism a further reason to interrogate them. In other words, because they were unquestionably major philosophers whose impact lives on outside the academy as well as in it, their racism has a particular claim to our attention.[28]

So too with the sexism of legal thinkers. Dicey not only said that women should not vote nor exercise other public powers, but he made it clear that the Individual or Person or subject who was at the heart of his theory was necessarily male. New biographical writing on Dicey and his theories (notably that of Mark Walters) does

[26] Gerda Lerner, *The Creation of Patriarchy* (New York, Oxford University Press, 1986) 220.
[27] Robert Bernasconi, 'Will the Real Kant Please Stand Up: The Challenge of Enlightenment Racism to the Study of the History of Philosophy' (2003) 117 *Radical Philosophy* 13, 13.
[28] ibid.

not deal with this.[29] Dicey is read selectively. Open scholarship demands that Dicey be read in the round and his theories assessed according to his full body of scholarship. John Finnis's theory of the Person deeply compromises the Personhood of women. And yet he declares that his basic goods of life are intended for everyone. This contradiction should raise profound concerns about the logic and legitimacy of his theory of natural law. HLA Hart and Ronald Dworkin put reproduction and women's reproductive lives outside of their general theories of law. What do their general theories look like if human reproduction is put right in?

V. Sidelining Women; Sidelining Feminism

The sidelining of feminist criticism, or treating its content as a sub or special issue, rather than as going to the general nature of law and its logic and integrity, is a cause for concern.[30] As Nicola Lacey has observed, 'the idea of feminist legal theory … suggests there is something not merely about particular laws or sets of laws, but rather, and more generally, about the very structure or method of modern law, which is hierarchically gendered'.[31] This is the stuff of general theory, to which Lacey herself has been a significant contributor. The feminist legal literature which makes this point is there to be read.

For example, a considerable literature has been generated by the Feminist Judgments Projects. These projects have produced a remarkable counterfactual history of law by means of the writing of hypothetical feminist judgments for landmark cases. They have shown another way the case law could have been done.[32] As Berger, Crawford and Stanchi explain:

> one central mission of rewriting court opinions from a feminist perspective is to demonstrate that judges can apply feminist theory and use feminist methods to advance the goals of equal justice, while still deciding issues in ways that are consistent with their judicial roles.[33]

The feminist judges 're-imagin[e] the reasoning of judicial opinions through the added insight of feminist theories and methods, while bound by the precedent and facts of the time'.[34]

[29] Mark D Walters, *AV Dicey and the Common Law Constitutional Tradition: A Legal Turn of Mind* (Cambridge, Cambridge University Press, 2020).

[30] See Joanne Conaghan, 'Jurisprudence/Legal Theory' in Rosemary Auchmuty (ed), *Great Debates in Gender and Law* (Palgrave Macmillan, 2018).

[31] Nicola Lacey, *Unspeakable Subjects* (Oxford, Hart Publishing, 1998) 2.

[32] On the purpose and methods of these projects, see Heather Roberts and Laura Sweeney, 'Why (Re) Write Judgments?: Australian Feminist Judgments: Righting and Rewriting Law' (2015) 37 *Sydney Law Review* 457; Rosemary Hunter, 'The Feminist Judgments Project: Legal Fiction as Critique and Praxis' (2015) 5 *International Critical Thought* 501; Linda Berger, Bridget Crawford and Kathryn Stanchi, 'Methods, Impact, and Reach of the Global Feminist Judgments Projects' (2018) 8 *Oñati Socio-legal Series* 1215.

[33] Berger, Crawford and Stanchi, ibid 1219.

[34] ibid 1218.

The resulting counterfactual judgments pay close attention to judicial norms, they draw on a deep understanding of the relevant law, they are numerous and international in scope and coverage.[35] And yet one senses that this impressive and extensive literature is often not read by mainstream legal scholars, or it is implicitly (or even explicitly)[36] deemed irrelevant to the broader project of general jurisprudence.[37] As Kristen Rundle notes, 'the woman problem of jurisprudence is better understood as a problem of under-acknowledgement rather than under-representation'.[38]

One way of keeping feminist legal criticism out or down has been to treat it as specialist not generalist, with a hint that it is ideological and political, rather than neutral and rigorous, and so lacking a reach across the whole of law. But it is the intellectual reach and concerns of prominent legal men that have been deliberately restricted and also self-focussed.[39] According to Erika Rackley and Rosemary Auchmuty, we need legal history that is fully rounded and complete, which has *both* women and men as its subjects; otherwise it is partial and stunted:

> Feminist legal history is also about the pursuit of accuracy and completeness. It does not simply produce alternative interpretations to sit alongside the conventional texts; it is not a niche companion to, or 'perspective on', the objective canon. Instead, it aims to write women (back) into legal history and thus force the discipline to confront the

[35] And they keep growing. For example, the Feminist Judgments Projects are making their way around the world. See Rosemary Hunter, Clare McGlynn and Erika Rackley (eds), *Feminist Judgments: From Theory to Practice* (Oxford, Hart Publishing, 2010); Rosemary Hunter, 'The Power of Feminist Judgments?' (2012) 20 *Feminist Legal Studies* 135; Erika Rackley, 'Why Feminist Legal Scholars Should Write Judgments: Reflections on the Feminist Judgments Project in England and Wales' (2012) 24 *Canadian Journal of Women and the Law* 389; Margaret Davies, 'The Law Becomes us: Rediscovering Judgment' (2012) 20 *Feminist Legal Studies* 167; Heather Douglas et al (eds), *Australian Feminist Judgments: Righting and Rewriting Law* (Oxford, Hart Publishing, 2014); Kathryn M Stanchi, Linda L Berger and Bridget J Crawford (eds), *Feminist Judgments: Rewritten Opinions of the United States Supreme Court* (Cambridge University Press, 2016); Máiréad Enright, Julie McCandless and Aoife O'Donoghue, *Northern/Irish Feminist Judgments: Judges' Troubles and the Gendered Politics of Identity* (Oxford, Hart Publishing, 2017); Elisabeth McDonald et al (eds), *Feminist Judgments of Aotearoa New Zealand: Te Rino: A Two-Stranded Rope* (Oxford, Hart Publishing, 2017); Bridget J Crawford, Kathryn Stanchi and Linda L Berger, 'Feminist Judging Matters: How Feminist Theory and Methods Affect the Process of Judgment' (2018) 47 *University of Baltimore Law Review* 167; Loveday Hodson and Troy Lavers, *Feminist Judgments in International Law* (Oxford, Hart Publishing, 2019); Sharon Cowan, Chloe Kennedy and Vanessa E Munro (eds), *Scottish Feminist Judgments: (Re)Creating Law from the Outside In* (Oxford, Hart Publishing, 2019); Vanessa E Munro, 'Feminist Judgments Projects at the Intersection' (2021) 29 *Feminist Legal Studies* 251.

[36] Leslie Green is quite explicit about it.

[37] See Joanne Conaghan, 'Gender and the Analytical Jurisprudential Mind: A Response to Leslie Green' (*The Modern Law Review Forum*, 20 August 2020), available at www.modernlawreview.co.uk/conaghan-green.

[38] Kristen Rundle, 'On Politics, Polemics and Performance' (2024) *Jurisprudence*, available at www.tandfonline.com/doi/full/10.1080/20403313.2024.2404356#d1e110.

[39] I expressed concerns about the male orientation, and hence poor scholarship, within criminological and legal theory, and the failure to address it, over a series of books. See Ngaire Naffine, *Female Crime: The Construction of Women in Criminology* (Sydney, Allen & Unwin, 1987); Ngaire Naffine, *Law and the Sexes: Explorations in Feminist Jurisprudence* (Sydney, Allen & Unwin, 1990); Ngaire Naffine, *Feminism and Criminology* (Philadelphia, Temple University Press, 1996); Naffine (n 2).

> issue of women's long exclusion and marginalisation. Women have always engaged with law, but knowledge of their achievements quickly disappears from public awareness.[40]

Women keep getting erased from the legal scholarship because they are theoretically awkward and encumbering.

> As long as feminist legal history is ghettoised, and its content not incorporated into mainstream historical accounts; as long as the legal curriculum and textbooks ignore history generally, or harness it only in the service of the status quo; as long as everything a woman does is regarded as less important than the actions of men (or entirely unimportant), then the knowledge and understandings that have been uncovered, publicised and become visible in one generation can and will disappear before the next comes along.[41]

Were law to be theorised and described using women's experience of law as the database, it would be vastly different from the law presented in the prevailing authoritative accounts, stretching over the centuries to the present day. Law would no longer look like a means, nor a set of values, for recognising individual self-expression and self-government or securing political participation. Instead law, based on women's experience of it, would appear repressive and rights denying; more a muzzle than a mouthpiece. It would be less a cathedral of light and reason and rights than a closed dark prison, or perhaps a place of non-being, or a locked door with the subjects on the outside. An integrated law of enlightened reason is not one that can be derived from the female experience of law. Dworkin's Helena rather than Hercules might describe a different law.

It would, admittedly, be a daunting task to make sense of law in this manner, with women fully factored in, including their historical treatment as partial or lesser legal subjects. And certainly law and its makers would come out much less well. And so perhaps it is not surprising that there is little appetite to do so within the jurisprudential mainstream. The solution has been to ignore it or cut it out.

VI. The Sexual and Reproducing Man of General Jurisprudence

We need to imagine Legal Persons living the lives of both women and men, socially, politically and biologically. Still, legal theory tends to imagine its Person in the public sphere and in the market and implicitly male.[42] One of the reasons that we know this is because this Person, as presently understood, has a sexual life and expects to reproduce but his reproductive role is not seen to impinge on his life

[40] Erika Rackley and Rosemary Auchmuty, 'The Case for Feminist Legal History' (2020) 40 *OJLS* 878, 902–03.

[41] ibid 903.

[42] I examined this character in Naffine, *Law and the Sexes* (n 39). So too did Katherine O'Donovan in her pathbreaking book *Sexual Divisions in Law* (London, Weidenfeld and Nicolson, 1985).

in the market and the public square. (The fact that there is another sex who operates differently is not put into general theory.) This still (male) paradigm Person can experience violence and do violence (we are not Hart's crabs), so John Stuart Mill's harm principle and Hart's minimal content of natural law are put in for good measure. A world is conjured up of male players, unspecified as male characters. Women need also to populate law's world and then we can truly see what it is like and what should be done about it.

Further evidence that women are still sidelined in legal thinking comes from the way in which criminal law is organised and analysed. Rape law, with its recent exemptions for husbands, and abortion law, with its exclusive application to women, tend to be treated as separate and special legal relations and laws. Hart and Dworkin conducted their liberal analyses of abortion law separately from their general theory. Finnis put it into his general theory, but then little was made of it by other scholars, and Finnis took full advantage of this fact, as we saw in chapter eight.

It should be recognised that law's Persons are still, in important ways, drawn from only half the population. Most clearly our Legal Person is never pregnant, but he does reproduce and he expects to reproduce. The male reproductive body is not of legal concern and the state does not seek to control its functions. The female reproductive body remains state controlled, poorly theorised and, in its legal treatment, most in breach of Mill's principle of self-government. When the Legal Individual is postulated in legal theory, he is almost never engaged in sex or reproduction. He tends to be a vaguely formulated being inhabiting a vaguely formulated public sphere. Thus, general jurisprudence has indeed taken little interest in what could be regarded as human existential problems. Legal theorists have been unhindered by these facts about the formation of Legal Persons, and so they are lacking vital information.

A form of life, a type of male being, has been imagined at the centre of theory but not discussed explicitly. Hart talked about the fact that we are not giant land crabs and that if we were, legal theory would be very different. Laws prohibiting violence were necessary for the sort of creatures we are, because a propensity for violence and a vulnerability to violence were presupposed. But the soft-skinned male beings who peopled the law of this transcendent theory were not physicalised more than this. They did and they did not engage in sex (for sex was generally not put into general theory); they did not reproduce with their own bodies (for the supposed wholeness and indivisibility of the person was presupposed and then put into theory).

The forceful and also the sexual and reproducing man remains (silently) at the heart of the concept of the Person. The right to sex (without a wife's consent) was put in the middle of male right by Matthew Hale and was carried through to the end of the twentieth century.[43] With it came a silent right to compel reproduction. And still when Individuals or Persons are theorised in modern legal theory, there

[43] See extended discussion in Naffine (n 2).

is silence about these basic unsavoury historical facts about law's Persons. Instead, these beings are implicitly engaged in market or political relations[44] or they might be under instruction from criminal law not to cheat or injure or steal from other Persons. They are not reproducing, nor are they trying not to reproduce. They are not caring for children.

Let us engage in a thought experiment involving a simple reversal of current legal thought about the nature of the Legal Person. What if the paradigmatic Legal Person were someone with the capacity for pregnancy, and the capacity for pregnancy was a major consideration in life decisions? What if the paradigmatic Person created future Persons within herself, that is, she was generative of Persons *and* this was a deeply esteemed capacity? There is actually a logic to treating the pregnant woman as the most bountiful, the fullest realisation of the human and then of the moral and Legal Person, and treating the man, who can never be pregnant,[45] as the lesser case of the Person. This would constitute a dramatic reversal of our most fundamental cultural thinking about Persons.

I am not meaning to suggest that the capacity for pregnancy is the defining feature of women. Rather this thought experiment is designed to show the extent to which patriarchy is constitutive of Persons. It is political and legal power that has made the (never-to-be pregnant) man the best and fullest realisation of the Person and it is legal power that has made the woman (with her potential capacity to reproduce) the more episodic and legally-impaired legal subject. Any treatise on Persons would do well to recognise the role of power in the formation of law's basic concept, the Legal Person. It needs to be seen that the concept has been conceived by those (men) with the power to define and explain it and this definitional and explanatory power has been tightly held.

VII. Female Legal Persons without Essentialism

We need to investigate the kind of being law is thought to be for. This has not been an explicit concern of jurisprudence.[46] Rather a human or Individual or Person has been inserted as the theoretical starting point, but with certain physiological features and propensities presupposed. Then theory of law has proceeded with this being as its subject. The untheorised nature of the Person, as a being implicitly of a particular sex, has left the doors open for the religious. It has permitted women's modes of sex and reproduction to remain odd and special and outside the tacit theory of the Person.

[44] See Carole Pateman, *The Sexual Contract* (Stanford, Stanford University Press, 1988) for the highly influential book-length treatment of this necessary feature of the social contract. See also Naffine, *Law and the Sexes* (n 39) for an account of the legal man of the market and the public square and also O'Donovan (n 42).

[45] Unless they are perhaps transmen and have retained a functional uterus.

[46] It was, however, the main concern of Naffine, *Law's Meaning of Life* (n 15).

There is still no strong standard, or sense, of female Legal Personhood (say self-directed, self-governing, other excluding and of course physically reproducing), or, to put it more prosaically, a sense of female lives, in all their diversity; a sense of women living free legal lives. All the clues and indicators of Personhood have come from men, or rather how men have conceived of men. If the concepts of the Person and the Individual are to have operational currency, as they do, then women need to be considered as Persons and as Individuals, not implicitly excluded when they assume normal and necessary (for the species) female states, that is, become pregnant. If these legal concepts are to be used, and powerfully so, then we need to consider how they operate in women's lives. What work do the concepts do to and for women?

I am not suggesting that there is such a thing as an essential female person (or an essential male person for that matter) waiting in the wings, and requiring discovery and who might act as a vital corrective to current thinking. On the contrary, legal and social Persons have been formed in relations and by relations, legally and socially.[47] These relations, with their pronounced sex hierarchies, are set in particular times and places and cultures and societies, and power is an important ingredient of the relational hierarchies thus produced. The conditions which have been thought culturally necessary for the development and protection of Personhood are themselves the products of a male-female hierarchy. So I am not suggesting that there is a prelegal female Person who, when identified, could stand alongside the male Person, or even replace him. I am not suggesting a need to look for the real woman and embed her in law: the real Female Person or the real Female Individual. This is essentialism (a search for essential meanings) and we have had enough of this and it is dangerous. It allows in ancient ways of thinking about the natures of men and women and religious absolutes.

VIII. The Personality of Law

What I am proposing represents a fundamental challenge to law because it may well go to law's very ontology. Male power within law has been so thorough that it has probably shaped law's very identity. It has been defining, existential. Once male power within law is acknowledged, law begins to look very different. Male power goes to the heart of law, and the powerful still make sure that it is sustained but not mentioned. (And not mentioning it helps to keep it so.)

Imagine another simple but hard reversal. Imagine a world in which women controlled the major institutions, in which they controlled the explanations of those institutions, in which they controlled the lives of men both publicly and privately, in which they controlled men's bodies and their sexuality. This is almost beyond contemplation. But the effort to imagine such a world tells us a lot, quickly,

[47] I examined this relationality in Naffine, *Law's Meaning of Life* (n 15) and also Ngaire Naffine, 'Who are Law's Persons? From Cheshire Cats to Responsible Subjects' (2003) 66 *MLR* 346.

about what has been going on all along and has been considered fair, neutral, natural and right. Men have supplied the safe pair of hands for law and in multiple ways. They have supplied and inhabited its characters and institutions, the very discipline of law: they have been its explainers, its authorities, its figures, its practitioners; and they have supported and promoted each other. They have suffused the law with themselves, while lacking the means (and motivation) to stand back from the institution of law, to acquire some distance and objectivity, and so to see that this is what they have made.

Maleness has formed a vital part of the very identity of English law which has spread itself around the common law world. Law and male identity have been fused together, a male identity that is taken to be rational, strong, principled and forceful. This helps to explain why male control has been thoroughgoing and viewed, by some leading legal figures, as necessary to law and state. As the South Australian Premier Don Dunstan declared in 1978,

> In our society women are still recognised as being different from men, in a non-biological sense, and they are still in the position of having to argue for rights as though they were a small, disadvantaged minority group with peculiar problems. The reality is, of course, that women make up 50% of our population, but in most areas of life they are treated as a subspecies, lacking influence and deprived of responsibility.[48]

Or as Gerda Lerner put it, '[w]omen are the majority, yet we are structured into social institutions as though we are a minority'.[49]

Honesty, credibility, respect and agency are meant to be important legal values, and law is said to recognise them in its subjects. Yet women have been treated as less than full Legal Persons and subjects. They have been characterised as weak or doubtful characters, and therefore ill-suited for full sustained Legal Personhood. This distrust of women, as lacking in character, fortitude and integrity (views espoused explicitly by Stephen, Dicey and Lords Loreburn and Birkenhead), has arguably carried through, so that it can be drawn upon in court, notably in the rape trial.[50] The problem of women being disbelieved (and the problem of women anticipating legal incredulity), when or if they complain of sexual abuse and violence, endures and it weakens justice.[51]

[48] Don Dunstan, *Women's Rights: The Challenge of Social Democracy* (Speech, Newcastle, 1978), quoted in Angela Woollacott, 'Being a Woman's Advisor at the State Level: Deborah McCulloch and Don Dunstan in 1970s South Australia' (2018) 33 *Australian Feminist Studies* 97, 98.

[49] Lerner (n 26) 5.

[50] See Joanne Conaghan and Yvette Russell, *Sexual History Evidence and the Rape Trial: A Multidisciplinary Critique* (Bristol University Press, 2023). See also L Ellison and Vanessa Munro, 'Educational Guidance and (Mock) Jurors' Assessments of Complainant Credibility in Rape Trials' (2010) 13 *Sexual Assault Report* 65, and the work of Vanessa Munro generally. The corroboration warning once required when women gave evidence of sexual assault is a clear illustration of this attitude of doubting women. See Constance Backhouse, 'Skewering the Credibility of Women: A Reappraisal of Corroboration in Australian Legal History' (2000) 29 *University of Western Australia Law Review* 79.

[51] See Deborah Tuerkheimer, *Credible: Why we Doubt Accusers and Protect Abusers* (Harper Wave, 2021); Benita Kolovos, '"Rape is Effectively Decriminalized": How Did Sexual Assault Become so Easy to Get Away With' *The Guardian* (Online, 31 January 2025), available at www.theguardian.com/

The sense of male entitlement, including entitlement to women, supported by law and documented in this book, may also have had a brutalising effect on (some) men. John Stuart Mill was alert to this possibility in the nineteenth century (see chapter three). Mill directly linked the power that men could lawfully exercise over their wives to the brutalisation of men and was met with a hostile reception when he put this in writing.[52] His observations were not received as valuable legal insights, important warnings about the failings of law and its commitment to equality and to the safety of all. On the contrary, the legally-endorsed power of men over women was positively supported by Mill's contemporaries, and by several of his successors.[53] The right of men to control women, through law, was considered an important and desirable part of male legal character, not something to be regretted or reconsidered.

This strong forceful male character, who once openly inhabited law, has been poorly acknowledged and scrutinised. He has not been critically examined, explicitly and systematically, within mainstream legal theory. It may be that we are still feeling the effects of this failure to take a hard, close, look at the historical character of the Legal Person and to do something about him. And women may well be getting the worst of it, still. Mill foreshadowed this. Male violence directed at women is an enduring problem.

The killing of women by men is, at the time of writing, a matter of great concern to governments. The Australian Government has called it a national emergency.[54] As criminologist Kate Fitz-Gibbon reported, 'in 2024, a woman ha[d] been killed by men's violence every four days, and, on average, 13 women [were] hospitalised each day in Australia because of family and domestic violence'.[55]

The Guardian is recording and acknowledging the women being killed in the United Kingdom (UK) by men. According to Topping, Banfield-Nwachi, Abdul and Hall, '[i]n recent years in the UK, a woman has been killed by a man every three days on average, yet most of their stories have gone unheard'.[56] With its

australia-news/ng-interactive/2025/jan/31/is-effectively-decriminalised-how-did-sexual-assault-become-so-easy-to-get-away-with-ntwnfb. And this has been a longstanding problem: see Mary Heath, 'Lack of Conviction: A Proposal to Make Rape Illegal in South Australia' (2007) 27 *Australian Feminist Law Journal* 175.

[52] I take up this point in Ngaire Naffine, 'Criminal Law and the Moral Education of Men' (2018) 11 *Fudan Journal of the Humanities and Social Sciences* 129.

[53] See my analysis of legal support for the husband's rape exemption in Naffine (n 2).

[54] 'On 28 April 2024, the Prime Minister declared that Australia faced a "national crisis" of violence against women, with one woman being killed every four days.': Australian Government, Department of the Prime Minister and Cabinet, 'A National Emergency – and an Ongoing National Priority', available at www.pmc.gov.au/resources/unlocking-prevention-potential/national-emergency-and-ongoing-national-priority. By the end of 2024 the situation had worsened. See Jessica Bahr, 'Is 2024 Australia's Worst Year Yet for Violence Against Women?' (*SBS News*, online, 29 December 2024), available at www.sbs.com.au/news/article/is-2024-australias-worst-year-for-violence-against-women/8rejzzpza. See also Kate Fitz-Gibbon, *Our National Crisis: Violence Against Women & Children* (Monash University Publishing, 2024).

[55] Kate Fitz-Gibbon, 'The Long Walk Continues' (*The Monthly*, online, November 2024), available at www.themonthly.com.au/issue/2024/november/kate-fitz-gibbon/long-walk-continues.

[56] Alexandra Topping et al, 'Killed Women Count: 80 Women Allegedly Killed by Men in UK in 2024' *The Guardian* (Online, 31 December 2024), available at www.theguardian.com/uk-news/

'Killed Women Count' of 2024, *The Guardian* has been reporting on 'every woman allegedly killed by a man, drawing on the work of campaigns such as Counting Dead Women, the Femicide Census and Killed Women.' By the end of 2024, 'the toll of women whose deaths … led to a man being charged' had reached 80.[57] Such violence may well be a legacy of insufficiently inspected (and condemned) male entitlement to women, and male entitlement to exclusive public power, once explicitly embedded in law and regarded as integral to the formation of law's central character.

IX. Thinking Afresh

Men have been regarded, by leading men of law, as innately superior beings – as more forceful, more credible, more rational, more naturally entitled – and so naturally equipped to be law's subjects and also equipped to assess the fitness of legal subjects. With right has come right. With non-right has come non-right. This needs to be recognised and to change, effortfully.

Thomas Kuhn once drew our attention to the problem of changing minds within scholarly communities when so much has been invested in a certain way of thinking and doing.

> The invention of … new theories regularly, and appropriately, evokes the same response from some of the specialists on whose area of competence they impinge. For these men [sic] the new theory implies a change in the rules governing the prior practice of normal science. Inevitably, therefore, it reflects upon much scientific work they have already successfully completed. That is why a new theory … is seldom or never just an increment to what is already known.[58]

When scientists are faced with evidence that refutes their standard disciplinary thinking, what may be needed is 'the reconstruction of prior theory and the re-evaluation of prior fact, an intrinsically revolutionary process'.[59] This does not happen quickly or easily and there is likely to be deep-seated resistance to change. But this is what I believe needs to happen in the practice of 'normal' law and theory, about our very Legal Subject, the Legal Person.

Once law operated, explicitly, with a basic division between preferred and unpreferred people: between men and women. Legal treatises and legal cases acknowledged the two groups, justified their very different rankings, and then went on to deal mainly with the law of the preferred people who exercised power,

ng-interactive/2024/dec/31/killed-women-count-a-project-highlighting-the-toll-and-tragedy-of-violence-against-women-in-the-uk.

[57] ibid. As the authors observe, '[n]one of these incidents are linked in any way other than that a woman has been killed and a man charged in connection with her death'.

[58] Thomas S Kuhn, *The Structure of Scientific Revolutions* (Chicago, University of Chicago Press, 1962) 7.

[59] ibid.

men, as if their law were the whole body of law. The less preferred people (women) generally ceased to be of interest. After all, because of their legal assignment, their portion, they had little role to play in the major public institutions or in the market. And certainly, they were not going to become law's officials: its makers, interpreters, enforcers.

When this partitioning of law was formally abandoned, over the course of the twentieth century, little was made of it and interest remained with the roles that had been inhabited by the preferred ones. It seems that the legal actor was released from his sex and yet he was not. Because of the silence about this history, the implication was that theory could proceed as if all this had never been the case. What I am proposing calls for much. It is difficult (but not impossible) to contemplate how to do things differently because the problem is deep, seemingly entrenched, and enduring. But truth and justice depend on it. Law and its theorists need a well-rounded, inclusive and robust conception of the Legal Person (or perhaps a plurality of Persons), that does not render the Personhood of women precarious, episodic and inferior. This entails effort, perhaps a radical rethinking of law, but law and theory can only benefit from it. As Thomas Nagel once reminded us: 'Pursuit of truth … requires a habitual readiness to attack one's own convictions.'[60] Then truth can form the reply to power.

[60] Thomas Nagel, *The View from Nowhere* (New York, Oxford University Press, 1986) 9.

BIBLIOGRAPHY

Articles/Books/Reports

Aquinas, Thomas, *Summa Theologica* vols IV–V (Fathers of the English Dominican Province trs, London, Burns Oates & Washbourne Ltd, 1922).

—— *The Summa Against the Gentiles* (Paul Sigmund tr, New York, WW Norton & Company, 1988).

Aristotle, *De Generatione Animalium* (JA Smith and WD Ross trs, Oxford, Clarendon Press, 1912).

—— *Generation of Animals* (AL Peck tr, London, William Heinemann Ltd, 1943).

Babie, Paul and Rochow, Neville (eds), *Freedom of Religion under Bills of Rights* (Adelaide, University of Adelaide Press, 2011).

Backhouse, Constance, 'Skewering the Credibility of Women: A Reappraisal of Corroboration in Australian Legal History' (2000) 29 *University of Western Australia Law Review* 79.

Bamforth, Nicholas and Richards, David AJ, *Patriarchal Religion, Sexuality, and Gender: A Critique of New Natural Law* (Cambridge, Cambridge University Press, 2008).

Berger, Linda, Crawford, Bridget and Stanchi, Kathryn, 'Methods, Impact, and Reach of the Global Feminist Judgments Projects' (2018) 8 *Oñati Socio-legal Series* 1215.

Bernasconi, Robert, 'Will the Real Kant Please Stand Up: The Challenge of Enlightenment Racism to the Study of the History of Philosophy' (2003) 117 *Radical Philosophy* 13.

Berns, Sandra S, 'Hercules, Hermes and Senator Smith: The Symbolic Structure of Law's Empire' (1988) 44 *Bulletin of the Australian Society of Legal Philosophy* 35.

Blackstone, William, *Commentaries on the Laws of England* vol 1 (Oxford, Clarendon Press, 1765).

Bond, Alma H, 'Virginia Woolf and Leslie Stephen: A Father's Contribution to Psychosis and Genius' (1986) 14 *Journal of the American Academy of Psychoanalysis and Dynamic Psychiatry* 507.

Bostick, Theodora, 'The Press and the Launching of the Women's Suffrage Movement, 1866–1867' (1980) 13 *Victorian Periodicals Review* 125.

Boutmy, Emile Gaston, *Etudes de droit Constitutionnel: France, Angleterre, États-Unis* (Paris, Plon, 1885).

—— *Studies of Constitutional Law: France, England, United States* (EM Dicey tr, London, Macmillan, 1891).

Brindis, Claire D et al, 'Health-Care Workforce Implications of the Dobbs v Jackson Women's Health Organization Decision' (2024) 403 *The Lancet* 2747.

—— 'Societal Implications of the Dobbs v Jackson Women's Health Organization Decision' (2024) 403 *The Lancet* 2751.

Burke, Edmund, *Correspondence of the Right Honourable Edmund Burke* (London, Rivington, 1844).

Bustamante, Thomas and Decat, Thiago Lopes (eds), *Philosophy of Law as an Integral Part of Philosophy: Essays on the Jurisprudence of Gerald J Postema* (Oxford, Hart Publishing, 2020).

Butler, Judith, *Gender Trouble: Feminism and the Subversion of Identity* (New York, Routledge, 1999).

Cane, Peter, *Responsibility in Law and Morality* (Oxford, Hart Publishing, 2002).

—— 'Taking Law Seriously: Starting Points of the Hart/Devlin Debate' (2006) 10 *The Journal of Ethics* 21.

—— (ed), *The Hart-Fuller Debate in the Twenty-First Century* (Oxford, Hart Publishing, 2010).

—— 'AV Dicey as Legal Theorist' (2022) 85 *MLR* 247.

Cannadine, David, 'David Cannadine: Interview' (2017) 31 *British Academy Review* 4.

Clark, Randall Baldwin, 'Platonic Love in a Colorado Courtroom: Martha Nussbaum, John Finnis, and Plato's Laws in Evans v Romer' (2000) 21 *Yale Journal of Law & the Humanities* 1.

Cohen, Felix, 'Transcendental Nonsense and the Functional Approach' (1935) 35 *Columbia Law Review* 809.
Conaghan, Joanne, *Law and Gender* (Oxford, Oxford University Press, 2013).
——, 'Jurisprudence/Legal Theory' in Rosemary Auchmuty (ed), *Great Debates in Gender and Law* (Palgrave Macmillan, 2018).
Conaghan, Joanne and Russell, Yvette, *Sexual History Evidence and the Rape Trial: A Multidisciplinary Critique* (Bristol University Press, 2023).
Connell, Raewyn, *Gender: In World Perspective*, 2nd edn (Cambridge, Polity, 2009).
Cowan, Sharon, Kennedy, Chloe and Munro, Vanessa E (eds), *Scottish Feminist Judgments: (Re)Creating Law from the Outside In* (Oxford, Hart Publishing, 2019).
Crawford, Bridget J, Stanchi, Kathryn and Berger, Linda L, 'Feminist Judging Matters: How Feminist Theory and Methods Affect the Process of Judgment' (2018) 47 *University of Baltimore Law Review* 167.
Criado-Perez, Caroline, *Invisible Women: Exposing Data Bias in a World Designed for Men* (London, Chatto & Windus, 2019).
Criminal Law Revision Committee, *Sexual Offences* (HMSO No 15, 1984).
Davies, Margaret, 'The Law Becomes us: Rediscovering Judgment' (2012) 20 *Feminist Legal Studies* 167.
—— *Law Unlimited* (Oxford, Routledge, 2017).
Davies, Margaret and Naffine, Ngaire, *Are Persons Property? Legal Debates about Property and Personality* (Aldershot, Ashgate, 2001).
Derham, DP, 'Theories of Legal Personality' in Leicester Webb (ed), *Legal Personality and Political Pluralism* (Carlton, Melbourne University Press, 1958) 1–19.
Dewey, John, 'The Historic Background of Corporate Legal Personality' (1926) 35 *Yale Law Journal* 655.
Dicey, AV, *Introduction to the Study of the Law of the Constitution*, 5th edn (London, Macmillan, 1897).
—— *Letters to a Friend on Votes for Women* (London, John Murray, 1909).
—— *Introduction to the Study of the Law of the Constitution*, 8th edn (London, MacMillan, 1915).
Douglas, Heather et al (eds), *Australian Feminist Judgments: Righting and Rewriting Law* (Oxford, Hart Publishing, 2014).
Duff, RA, *Answering for Crime: Responsibility and Liability in the Criminal Law* (Oxford, Hart Publishing, 2007).
Dworkin, Ronald, *Taking Rights Seriously* (London, Duckworth, 1977).
—— *Law's Empire* (London, Fontana Press, 1986).
—— 'The Great Abortion Case' (1989) 36 *The New York Review of Books* 49.
—— *Life's Dominion: An Argument about Abortion, Euthanasia, and Individual Freedom* (New York, Alfred A Knope, 1993).
Ellison, L and Munro, Vanessa, 'Educational Guidance and (Mock) Jurors' Assessments of Complainant Credibility in Rape Trials' (2010) 13 *Sexual Assault Report* 65.
Enright, Máiréad, McCandless, Julie and O'Donoghue, Aoife, *Northern/Irish Feminist Judgments: Judges' Troubles and the Gendered Politics of Identity* (Oxford, Hart Publishing, 2017).
Evans, Jonathan and Johnson-Laird, Philip, 'Editorial Obituary: Peter Wason (1924–2003)' (2003) 9 *Thinking and Reasoning* 177.
Evans, Richard J, *Altered Pasts: Counterfactuals in History* (Chicago, Brandeis University Press, 2014).
Farmer, Lindsay, *Making the Modern Criminal Law: Criminalization and Civil Order* (Oxford, Oxford University Press, 2016).
Feinberg, Joel, *The Moral Limits of the Criminal Law* vols 1–4 (New York, Oxford University Press, 1984–88).
Finnis, John, 'Abortion and Legal Rationality' (1970) 3 *Adelaide Law Review* 431.
—— 'The Rights and Wrongs of Abortion: A Reply to Judith Thomson' (1973) 2 *Philosophy & Public Affairs* 117.
—— *Natural Law and Natural Rights*, 1st edn (Oxford, Clarendon Press, 1980).
—— 'The Legal Status of the Unborn Baby' (1992) 43 *Catholic Medical Quarterly* 5.

—— 'Law, Morality, and "Sexual Orientation"' (1994) 69 *Notre Dame Law Review* 1049.
—— 'The Good of Marriage and the Morality of Sexual Relations: Some Philosophical and Historical Observations' (1997) 42 *American Journal of Jurisprudence* 97.
—— *Aquinas: Moral, Political, and Legal Theory* (Oxford, Oxford University Press, 1998).
—— 'Public Reason, Abortion, and Cloning' (1998) 32 *Valparaiso University Law Review* 361.
—— 'Abortion, Natural Law and Public Reason' in Robert P George and Christopher Wolfe (eds), *Natural Law and Public Reason* (Washington, Georgetown University Press, 2000) 75–106.
—— 'The Priority of Persons' in Jeremy Horder (ed), *Oxford Essays on Jurisprudence* (Oxford, Oxford University Press, 2000) 1–15.
—— '"The Thing I Am": Personal Identity in Aquinas and Shakespeare' in Ellen Frankel Paul, Fred D Miller Jr and Jeffrey Paul (eds), *Personal Identity* (Cambridge, Cambridge University Press, 2005) 250–82.
—— 'Marriage: A Basic and Exigent Good' (2008) 91 *The Monist* 388.
—— *Intention and Identity: Collected Essays* vol 2 (Oxford, Oxford University Press, 2011).
—— *Natural Law and Natural Rights*, 2nd edn (Oxford University Press, 2011).
—— 'The Priority of Persons Revisited' (2013) 58 *The American Journal of Jurisprudence* 45.
Finnis, John and George, Robert P, 'Equal Protection and The Unborn Child: A Dobbs Brief' (2022) 45 *Harvard Journal of Law & Public Policy* 927.
Fitz-Gibbon, Kate, *Our National Crisis: Violence Against Women & Children* (Monash University Publishing, 2024).
Fitzgerald, Sharron and Carline, Anna, 'Problematising the "Man Problem" in the Domestic Abuse Act: Discursive Co-option and the (In)Visibility of Gender' (2024) *Social and Legal Studies*, journals.sagepub.com/doi/epub/10.1177/09646639241288528.
Fricker, Miranda, *Epistemic Injustice: Power and the Ethics of Knowing* (Oxford, Oxford University Press, 2007).
Friedman, Lawrence, 'Is there a Modern Legal Culture?' (1994) 7 *Ratio Juris* 117, 125.
Fuller, Lon L, *Legal Fictions* (Stanford, Stanford University Press, 1967).
Funder, Anna, *Wifedom: Mrs Orwell's Invisible Life* (Hamish Hamilton, 2023).
Geis, Gilbert and Bunn, Ivan, *A Trial of Witches: A Seventeenth-Century Witchcraft Prosecution* (London, Routledge, 1997).
Gilbert, Scott F, 'Pseudo-Embryology and Personhood: How Embryological Pseudoscience Helps Structure the American Abortion Debate' (2023) 3(1) *Natural Sciences*, onlinelibrary.wiley.com/doi/epdf/10.1002/ntls.20220041.
—— '"When Does Human Life Begin?" Teaching Human Embryology in the Context of the American Abortion Debate' (2024) 515 *Developmental Biology* 102.
Gleeson, Kate, 'The Problem of *Clarence*, Brutal at his Best: James Fitzjames Stephen and the Doctrine of Sexual Inequality' (2005) 14 *Nottingham Law Journal* 1.
Gorsuch, Neil, *The Future of Assisted Suicide and Euthanasia* (Princeton, Princeton University Press, 2006).
Grabham, Emily, *Brewing Legal Times: Things, Form and the Enactment of Law* (Toronto, University of Toronto Press, 2016).
Great Britain Home Office, *Report of the Advisory Group on the Law of Rape* (London, CMND No 6352, 1976).
Green, Leslie, 'Gender and the Analytical Jurisprudential Mind' (2020) 83 *MLR* 893.
Hale, Matthew, *Historia Placitorum Coronae* vol 1 (PR Glazebrook ed, London, Professional Books, 1971).
Hamilton, Sheryl N, *Impersonations: Troubling the Person in Law and Culture* (Toronto, University of Toronto Press, 2009).
Hart, HLA, *Definition and Theory in Jurisprudence: An Inaugural Lecture Delivered Before the University of Oxford on 30 May 1953* (Oxford, Clarendon Press, 1953).
—— 'Positivism and the Separation of Law and Morals' (1958) 71 *Harvard Law Review* 593.
—— *The Concept of Law* (Oxford, Clarendon Press, 1961).

—— 'Abortion Law Reform: The English Experience' (1972) 8 *Melbourne University Law Review* 388.
—— *Essays in Jurisprudence and Philosophy* (Oxford, Clarendon Press, 1983).
Harvie, Christopher, 'Revolution and the Rule of Law (1789–1851)' in Kenneth O Morgan (ed), *The Oxford Illustrated History of Britain* (Oxford, Oxford University Press, 1986) 419–62.
Heath, Mary, 'Lack of Conviction: A Proposal to Make Rape Illegal in South Australia' (2007) 27 *Australian Feminist Law Journal* 175.
Hekman, Susan, 'Backgrounds and Riverbeds: Feminist Reflections' (1999) 25 *Feminist Studies* 427.
Heller, Joseph, *Catch-22* (London, Jonathan Cape, 1967).
Henderson, Lynne, 'Whose Nature? Practical Reason and Patriarchy' (1990) 38 *Cleveland State Law Review* 169.
Heuston, RFV, *Lives of the Lord Chancellors 1940–1970* (Oxford, Clarendon Press, 1987).
Hodgson, Geoffrey M, 'Meanings of Methodological Individualism' (2007) 14 *Journal of Economic Methodology* 211.
Hodson, Loveday and Lavers, Troy, *Feminist Judgments in International Law* (Oxford, Hart Publishing, 2019).
Hohfeld, Wesley Newcomb, 'Fundamental Legal Conceptions as Applied in Judicial Reasoning' (1916) 26 *The Yale Law Journal* 710.
Holdcroft, Anita, 'Gender Bias in Research: How Does it Affect Evidence Based Medicine?' (2007) 100 *Journal of the Royal Society of Medicine* 2.
Holton, Sandra Stanley, 'State Pandering, Medical Policing and Prostitution: The Controversy within the Medical Profession Concerning the Contagious Diseases Legislation 1864–1886' (1988) 9 *Research in Law, Deviance and Social Control* 149.
—— 'Challenging Masculinism: Personal History and Microhistory in Feminist Studies of the Women's Suffrage Movement' (2011) 20 *Women's History Review* 829.
Honoré, AM, 'Ownership' in AG Guest (ed), *Oxford Essays in Jurisprudence* (Oxford, Oxford University Press, 1961) 107–47.
Horder, Jeremy (ed), *Oxford Essays on Jurisprudence* (Oxford University Press, 2000).
Hunter, Rosemary, 'The Power of Feminist Judgments?' (2012) 20 *Feminist Legal Studies* 135.
—— 'The Feminist Judgments Project: Legal Fiction as Critique and Praxis' (2015) 5 *International Critical Thought* 501.
Hunter, Rosemary, McGlynn, Clare and Rackley, Erika (eds), *Feminist Judgments: From Theory to Practice* (Oxford, Hart Publishing, 2010).
Huq, Aziz Z, 'What We Ask of Law' (2022) 132 *Yale Law Journal* 487, 539.
Jackson, Gabrielle, *Pain and Prejudice: A Call to Arms for Women and their Bodies* (Sydney, Allen & Unwin, 2019).
James, William, *The Principles of Psychology* (New York, Henry Holt and Company, 1890).
Jex-Blake, Sophia, *Medical Women* (Edinburgh, William Oliphant & Co, 1872).
Jose, Jim and McLoughlin, Kcasey, 'John Stuart Mill and the Contagious Diseases Acts: Whose Law? Whose Liberty? Whose Greater Good?' (2016) 34 *Law and History Review* 249.
Judiciary United States Senate, *Confirmation Hearing on the Nomination of Hon Neil M Gorsuch to be an Associate Justice of the Supreme Court of the United States* (No J-115-6, March 2017).
Kahan, Dan M and Braman, Donald, 'The Self-Defence Cognition of Self Defence' (2008) 45 *American Criminal Law Review* 1.
Kahan, Dan M et al, '"They Saw a Protest": Cognitive Illiberalism and the Speech-Conduct Distinction' (2012) 64 *Stanford Law Review* 851.
Kelsen, Hans, *General Theory of Law and State* (Anders Wedberg tr, New York, Russell and Russell, 1945).
Keown, John and George, Robert P (eds), *Reason, Morality, and Law: The Philosophy of John Finnis* (Oxford, Oxford University Press, 2013).
Kerruish, Valerie, 'Philosophical Retreat: A Criticism of John Finnis' Theory of Natural Law' (1983) 15 *University of Western Australia Law Review* 224.
—— *Jurisprudence as Ideology* (London, Routledge, 1991).

Khan, Naveeda, *River Life and the Upspring of Nature* (Durham, Duke University Press, 2023).
Kramer, Matthew et al (eds), *The Legacy of HLA Hart: Legal, Political, and Moral Philosophy* (Oxford, Oxford University Press, 2008).
Kuhn, Thomas S, *The Structure of Scientific Revolutions* (Chicago, University of Chicago Press, 1962).
Kuhse, Helga (ed), *Unsanctifying Human Life: Essays on Ethics* (Oxford, Blackwell Publishing, 2002).
Kurki, Visa AJ, *A Theory of Legal Personhood* (Oxford, Oxford University Press, 2019).
—— *Legal Personhood* (Cambridge, Cambridge University Press, 2023).
Lacey, Nicola, *Unspeakable Subjects* (Oxford, Hart Publishing, 1998).
—— '"Philosophical Foundations of the Common Law" Social not Metaphysical' in Jeremy Horder (ed), *Oxford Essays in Jurisprudence*, 4th edn (Oxford, Oxford University Press, 2000) 17–39.
—— *A Life of HLA Hart: The Nightmare and the Noble Dream* (Oxford, Oxford University Press, 2006).
—— 'Philosophy, Political Morality, and History: Explaining the Enduring Resonance of the Hart-Fuller Debate' (2008) 83 *New York University Law Review* 1059.
—— *In Search of Criminal Responsibility Ideas, Interests, and Institutions* (Oxford, Oxford University Press, 2016).
Langer, Susanne K, *Philosophy in a New Key: A Study in the Symbolism of Reason, Rite, and Art*, 3rd edn (Cambridge, Harvard University Press, 1971).
Larcombe, Wendy and Heath, Mary, 'Developing the Common Law and Rewriting the History of Rape in Marriage in Australia: PGA v The Queen' (2012) 34 *Sydney Law Review* 785.
Law Commission, 'Rape within Marriage' (1990) Law Commission Working Paper No 116; Law Commission, *Criminal Law: Rape within Marriage* (HMSO No 205, 1992).
Lawson, FH, 'The Creative Use of Legal Concepts' (1957) 32 *New York University Law Review* 907.
Leader-Elliott, Ian, 'A Critical Reading of Duff Answering for Crime' (2010) 31 *Adelaide Law Review* 47.
Lerner, Gerda, *The Creation of Patriarchy* (New York, Oxford University Press, 1986).
Lesses, Kos, 'PGA v The Queen: Marital Rape in Australia: The Role of Repetition' (2014) 37 *Melbourne University Law Review* 786.
Lincoln, Bruce, *Discourse and the Construction of Society: Comparative Studies of Myth, Ritual, and Classification* (Oxford, Oxford University Press, 1989).
Lino, Dylan, 'The Rule of Law and the Law of Empire: AV Dicey in Imperial Context' (2018) 81 *MLR* 739.
Locke, John, *An Essay Concerning Human Understanding* (London, Ward, Lock, & Co, 1689).
Loughlin, Martin, 'AV Dicey and the Making of Common Law Constitutionalism' (2022) 42 *OJLS* 366.
Lukes, Steven, 'Methodological Individualism Reconsidered' (1968) 19 *British Journal of Sociology* 119.
—— *Individualism* (Oxford, Basil Blackwell, 1973).
Malik, Maleiha, 'Faith and the State of Jurisprudence' in Peter Oliver, Sionaidh Douglas Scott and Victor Tadros (eds), *Faith in Law: Essays in Legal Theory* (Oxford, Hart Publishing, 2000) 129–49.
Marguerite, Ritchie E, 'Alice Through the Statutes' (1975) 21 *McGill Law Journal* 685.
Matthew, HCG, 'The Liberal Age (1851–1914)' in Kenneth O Morgan (ed), *The Oxford History of Britain* (rev ed, Oxford, Oxford University Press, 1988) 463–522.
McCarthy, Justin, *Modern Leaders: Being a Series of Biographical Sketches* (New York, Sheldon & Company, 1872).
McDonald, Elisabeth et al (eds), *Feminist Judgments of Aotearoa New Zealand: Te Rino: A Two-Stranded Rope* (Oxford, Hart Publishing, 2017).
McGilchrist, Ian, *The Master and his Emissary: The Divided Brain and the Making of the Western World* (New Haven, Yale University Press, 2009).
Merone, Lea et al, 'Sex Inequalities in Medical Research: A Systematic Scoping Review of the Literature' (2022) 3 *Women's Health Reports* 49.
Mill, John Stuart, *On Liberty* (London, John W Parkers and Son, 1859).
—— *The Subjection of Women* (London, Longmans, Green, Reader and Dyer, 1869).
—— *Autobiography* (London, Longmans, Green, Reader and Dyer, 1873).
—— *On Liberty* (Stefan Collini ed, Cambridge, Cambridge University Press, 1989).
—— *On Liberty* (John Gray ed, Oxford, Oxford University Press, 1991).

Miller, Ian, *A History of Force Feeding: Hunger Strikes, Prisons and Medical Ethics, 1909–1974* (Basingstoke, Palgrave Macmillan, 2016).
Moore, GCG, *Leslie Stephen and the Clubbable Men of Radical London: An Essay in Honour of John King's Retirement* (Virginia, George Mason University, 2007).
Munro, Vanessa E, 'Feminist Critiques of the Rule of Law' in Jens Meierhenrich and Martin Loughlin (eds), *The Cambridge Companion to the Rule of Law* (Cambridge, Cambridge University Press, 2021) 340–56.
—— 'Feminist Judgments Projects at the Intersection' (2021) 29 *Feminist Legal Studies* 251.
Naffine, Ngaire, *Female Crime: The Construction of Women in Criminology* (Sydney, Allen & Unwin, 1987).
—— *Law and the Sexes: Explorations in Feminist Jurisprudence* (Sydney, Allen & Unwin, 1990).
—— *Feminism and Criminology* (Philadelphia, Temple University Press, 1996).
—— 'The Body Bag' in Ngaire Naffine and Rosemary J Owens (eds), *Sexing the Subject of Law* (London, Sweet & Maxwell, 1997) 79–93.
—— 'The Legal Structure of Self-Ownership: Or the Self-Possessed Man and the Woman Possessed' (1998) 25 *Journal of Law and Society* 193.
—— 'Who are Law's Persons? From Cheshire Cats to Responsible Subjects' (2003) 66 *MLR* 346.
—— 'How Religion Constrains Law and the Idea of Choice' (2009) 30 *Adelaide Law Review* 15.
—— *Law's Meaning of Life: Philosophy, Religion, Darwin, and the Legal Person* (Oxford, Hart Publishing, 2009).
—— 'The Common Discourse of Hart and Fuller' in Peter Cane (ed), *The Hart-Fuller Debate in the Twenty-First Century* (Oxford, Hart Publishing, 2010) 217–25.
—— 'Women and the Cast of Legal Persons' in Jackie Jones et al (eds), *Gender, Sexualities and Law* (Routledge, 2011) 24–34.
—— 'Postema's Persons' (2017) 8 *Jurisprudence* 588.
—— 'Criminal Law and the Moral Education of Men' (2018) 11 *Fudan Journal of the Humanities and Social Sciences* 129.
—— *Criminal Law and the Man Problem* (Oxford, Hart Publishing, 2019).
—— 'Hidden Presuppositions and the Problem of Paradigm Persons: Visa AJ Kurki's "A Theory of Legal Personhood"' (2021) 44 *Revus* 127.
—— 'Policing the Legal Person: How John Finnis and Other Jurisprudential Figures Continue to Unperson Women' (2024) 45 *Adelaide Law Review* 21.
Naffine, Ngaire and Rosemary J Owens (eds), *Sexing the Subject of Law* (Law Book Company, 1997).
Nagel, Thomas, *The View from Nowhere* (New York, Oxford University Press, 1986).
Nedelsky, Jennifer, 'Reconceiving Autonomy: Sources, Thoughts and Possibilities' (1989) 1 *Yale Journal of Law & Feminism* 7.
—— 'Law, Boundaries and the Bounded Self' (1990) 30 *Representations* 162.
—— *Private Property and the Limits of American Constitutionalism: The Madisonian Framework and its Legacy* (Chicago, University of Chicago Press, 1990).
—— *Law's Relations: A Relational Theory of Self, Autonomy, and Law* (Oxford, Oxford University Press, 2011).
Nekam, Alexander, *The Personality Conception of the Legal Entity* (Cambridge, Harvard University Press, 1938).
Nickerson, Raymond, 'Confirmation Bias: A Ubiquitous Phenomenon in Many Guises' (1998) 2 *Review of General Psychology* 175.
Norrie, Alan, *Crime, Reason and History: A Critical Introduction to Criminal Law*, 3rd edn (Cambridge, Cambridge University Press, 2014).
Note, 'What We Talk About When We Talk About Persons: The Language of a Legal Fiction' (2001) 114 *Harvard Law Review* 1746.
—— 'The Legacy of John Finnis: Contemporary Engagements and Developments' (2022) 67 *American Journal of Jurisprudence* 141.
Nye Jr, Joseph S, 'Soft Power' (1990) 80 *Foreign Policy* 153.

—— 'Soft Power: The Origins and Political Progress of a Concept' (2022) 28 *Journal of International Communication* 1.

O'Donnell, Erin L, *Legal Rights for Rivers: Competition, Collaboration and Water Governance* (London, Routledge, 2018).

O'Donnell, Erin L and Talbot-Jones, Julia, 'Creating Legal Rights for Rivers: Lessons from Australia, New Zealand, and India' (2018) 23 *Ecology and Society* 7.

O'Donovan, Katherine, *Sexual Divisions in Law* (London, Weidenfeld and Nicolson, 1985).

Orwell, George, *Animal Farm* (London, Secker & Warburg, 1945).

Pataki, Tamas, *Against Religion* (Melbourne, Scribe Short Books, 2007).

Pateman, Carole, *The Sexual Contract* (Stanford, Stanford University Press, 1988).

Paulson, Richard J, 'The Unscientific Nature of the Concept that "Human Life Begins at Fertilization," and Why it Matters' (2017) 107 *Fertility and Sterility* 566.

Pearson, Rose and Sachs, Albie, 'Barristers and Gentlemen: A Critical Look at Sexism in the Legal Profession' (1980) 43 *MLR* 400.

Plevkova, J et al, 'Various Aspects of Sex and Gender Bias in Biomedical Research' (2020) 69 *Psychological Research* 367.

Pollock, Frederick and Maitland, Frederic William, *History of English Law* vol 1 (Cambridge, Cambridge University Press, 1895).

Postema, Gerald J, 'On the Moral Presence of the Past' (1991) 36 *McGill Law Journal* 1153.

—— *Legal Philosophy in the Twentieth Century: The Common Law World* (Carolina, Springer, 2011).

—— 'Jurisprudence, the Sociable Science' (2015) 101 *Virginia Law Review* 869.

—— 'Philosophical Jurisprudence: A Vision' (2021) UNC Legal Studies Research Paper, 8.

Rackley, Erika, 'When Hercules Met the Happy Prince: Re-Imagining the Judge' (2005) 12 *Texas Wesleyan Law Review* 213.

—— 'Why Feminist Legal Scholars Should Write Judgments: Reflections on the Feminist Judgments Project in England and Wales' (2012) 24 *Canadian Journal of Women and the Law* 389.

Rackley, Erika and Auchmuty, Rosemary (eds), *Women's Legal Landmarks: Celebrating the History of Women and Law in the UK and Ireland* (Oxford, Hart Publishing, 2018).

Rackley, Erika and Auchmuty, Rosemary, 'The Case for Feminist Legal History' (2020) 40 *OJLS* 878.

Reeves, Richard, 'John Stuart Mill' (2007) 153–4 *Salmagundi* 47.

Richards, Eric, 'History from Below' (1975) 1 *Journal of the Historical Society of South Australia* 1.

Richette, Lisa Aversa, 'Book Review: Sexism and the Law: A Study of Male Beliefs and Legal Bias in Britain and the United States by Albie Sachs and Joan Hoff Wilson' (1979) 6 *Women's Rights Law Reporter* 145.

Richter, Melvin, *The Politics of Conscience: TH Green and his Age* (London, Weidenfeld and Nicolson, 1964).

Roberts, Heather and Sweeney, Laura, 'Why (Re)Write Judgments?: Australian Feminist Judgments: Righting and Rewriting Law' (2015) 37 *Sydney Law Review* 457.

Rundle, Kristen, *Revisiting the Rule of Law* (Cambridge University Press, 2022).

—— 'On Politics, Polemics and Performance' (2024) *Jurisprudence*, www.tandfonline.com/doi/full/10.1080/20403313.2024.2404356.

Russell, Bertrand, 'On AntiSuffragist Arguments' in Jeff McLaughlin (ed), *The Originals: Classic Readings in Western Philosophy* (Yukon, British Columbia, Press Books, 2017) 380–7.

Sachs, Albie, 'The Myth of Judicial Neutrality: The Male Monopoly Cases' (1975) 23 *The Sociological Review* 104.

Sachs, Albie and Hoff Wilson, Joan, *Sexism and the Law: A Study of Male Beliefs and Legal Bias in Britain and the United States* (Oxford, Martin Robertson, 1978).

Sallmann, PA and Chappell, Duncan, *Rape Law Reform: A Study of the South Australian Experience* (Adelaide Law Review Research Paper No 3, 1982).

Selden, John, *Ioannis Seldeni De Synedriis & Præfecturis Iuridicis Veterum Ebræorum Liber Secundus* (London, Prostant apud Cornelium Bee, 1653).

Seligman, David B, 'Wittgenstein on Seeing Aspects and Experiencing Meanings' (1976) 37 *Philosophy and Phenomenological Research* 205.

Sharpe, Robert J, 'The Persons Case and the Living Tree Theory of Constitutional Interpretation' (2013) 64 *University of New Brunswick Law Journal* 1.

Sharpe, Robert J and McMahon, Patricia I, *The Persons Case: The Origins and Legacy of the Fight for Legal Personhood* (Toronto, University of Toronto Press, 2007).

Sheldon, Sally, 'The Decriminalisation of Abortion: An Argument for Modernisation' (2016) 36 *OJLS* 334.

Sheldon, Sally et al, *The Abortion Act of 1967: A Biography of a UK Law* (Cambridge University Press, 2023).

Shyam, Geeta, 'Is the Classification of Animals as Property Consistent with Modern Community Attitudes?' (2018) 41 *University of New South Wales Law Journal* 1418.

Sloman, Steven and Fernbach, Philip, *The Knowledge Illusion: Why we Never Think Alone* (New York, Riverhead Books, 2017).

Smalley, George W, *Society in London, by a Foreign Resident* (London, Chatto & Windus, 1885).

Smith, KJM, *James Fitzjames Stephen: Portrait of a Victorian Rationalist* (Cambridge, Cambridge University Press, 1988).

Stanchi, Kathryn M, Berger, Linda L and Crawford, Bridget J (eds), *Feminist Judgments: Rewritten Opinions of the United States Supreme Court* (Cambridge University Press, 2016).

Stephen, James Fitzjames, *A General View of the Criminal Laws of England* (London, Macmillan and Co, 1863).

—— *Liberty, Equality and Fraternity* (New York, Holt and Williams, 1873).

—— *A Digest of the Criminal Law*, 4th edn (London, Macmillan and Co, 1877).

—— *A History of the Criminal Law of England* vols 1–3 (London, Macmillan and Co, 1883).

—— *Liberty, Equality, Fraternity* (Stuart D Warner ed, Indianapolis, Liberty Fund, 1993).

Stretton, Tim, 'Coverture and Unity of Person in Blackstone's Commentaries' in Wilfrid R Prest (ed), *Blackstone and His Commentaries: Biography, Law, History* (Oxford, Hart Publishing, 2009) 111–27.

Stretton, Tim and Kesselring, Krista (eds), *Married Women and the Law: Coverture in England and the Common Law World* (Montreal, McGill-Queen's University Press, 2013).

Sutherland, Duncan, 'Peeresses, Parliament and Prejudice: The Admission of Women to the House of Lords, 1918–1963' (2010) 20 *Parliaments, Estates and Representation* 215.

—— 'Ladies in a Lords' House: Women in the House of Lords Since 1958' in Bruce Kinzer, Molly Baer Kramer and Richard Trainor (eds), *Reform and its Complexities in Modern Britain: Essays Inspired by Sir Brian Harrison* (Oxford, Oxford University Press, 2022) 203–26.

Tamanaha, Brian Z, *A General Jurisprudence of Law and Society* (Oxford, Oxford University Press, 2001).

Thomas, Tobi, 'Outrage at Jail Sentence for Woman who Took Abortion Pills Later than UK Limit' *The Guardian* (London, 13 June 2023).

Thompson, EP, *The Making of the English Working Class* (London, Victor Gollancz, 1963).

Tosh, John, 'What Should Historians do with Masculinity? Reflections on Nineteenth-century Britain' (1994) 38 *History Workshop* 179.

Tuerkheimer, Deborah, *Credible: Why we Doubt Accusers and Protect Abusers* (Harper Wave, 2021).

Turner, JW Cecil, *Kenny's Outlines of Criminal Law*, 18th edn (Cambridge, Cambridge University Press, 1962).

Voules, F Minchin, 'Beresford-Hope v Sandhurst' (1889) 1 *County Council Magazine* 231.

Wacks, Raymond, *Understanding Jurisprudence*, 4th edn (Oxford, Oxford University Press, 2015).

Walters, Mark D, 'Dicey's Law of the Constitution' (2012) 32 *OJLS* 21.

—— *AV Dicey and the Common Law Constitutional Tradition: A Legal Turn of Mind* (Cambridge University Press, 2020).

Wason, PC, 'On the Failure to Eliminate Hypotheses in a Conceptual Task' (1960) 12 *Quarterly Journal of Experimental Psychology* 129.

Wells, Celia and Quick, Oliver, *Lacey, Wells and Quick, Reconstructing Criminal Law: Text and Materials*, 4th edn (Cambridge, Cambridge University Press, 2010).

Whitehead, Alfred North, *Science and the Modern World* (Cambridge, Cambridge University Press, 1925).

Wijngaards, John, *The Ordination of Women in the Catholic Church: Unmasking a Cuckoo's Egg Tradition* (London, Darton, Longman & Todd, 2001).

Wilkes, Kathleen, *Real People: Personal Identity without Thought Experiments* (Oxford, Oxford University Press, 1988).

Wise, Steven, *Drawing the Line: Science and the Case for Animal Rights* (Cambridge, Perseus Publishing, 2002).

Wittgenstein, Ludwig, *Philosophical Investigations*, 3rd edn (GEM Anscombe trs, New York, MacMillan Publishing, 1958).

—— *On Certainty* (Oxford, Basil Blackwell, 1969).

—— *Philosophical Investigations* (GEM Anscombe, PMS Hacker and Joachim Schulte trs, Oxford, Blackwell, 2009).

Wolgast, Elizabeth H, *Ethics of an Artificial Person: Lost Responsibility in Professions and Organizations* (Stanford, Stanford University Press, 1992).

Woolf, Virginia, *A Room of One's Own* (London, Hogarth Press, 1929).

—— *Three Guineas* (London, Hogarth, 1938).

Woollacott, Angela, 'Being a Woman's Advisor at the State Level: Deborah McCulloch and Don Dunstan in 1970s South Australia' (2018) 33 *Australian Feminist Studies* 97.

Wright, Charles Alan, 'A Modern Hamlet in the Judicial Pantheon' (1995) 93 *Charles Michigan Law Review* 1841.

Ziegler, Mary, 'Personhood: The New War over Reproduction' (Yale University Press, 2025).

Dictionaries/Encyclopedias

Bauer, Patricia, 'My Fair Lady' (*Britannica*, 17 January 2024), www.britannica.com/topic/My-Fair-Lady-film-by-Cukor.

Brink, David, 'Mill's Moral and Political Philosophy', *The Stanford Encyclopedia of Philosophy* (Edward N Zalta and Uri Nodelman eds, Fall edn, 2022), https://plato.stanford.edu/archives/fall2022/entries/mill-moral-political/.

Campbell, John, 'Smith, Frederick Edwin, First Earl of Birkenhead' (*Oxford Dictionary of National Biography*, 17 September 2015), www.oxforddnb.com/display/10.1093/ref:odnb/9780198614128.001.0001/odnb-9780198614128-e-36137?rskey=UuDw8o&result=4.

Casad, Bettina J and Luebering, JE, 'Confirmation Bias' (*Britannica Encyclopedia*, 17 December 2024), www.britannica.com/science/confirmation-bias.

John, Angela V, 'Thomas, Margaret Haig, 2nd Viscountess Rhondda (1883–1958), Suffragette, Editor, Author and Businesswoman' (*Dictionary of Welsh Biography*, 11 June 2021), biography.wales/article/s12-THOM-HAI-1883.

Law, Jonathan and Martin, Elizabeth A, *A Dictionary of Law*, 7th edn (Oxford, Oxford University Press, 2009).

Lentin, A, 'Reid, Robert Threshie, Earl Loreburn' (*Oxford Dictionary of National Biography*, 25 May 2006), www.oxforddnb.com/display/10.1093/ref:odnb/9780198614128.001.0001/odnb-9780198614128-e-35719?rskey=VtoQ5a&result=2.

Loughlin, Martin, 'Dicey, Albert Venn (1835–1922)' (*Routledge Encyclopedia of Philosophy*, 1998), www.rep.routledge.com/articles/biographical/dicey-albert-venn-1835-1922/v-1.

Macleod, Christopher, 'John Stuart Mill' (*The Stanford Encyclopedia of Philosophy*, Summer edn, 2020), plato.stanford.edu/entries/mill/.

Unattributed, 'Dame Elizabeth Kathleen Lane' (*Britannica*), www.britannica.com/topic/legal-education/Study-and-practice.

—— 'Sir Leslie Stephen: British Critic' (*Britannica*, 2024), www.britannica.com/biography/Leslie-Stephen.

—— 'Thomas Aquinas' (*Stanford Encyclopedia of Philosophy*, 7 December 2022), plato.stanford.edu/entries/aquinas/#:~:text=Between%20antiquity%20and%20modernity%20stands,of%20the%20newly%20founded%20universities.

Uglow, Jennifer (ed), *The Macmillan Dictionary of Women's Biography*, 2nd edn (London, Macmillan, 1989).

Other

Allen, Kevin, 'Professor Emeritus John Finnis Made a Commander of the Order of the British Empire' (*University of Notre Dame*, 6 January 2023), law.nd.edu/news-events/news/professor-john-finnis-2023-commander-order-british-empire/.

Australian Government, Department of the Prime Minister and Cabinet, 'A National Emergency – and an Ongoing National Priority', www.pmc.gov.au/resources/unlocking-prevention-potential/national-emergency-and-ongoing-national-priority.

Badger, Emily, Sanger-Katz, Margot and Miller, Clarie Cain, 'States with Abortion Bans are Among Least Supportive for Mothers and Children' *New York Times* (Online, 28 July 2022), www.nytimes.com/2022/07/28/upshot/abortion-bans-states-social-services.html.

Bahr, Jessica, 'Is 2024 Australia's Worst Year Yet for Violence Against Women?' (*SBS News*, online, 29 December 2024), www.sbs.com.au/news/article/is-2024-australias-worst-year-for-violence-against-women/8rejzzpza.

Barkham, Patrick, 'Should Rivers Have the Same Rights as People?' *The Observer* (London, 21 July 2021).

Becker, Lydia E, 'Election Intelligence' *Women's Suffrage Journal* (Manchester, 1 December 1873).

Cannadine, David, 'Lord Bounder' *London Review of Books* (London, 19 January 1984), www.lrb.co.uk/the-paper/v06/n01/david-cannadine/lord-bounder.

Conaghan, Joanne, 'Gender and the Analytical Jurisprudential Mind: A Response to Leslie Green' (*The Modern Law Review Forum*, 20 August 2020), www.modernlawreview.co.uk/conaghan-green.

Davis, Dena, 'Neil Gorsuch, Aid in Dying, and Roe v Wade' (*The Hastings Center*, 24 March 2017), www.thehastingscenter.org/neil-gorsuch-aid-dying-roe-v-wade/.

Dunstan, Don, *Women's Rights: The Challenge of Social Democracy* (Speech, Newcastle, 1978).

Finnis, John, 'Abortion is Unconstitutional' (*First Things*, online, April 2021), www.firstthings.com/article/2021/04/abortion-is-unconstitutional.

Finnis, John and George, Robert, 'Brief of Amici Curiae Scholars of Jurisprudence John M Finnis and Robert P George in Support Of Petitioners Amicus Brief', Submission in *Dobbs v Jackson Women's Health* Organization 597 US 215 (2022), 29 July 2021.

Fitz-Gibbon, Kate, 'The Long Walk Continues' (*The Monthly*, online, November 2024), www.themonthly.com.au/issue/2024/november/kate-fitz-gibbon/long-walk-continues.

Government Legal Department, 'The Sex Disqualification (Removal) Act 1919: 100 Years ago the Sex Disqualification (Removal) Act was Given Royal Assent' (*Gov.UK*, online, 24 December 2019), www.gov.uk/government/news/the-sex-disqualification-removal-act-1919.

Hale, Brenda, 'Beanstalk or Living Instrument? How Tall can the European Convention on Human Rights Grow?' (Gray's Inn Reading, 16 June 2011).

Heilbron, Hilary, 'Women at the Bar: An Historical Perspective' (*Counsel*, online, 31 May 2013), www.counselmagazine.co.uk/articles/women-the-bar-historical-perspective.

Hennessy, Kathleen, 'You've Come a Long Way, Jenny' *The Guardian* (Online, 18 April 2004), www.theguardian.com/money/2004/apr/18/womenandmoney.observercashsection.

Hessel, Katy, '"What if Women Ruled the World?" Judy Chicago's Latest Show Feels Very Timely' *The Guardian* (Online, 6 November 2023), www.theguardian.com/artanddesign/2023/nov/06/women-ruled-world-judy-chicago-herstory-covid.

HM Revenue & Customs, 'Residence, Domicile and Remittance Basis Manual' (*Gov.com*, 15 May 2024), www.gov.uk/hmrc-internal-manuals/residence-domicile-and-remittance-basis/rdrm22240.

Hodgson, Godfrey, 'Ronald Dworkin Obituary' *The Guardian* (Online, 15 Feb 2013), www.theguardian.com/law/2013/feb/14/ronald-dworkin.

Jackson, Gabrielle, 'The Female Problem: How Male Bias in Medical Trials Ruined Women's Health' *The Guardian* (Online, 14 November 2019), www.theguardian.com/lifeandstyle/2019/nov/13/the-female-problem-male-bias-in-medical-trials.

Kagan, Dion, 'Diminished Patriarchal Dividend' (*Meanjin*, 18 July 2022), meanjin.com.au/books/diminished-patriarchal-dividend/.

Kasdan, Diana, 'Two Years After Dobbs: Pregnant Peoples' Lives are Still on the Line and the Texas Supreme Court Looks Away' (*American Bar Association*, 23 June 2024), www.americanbar.org/groups/crsj/publications/crsj-featured-articles/two-years-after-dobbs/.

Kohlbert, Elizabeth, 'Why Facts Don't Change our Minds' *The New Yorker* (Online, 19 February 2017), www.newyorker.com/magazine/2017/02/27/why-facts-dont-change-our-minds.

Kolovos, Benita, '"Rape is Effectively Decriminalized": How Did Sexual Assault Become so Easy to Get Away With' *The Guardian* (Online, 31 January 2025), www.theguardian.com/australia-news/ng-interactive/2025/jan/31/is-effectively-decriminalised-how-did-sexual-assault-become-so-easy-to-get-away-with-ntwnfb.

Lamon, Severine and Knowles, Olivia, 'Why are Males Still the Default Subjects in Medical Research?' (*The Conversation*, online, 4 October 2021), theconversation.com/why-are-males-still-the-default-subjects-in-medical-research-167545.

Laughland, Oliver and Redden, Molly, 'Neil Gorsuch Distances Himself from Mentor who Compared Gay Sex to Bestiality' *The Guardian* (Online, 22 March 2017), www.theguardian.com/law/2017/mar/21/neil-gorsuch-hearing-legal-mentor-gay-sex-bestiality.

May, Natasha, 'Learning CPR on Manikins Without Breasts Puts Women's Lives at Risk, Study Finds' *The Guardian* (Online, 22 November 2024), www.theguardian.com/australia-news/2024/nov/21/learning-cpr-on-manikins-without-breasts-puts-womens-lives-at-risk-study-finds.

National Police Chiefs Council, 'Violence Against Women and Girls' (March 2024), www.npcc.police.uk/our-work/violence-against-women-and-girls/.

Pentin, Edward, 'John Finnis to Pontifical Academy for Life: Church's Infallible Teaching Against Contraception Is "Certainly True"' (*National Catholic Register*, Vatican, 26 January 2023), www.ncregister.com/news/john-finnis-to-pontifical-academy-for-life-church-s-infallible-teaching-against-contraception-is-certainly-true.

Purvis, Jane, 'What was the Cat and Mouse Act? The Reason why Suffragettes were Force-Fed' (*History Extra*, online, 10 July 2024), www.historyextra.com/period/edwardian/cat-mouse-force-feeding-suffragettes-hunger-strike/.

Rix, Kathryn, '"The First Humble Beginnings of an Agitation": The Women's Suffrage Petition of 7 June 1866' (*The Victorian Commons*, 7 June 2016), victoriancommons.wordpress.com/2016/06/07/the-first-humble-beginnings-of-an-agitation-the-womens-suffrage-petition-of-7-june-1866/.

Sandhu, Serina, 'The Court Case that Legally Denied Women the Vote – and the Women who Voted Anyway' (*The iPaper*, London, 6 February 2018), inews.co.uk/news/uk/court-case-legally-denie d-women-vote-women-voted-anyway-116375.

Sedley, Stephen, 'Persons Aggrieved' (*London Review of Books*, London, 22 May 1997), www.lrb.co.uk/the-paper/v19/n10/stephen-sedley/persons-aggrieved.

Sherman, Carter, 'States Push "Fetal Personhood" Bills Despite Outrage at Alabama IVF Ruling' *The Guardian* (Online, 20 March 2024), www.theguardian.com/society/2024/mar/20/states-fetal-personhood-bill.

Stephen, Leslie, 'The Late John Stuart Mill' (*The Nation*, 5 June 1873).

Topping, Alexandra et al, 'Killed Women Count: 80 Women Allegedly Killed by Men in UK in 2024' *The Guardian* (Online, 31 December 2024), www.theguardian.com/uk-news/ng-interactive/2024/dec/31/killed-women-count-a-project-highlighting-the-toll-and-tragedy-of-violence-against-women-in-the-uk.

Unattributed, 'Human Rights Crisis: Abortion in the United States After Dobbs' (18 April 2023), www.hrw.org/news/2023/04/18/human-rights-crisis-abortion-united-states-after-dobbs.
—— 'John Stuart Mill Amendment' (*UK Parliament*), www.parliament.uk/about/living-heritage/evolutionofparliament/houseofcommons/reformacts/from-the-parliamentary-collections/collections-reform-acts/great-reform-act112/.
—— 'List of Fellows of the Royal Society 1660–2007: A–J' (*The Royal Society*, 2007).
—— 'Presenting the 1866 Petition' (*UK Parliament*), www.parliament.uk/about/living-heritage/transformingsociety/electionsvoting/womenvote/parliamentary-collections/1866-suffrage-petition/presenting-the-petition/.
—— 'Professor Dicey's Letters on Woman Suffrage' *The Spectator* (19 June 1909).
—— 'Statement by the Secretary of Health and Human Services on the Second Anniversary of Dobbs v Jackson Women's Health Organization' (*US Department of Health and Human Services*, 24 June 2024), www.hhs.gov/about/news/2024/06/24/statement-secretary-health-and-human-services-second-anniversary-dobbs-v-jackson-womens-health-organization.html.
—— 'WEH Stanner and the Great Australian Silence' (*ABS Radio National*, 26 March 2009), www.abc.net.au/listen/programs/latenightlive/weh-stanner-and-the-great-australian-silence/3143396.
—— 'Women's Suffrage in Australia' (*Parliament of Australia*), aph.gov.au/Visit_Parliament/Art/Stories_and_Histories/Womens_Suffrage_in_Australia.
Weaver, Matthew, '"Absence of Humanity": Helen MacNamara's Evidence to Covid Inquiry' *The Guardian* (Online, 2 November 2023), www.theguardian.com/uk-news/2023/nov/01/absence-of-humanity-helen-macnamara-evidence-to-covid-inquiry.
Williams, Blair, 'I Studied 31 Australian Political Biographies Published in the Past Decade – Only 4 were About Women' (*The Conversation*, online, 14 September 2021), theconversation.com/i-studied-31-australian-political-biographies-published-in-the-past-decade-only-4-were-about-women-167448.
World Health Organization, 'Violence Against Women' (25 March 2024), www.who.int/news-room/fact-sheets/detail/violence-against-women.
Ziegler, Mary, 'The Endgame in the Battle Over Abortion: The Arc of the Fetal Personhood Movement Signals where Republicans may be Headed' (*Politico Magazine*, online, 24 March 2024), www.politico.com/news/magazine/2024/03/24/personhood-abortion-legal-fight-00147138.

INDEX

www.ingramcontent.com/pod-product-compliance
Ingram Content Group UK Ltd.
Pitfield, Milton Keynes, MK11 3LW, UK
UKHW022109071026
476420UK00001B/90

9 781509 983476